David,

Pucked

Rachel Walter

I hope you always have a light in the dark.

♡

R Walter

CREATESPACE EDITION

*****

Pucked

ISBN:1514203111
ISBN-13: 978-1514203118

Cover Design: Regina Wamba © Mae I Design

Editor: Maria DeSouza

Proofreader: Kathalene Miller

Dedication

To anyone affected by Parental Alienation

"The power of love and knowledge is your best effort at establishing the relationship or reestablishing one. Know what to look for, know what to say, know what to do, but firstly, do all things in love. Show love."

\- Rachel Walter

Sweet 16 Years

Audrey & Riley

Chapter 1

Audrey

The last five minutes of study hall are always the slowest, but today, the hands on Mr. Theiss's old-fashioned clock seem to stand still. I stare out the window, waiting, wishing I were free from this place and already home.

The sun peeks out from behind the gray clouds that have cast our little town in the shadows for days.

Life is like the weather. Rain, like our emotions, builds up along the streets of our hearts, softening the earth of our souls, creating mud. Though messy, mud is the glue of our decisions. It cements our personal changes. It's not permanent, because when it rains again, you'll need to restructure, rebuild, change, and just like our decisions in life, nothing lasts forever.

But in the mud, there's freedom, relief, hope, and even a sense of peace - a mask.

Hiding behind masks is human nature. Even I hide behind a mask to keep others out, to shield my feelings and thoughts.

When it rains, for me, it's a time to reflect, and

when the sun shines, drying the residue and warming my soul, I know I'll begin to heal. Temporary or not, it's still a relief to know that even a small solution is on the way.

The bell shrills, startling me from my thoughts. I burst from my seat and work my way to the door.

It's been raining for two days straight on this side of the Susquehanna River. School just ended, and the brightness of the sun feels like a long lost friend has finally come home, making an unusually warm autumn day.

"Aud!" My friend Alice's voice carries over the chatter of the student body. I wave my hand in the direction of her voice as I weave between the other students in my school, ignoring her as she hollers for me again. I'll call her later. I have to get home and I'm still mad at her for making me waste my paycheck on these uncomfortable jeans I'm wearing. I should've stuck with my tried and true Levi's and not listened to her fawning over the latest "in" style fashion guide.

A backpack slams into my side as I turn the last corner before the glass doors of freedom. "Omph," I gasp.

"Sorry, Audrey," Collin mutters, not slowing his jog to the band room.

Rolling my eyes, I run through the doors and gently rub my side as I cross the parking lot.

Rain makes mud. And mud is enjoyable for more than just a metaphor.

I wiggle my keys out of the small pocket of these jeans that feel plastered on. Alice was so wrong about the comfort level of skinny jeans. My keys jingle and clank together, finally free from the vice-gripped pocket. I unlock my door, tossing my backpack into the passenger seat at the same time as I drop onto the driver's seat.

I allow myself to catch my breath before cranking the engine and maneuvering out of the student lot. This place is insane this time of day, overflowing with crazed students rushing to their cars like ravenous wolves chasing their dinner. One by one, we file down the one-way lane that leads to the road at a snail's pace.

Messing with the radio, I find a station with decent music while I wait.

Two songs later, it's my turn, and I don't take my time leaving Dalesburg High campus. My tires screech as I stomp on the gas pedal. Rain is a Good Thing by Luke "Nice Butt" Bryan comes on the radio. I turn the volume up and shout the lyrics as I drive home like a NASCAR driver.

The tires spray gravel on the undercarriage and behind me as I turn onto my street. Slowing down so my parents don't yell at me again, I carefully park in my spot, grab my stuff, and launch out of my car. My chucks slide in the grass as I run to the porch and I smile to myself.

Everything's perfect.

I fling the front door open. "Mom! Dad!" I yell, dumping my book bag and car keys on the couch on my way to my bedroom. "I'm headin' out!" I shut my door to change. Mom would tear me a new one if I "mud up" any more school clothes. I wiggle and kick out of those stupid jeans.

"Game doesn't start for another three hours Audrey, where you going?" My dad hollers.

Pulling my stained jeans up and over my hips, I shimmy to line the seams perfectly before buttoning them. "It rained!" I shout my answer.

Dad knows exactly what I'm up to. He's the one who has told me since I was little; *Audrey, there's peace in the mud. It centers your soul, and anything you can do to get closer to it brings you closer to your true self. And it's fun to throw at your brothers.* So I'm not sure why he's asking now.

"Yes, Paul. It rained! You're the one who shared your love of mud with her. How could you forget?" my mom answers for me, dryly.

Giggling at her sarcasm, I pull a long sleeved long john shirt over my head, followed by Luca's, my oldest brother, stained Scooby shirt. I pretty much swim in it, but it's the shirt he always wore when he went muddin', before he left for college in New York City anyway. He claimed Scooby kept him from bogging out. I know it's because he didn't full throttle like Greg, our other brother. It doesn't stop me from wearing it, and rub Greg's face in the fact that I'm wearing Luca's lucky shirt.

"Denise, she's my only girl. She could've been going shopping!"

Opening my door and skipping down the hall to the kitchen where my parents are, I laugh. "Give me forty bucks, and I can improve my wardrobe, Daddy!"

He tilts his head toward me and smirks as I lean against the counter. "Detail my truck and you've got a deal."

I brush my fingers through my long, light brown hair, separating the strands into three locks to braid as I think over his offer. Maybe cleaning dad's truck would be worth it, I could go for a few new pairs of jeans from the Goodwill.

"When was the last time it's been cleaned?"

My dad's smirk turns into a full grin, exposing his slightly crooked teeth, which is something he rarely does. Mom says he's embarrassed by his top teeth. When he was about my age, he was told that the unevenness wasn't enough for braces. I have his mouth, so my mom says, but I don't mind it as much as he does.

"Baby girl, there's at least a full load of work clothes between your brother and me in the back cab," he says with hearty laugh.

I scrunch my nose, wrapping the rubber band around the end of my braid. I know what the smell of their dirty work clothes smells like, and it's not pleasant.

"No thanks, keep your money today, I'm goin' muddin'." I leave my parents chuckling in the kitchen as I dart out the backdoor, only stopping to step into my boots and tie the laces.

Mom pokes her head out the door, "Take mine." Her green eyes twinkle with mischief. "Your brother and Billy took his and yours out about ten minutes ago. If you hurry, you might catch them. Give Greg hell and see to it that he's dirtier than you."

"You know he'll be covered without my help," I remind her as I take the key from her extended palm.

"I'll leave towels and the hose out. Just be sure to unhook it and hang it in the garage before you leave for the game. The weatherman said the temperature is supposed to dip low tonight," she orders as I start backing my way out the door. "Be careful!" she yells, her concern seeping into her tone.

“I will! Bye, Ma!” I let the door clang shut and run for the garage, only slipping once as I dodge around Greg’s car. Bursting through the rickety wooden door, paint chips skitter to the cement floor. I jog around Dad’s black ATV to Mom’s forest green one.

Sawdust and grease invade my senses. It’s one of my favorite scents. I smile widely in happiness and anticipation.

After checking to make sure the gas tank is full, I snap the latch behind the seat and pop it off before spinning to grab the WD-40 from the workbench. I do a quick once-over of the radiator and airbox, making sure everything is sealed and then lube all the necessary parts.

Finally, after several long minutes of prepping for mud, I fire the engine and take off for the field across the street.

Years ago, my oldest brothers and my dad turned the grassy field across the street into the perfect muddin’ field. They spent all their free time there, and Dad rented a backhoe to help clear it out and flatten areas. They even made one hole with a launching ramp on it, mostly because one of my brothers enjoyed doing tricks on his dirt bike more than muddin’.

I round the tree line and spot my brother and his friend, Billy. With the wind pushing the loose hair that fell from my braid out of my face, I fly across the field, flinging a spray of mud behind me.

Just ahead, my brother stands on his 4-wheeler, rocking and wiggling, trying to get unstuck. His height and muscle give him a slight advantage, and he can usually stop from stalling out, but I don’t think he’ll be able to muscle his way out of this one.

Billy sits off to the side, laughing, his rust red and torn hat shielding his eyes as he throws his head back. Billy is shorter than my brother by nearly a foot, only an inch or two taller than my five foot three inch frame. But Billy is probably just as strong as my brother, if not stronger.

I test the dip in the field, not exactly smart on my part, but I gotta get Greg at least once if this is his stopping point.

Getting closer to my almost stalled brother, I head straight for him. I turn the bar and lean into the curve, hoping to keep my momentum, I rev at the same time.

"Damn you, Audrey!" My brother garbles through the mud that I just kicked at him.

I laugh and steer further away, enjoying the spray of the mud and the wind in my face.

"Audrey Hepburn!" Billy wails behind me. "Dahling, wait up!"

I roll my eyes as I slow down. "Billy Madison? That you?"

He grins. "Billy got the girl he wanted at the end of that movie."

I laugh. "This is true."

This is what Billy does. He teases me relentlessly because my parents named me after Audrey Hepburn. My parents, more my mom, love Audrey Hepburn. In fact, my brothers were even named for her family as well. My oldest brothers, twins, are named for Audrey's children, Sean and Luca, and Greg was named after her lifelong friend, Gregory Peck.

Since my mom mentioned this fact a few years ago, Billy has done nothing but crack jokes. It's not even that I look or even act like her in any way. She was a beautiful woman; tall, slender, dark hair, and from what my dad says, "She could make anything a beautiful class of sexy." I'm nearest to her opposite. I'm short, have light brown hair, and I'm "cute" Or so I'm told. "Aw, Audrey, you look so cute and innocent." It's annoying and probably not something Audrey Hepburn was ever told. Although, someone could've told her that, but it's not like I would know.

Even with the differences, it doesn't stop Billy from teasing me. So in return, I find as many "Billy" actors, movies, and quotes that I can find just to get back at him.

"How's Sarah these days?" I ask him about his girlfriend.

"She's alright I guess, filling out applications for college and what not," he says, circling me and spraying mud in my direction.

I rev when he's directly behind me to pay him back.

"So she kicks you out because you distract her?" I turn toward him and laugh, seeing the mud splashed across his mouth, clinging to his beard.

He pulls a blue and white handkerchief from his back pocket and wipes his round face. "Well, there is that, and she knows I'm not goin' to college. I've got my career already."

Billy, Greg, and my dad are masons. It's a hard, laboring job that sometimes pulls them away from home and winter months are always the hardest, but it's something they all love and keeps them active and healthy. My mom does Yoga, Pilates, and Zumba weekly. She says she has to stay fit like Dad, and at her age, it's harder to keep fit, especially in her line of work. She's a secretary and a sports photographer for the Susquehanna Daily Record.

"Is she staying around here?" I ask, hoping that she does. Sarah is a gorgeous blonde, cheerleader type of person, but she's just like me and would choose mud over makeup any day. She's the only girl I know who I can shop with, though I still attempt shopping with my fashionista friend, Alice, and allow the torture from time to time. Sarah's hippy style matches my own, and she can throw a punch to keep Billy from being a dumb boy when she has to.

Billy stuffs his handkerchief in his back pocket. "She hasn't decided. She said she's waiting to hear back from colleges before deciding where to go. Doesn't want to be disappointed." He drives my ATV close to my mom's, gently pushing the front tire.

That sounds like her, but I'm willing to bet she's got one college picked that she'd go to no matter how many other colleges accepted her. "What if she goes to a college across the country?" I ask, shifting directions to run side by side, back to where Greg is still stuck in the mud. He's off the seat and trying to push the backend to shove out of the mud.

"We'll cross that bridge when we get that news, but I don't think she'll go that far. Even if she does, she's the only one for me." He shrugs a thick shoulder as we veer to the left near the still grassy ground.

I smile at his promise. They've been together for as long as I can remember. Everyone thought Billy would leave her when he graduated last year, but he didn't. I have to admit that even I was surprised. He and Sarah are such an unlikely pair but maybe that's what makes them special. They don't have an easy relationship; Billy is Billy. He's hardheaded and has the temper of a Papa Bear who's protecting his cubs. She's hotheaded and demanding. But they make it work.

"Greg, man. You *always* get stuck first," Billy teases as he parks in a grassy patch.

"Ain't my fault," he mutters as he tries once more, shoving on his own.

"Did you do the checks like Dad taught us?" I ask, parking next to Billy.

He grunts with the force of his shove, sinking deeper in the mud, standing knee deep in the muddy pit. "I swear I did," he says gruffly, wiping the back of his hand across his forehead, smearing more mud on his face.

Billy laughs. "I watched you, you didn't do squat. You even teased me for checkin' Audrey's and "wasting time." Audrey would kick my ass if I got hers stuck."

"No matter how much you check there's still a chance of getting stuck," Greg argues.

I chuckle at them. Both would be right, but Dad taught us to take care of our vehicles. "Come on, let's get you unstuck," I cheer as I wade through the sloppy mud.

"Love it when girls get dirty!" Billy shouts, jumping into the mud bog.

"That girl is my sister, prick," Greg sneers, flinging a gob of mud at him.

Billy dodges the mud wad. "No shit, Sherlock. Scoot over, let's get your baby free."

I use Greg's arm to help get me closer to the front of his ATV where I start digging mud away from the tires. "And hurry up! I gotta go to Riley's game in a few hours!" I yell, trying to hustle them. If these dorks make me late, someone will take my favorite seat - right behind home bench in the center.

Chapter 2
Riley

Gliding across the ice to the face-off in Cougar's zone, I focus on the play I need to complete. For as small of a town as Dalesburg Pennsylvania is, our community really pulls through on game nights. In other districts, football usually has the largest turnout, but for Dalesburg, football and hockey are neck and neck with attendance. Tonight is no different. Everyone's dressed in red and black, which are our school colors. The stands are filled with parents and classmates. They're all shouting and chanting, "Here we go Warriors! Here we go!" louder than I can think.

If I can tip the puck to my teammate, we have a chance to win this and not end up with a tie. There's eighteen seconds left in the last period with the score tied at two. I hunch, holding my stick in front of me, stopping on the edge of the face-off marker across from my opponent, Emanuel Draggah.

I breathe in the ice and chants, and the play becomes clearer in my mind, like locking a puzzle piece in the correct spot.

Waiting for the ref to drop the puck, I let the ice settle comfortably around my features. My heart and lungs hug the ice and I feel it fill me up, freezing everything inside of me in the best way possible as I wait for the puck to drop.

The ref's eyes flit from player to player, slowly raising the hand that's grasping the puck.

I count the seconds.

One

Draggah twitches his stick.

Two

I slap mine to the ice.

Three

The puck drops.

Both of us fight to tip it to our own teammates.

I dig my blade into the ice and check my shoulder into Draggah's chest, slapping the puck behind me and to the right. My Center, Rob Hopkins, is awaiting my pass and, thankfully, receives the puck and immediately gets the jump on the Cougars. He weaves between our opponents, getting closer to the goal, as they scramble to stop him.

"Go, go!" I yell around my mouth guard.

Sliding to the left, I run into Draggah. He's blocking me with a threatening smile.

Down the ice, Allen Humphrey is unguarded and open. But it's Allen. He's not paying attention, like usual. Why coach put him in, I'll never know.

"Look alive, Allen!" I shout, hoping he hears me.

"Shoot! Shoot! Shoot!" people in the stands cheer.

I head deke to the left, but Draggah knows what I'm up to and isn't fooled by my fake, blocking me the right side with his arm and foot.

Rob passes to Allen. I hold my breath and push against Draggah, trying to get around him or bowl through him.

Four seconds left.

I'm able to slide Draggah backwards.

Suddenly, Allen comes to life like he's borrowing the talent of Mario Lemieux. He readies like a pro and pushes forward, shooting with his wrist. The light above the net flashes a second before the end of game buzzer sounds, the crowd roars even louder.

I shove around my shocked opponent, flying the last few feet to Allen and ram into him, slapping his helmet. Flipping my mouth guard to hang in the corner of my mouth, I congratulate Allen. "Holy shit, Hump! You made it!" I shout close to his head.

With his eyes crinkling, his face splits into the widest smile I've seen on him yet. He drops his mouth guard into his gloved hand. "Coach and Rob have been workin' with me."

His words are a subtle reminder that as captain of the team, I should know these things at the very least. But that's hard to accomplish these days. I swallow the onslaught of guilt threatening to lay me out and remind myself that I'm doing what's best for my baby sister, Hannah.

The rest of the team joins us on the ice, followed by Coach Page, who rallies us to shake hands with our opponents.

I steel my face into what the team, and the school, has deemed the *Frozen Silk* death glare. Leading the team to center ice, I begin the line of sportsmanship, and without removing my glove, I tap each hand of the opponents and their coaches.

At the end of the line, I circle around the ice, raising my stick in the air to celebrate with everyone. A familiar tap on the safety glass catches my attention when I stop at the exit door.

A girl with light brown hair piled on top of her head in a wet mess waits on the other side. A light dusting of freckles shadow her cheeks and the dimple in her right cheek is out with her full-fledged smile.

Audrey.

I can't help but grin at her. She never misses a game.

Pulling a glove off and stuffing it under my arm, I slice to a stop right in front of her.

"You won!" she screams as she bounces, tapping the glass again.

I laugh. "See you soon!" I press my hand to the safety glass board with two fingers raised. Each finger marking how many years of school left until graduation, and she holds up the same two.

She's my best friend, closer to me than any of my teammates. Even closer than Todd Van Luit, my goalie and neighbor, and we've been best friends since we were in diapers.

She winks and points to the hall going back to the showers before waving a hand in front of her face. "Shower up!" A strand of her hair falls from the messy bun with her movements, revealing some drying mud.

I laugh again. "You still got mud in your hair, Aud!"

She groans and closes her eyes. "I'll explain later!"

Pushing off the ice, I wait until Todd exits and cut in behind him, before Coach and the trainers.

"You made some good saves tonight, Todd," I say, clapping his padded shoulders.

He yanks off his helmet, cracking it on the butt of his stick before turning his head toward me. "Naw, I left two in. I need more practice. These first few games have been too damn close." His green eyes are usually filled with an unbridled happiness, one way to know that his life has been, so far, untouched by life's bullshit. But tonight, they're filled with disappointment and anger.

I shake my head at him. "We still won. We'll work on your saves tomorrow."

His head drops back, staring at the ceiling for a moment. "You're right, we did." Grinning, he turns to me and points through the locker room doors, "Allen's kind of a hero tonight." We both smile as we watch our teammates hoisting a peacefully happy Allen into the air.

"Alright guys!" Coach yells over the team's shouts.

Dan, the trainer, puts his fingers in his mouth and screams out a loud whistle. "Listen up, Warriors!"

Everyone goes silent and turns to Coach. I glance

around the room, checking to make sure they're all listening. When I'm satisfied, I turn my attention to the man who has coached me for almost ten years. His hair is graying, but aside from that he looks just the same as I remember him when I was six; a tall man with a scary, intimidating presence.

He takes his glasses off, leaving his face devoid of emotion as he glances to each of us. "We've still got work to do if we want a successful season. Allen, you picked up being the secret weapon as good as I'd hoped you'd be, but the lack of focus throughout the rest of the game is not acceptable. There were a few of you," he stops to glare at someone I can't see, "I won't name names, who thought flirting and showing off would help the team...you played loose because of it. We've got to work on the run game. Take tonight to celebrate the win, but be ready tomorrow morning for practice at ten!" He claps his hands together and dismisses us to the showers.

As I watch everyone resume their cheering, Coach Page catches my eye. His jaw ticks as we lock eyes. I know he wants me to come to him and tell him how things are going at home. This is the man who's been more of a father to me than a coach. I give him a small nod, silently letting him know I'll try to make time to speak with him before I flee from his knowing eyes and rush to my locker.

After my shower, I sit on the bench and pull my socks on.

"Dude, did you see Audrey tonight?" Alex, second-string wing, whistles his apparent appreciation. My hands still as I fold the cuff of my sock, and slowly, I turn my face towards him. He doesn't notice me sitting here, or he'd probably run off. "Man, she's smokin' hot!" He continues. "Even with that mud in her hair!"

Luckily for him, his buddy Jimmy, another second-string, sees me and the look on my face. Jimmy smacks him to shut him up.

"Wonder if Silk's hit that yet? I certainly wouldn't wait."

I rise from the bench, anger fueling me more than anything.

Jimmy shakes his head, closes his eyes, and turns away. "You're on your own, dude."

"What?" Finally Alex turns my way. His eyes widen and his dark skin turns a lighter shade of tan. Before I manage to say a word, he takes off running the opposite way, barreling into Todd in the process.

Todd chuckles as he steadies Alex before letting him go. "What you say to the little guy?" I turn my glare toward him, still reeling from what the kid was saying. His brown hair is still damp, clinging to the side of his face. "Hey, I didn't do anything! What happened?"

I take a calming breath and sit back down on the bench to put my other sock on. "Just a little prick talkin' 'bout things he shouldn't."

"He said somethin' about Audrey, didn't he?" He asks as he pulls his shirt over his head.

I don't answer him. I pull my boxers on, drop the towel, and finish getting dressed in silence.

I'm going to try to come in early tomorrow to talk to Coach. My anger wouldn't impress Coach at this point and I'd have to keep Audrey waiting for longer than necessary.

"I'll see you in the morning. Audrey's giving me a

ride home."

"You guys goin' for milkshakes? We did win." He smiles wide, showing off his perfectly straight teeth.

"Probably." I shrug. "Wouldn't wanna break that tradition this early in the season." I grab my gear bag and head for the door.

Alex is heading for the door too, but he stops at the end of the row of lockers, busying himself with his shoe.

If he wasn't a teammate, I might've decked him for talking foully about my best friend. But he is a teammate. I'll just let him shake in his boots through practice tomorrow and then have a little chat with him after. Releasing a harsh breath, I force myself to continue to the door.

Chapter 3
Audrey

Picking the dirt from under my fingernails with my house key on my keychain as I wait for Riley, I wonder how much dirt I missed tonight. I didn't have time to shower, so I rinsed off best I could with the unbelievably freezing hose water. I'll get Greg back for getting stuck that bad tomorrow.

The locker room door bangs open. I jump, and luckily, I don't stab myself with the key. Turning toward the doors, I spy a very pissed off Riley stalking out. I can tell from the glare on his face that he's not really seeing what's in front of him. His square jaw is set, lips thinned, brows firm, and eyes frozen. Not to mention his free hand fisted at his side and anger seems to be rolling off him in visible waves. Anyone else would walk or run in the opposite direction seeing this face on him. He's built like a machine compared to most sixteen year old boys. Thanks to two summers worth of lifting weights and workouts. When he looks all scary like that, people know he's got what it takes to back himself up, so they cower.

But I'm not them. I *know* Riley better than they do.

"Ri," I shout to get his attention.

His steps falter before a beautiful smile splits across his face. "Hey Aud," he says, taking the steps two at time to where I'm sitting.

"What was that look all about? You guys did pretty awesome tonight, and you won."

He drops his duffel down and slumps next to me on the bleachers. "Second-string has me pissed."

I choke back my smile. Second-stringers always get under his skin with their cockiness. "I thought you were workin' on bein' their friend this year, Mister Captain." I elbow him lightly in the ribs.

He tilts his head at me and smirks. "I tried bein' the little prick's friend, but he-," he cuts himself off with a deep breath. "Nothin', you wouldn't understand." The pissed off, *Frozen Silk* look comes back. The look that turns his iceberg blue eyes into sheets of steel. The same look that my dad says is rage turned to stone. But it doesn't scare me on Riley.

"Ri, come on. It's me," I say, smacking his bicep, proving to him that his look doesn't affect me. "You tell me everything. What's really goin' on?"

He shakes his head again.

Lovely. He's trying to freeze me out. It's been a while since this happened.

The locker room door bangs open again, and on instinct, I turn to see who it is. Todd exits into the hallway with his usual charming smile. He's a little shorter than Riley and smaller built, but being a net minder, he needs to be limber and smaller. His brown hair, still damp, hangs over his left eye.

"Hey, brown eyes!" He sings with a grin.

"Hi, Todd. You looked good out there tonight!" I admit and push some drying, mud-caked hair behind my ear.

"So did you!" He grins. "I saw you cheerin' us on the whole time."

Riley groans and leans back, locking his fingers behind his head, his blond hair falling away from his face in the process.

"I'm always cheering you guys on. If I don't, you let everything flying at you go into the net," I tease.

"Maybe I should keep you by my side on the ice and off," he teases with a wink.

"It'll cost you," I warn.

"Name it," he breathes.

I look him over, head to toe, and watch as a gentle blush creeps up his neck and practically makes his long ears glow. "It'll cost your stick." His eyes widen, and Riley groans beside me. "I've always wanted to beat someone over the head with a goalie's stick."

Riley bursts out laughing. I take my eyes off Todd, watching Riley from the corner of my eye. I absolutely love when he lets loose like this. His life isn't conventional for a teenager, and I always find myself trying to give him the release he needs. The more he smiles and laughs, the less chance I have at being frozen out again.

I smile proudly, knowing I've eased some of his pain for the moment.

"Really?" Todd groans, pulling my attention from Riley back to him.

"Well, I could've said it'll cost your life, but I'm not that mean. Although, I could use a lifetime servant, you know, someone to clean my dad's truck for me, but I still get paid for it," I add and glance out to the rink wondering if I'll see Mr. Hare on the zamboni tonight.

"I'm not touchin' that. You two have fun, and Audrey?"

I look back up to his forest green eyes. "Yes?"

"I'll see you Monday," he says quietly, tapping his palm on the railing before backing away.

"Why do you do that?" Riley asks after Todd disappears through the doors to the parking lot.

"Do what?"

His eyes lock with mine. "Why do you flirt with everyone?"

"You're just jealous because I flirt with everyone except you," I accuse with a smile.

He shakes his head. "Nah, you flirt with me. But I'm used to it. Everyone else isn't, and it leads them to think they have a shot with you."

I laugh, probably harder than I should. "I think you've been takin' pucks to the head for too long, Ri."

He stands. "Come on, lets go get our milkshakes, I'm tired of bein' here for the day."

This isn't anything new. Since last summer he's wanted to spend less and less time at the rink, at school, anywhere really. He doesn't like being home either, but that's where he needs to be for Hannah.

I follow behind him and snatch his helmet off his stick. Pulling it over my head, I pray it'll fit with my hair up in a bun. It slides on with ease. I guess he's got a bigger head than I thought. I pause just before the steps and lower the visor before clipping the chin strap dangling under my chin.

He reaches the bottom of the steps and starts to cross the hallway to leave before he realizes I'm not right behind him. "What's-," he stops talking as he turns around, laughing when he sees me.

I mimic his signature glare as best I can, trying to look threatening.

"I might piss myself if you don't take that off," he laughs.

"'Cause you're scared, right?" I hold my face in what feels like a glare.

He leans on the railing. "No, because you look like a constipated chicken!"

I pout and stomp down two of the steps. "No fair. You could've at least lied."

His eyes roam my face, lingering on my protruded lip. "You are the scariest chick wearing a too big helmet that I've ever seen in my life. Pretty, but scary."

As much as I hate it, his lie burns inside. He didn't have to add "pretty" in his lie. I try unhooking the chin strap but my fingers fumble.

"I'll get it," he whispers, taking a step towards me. As he brushes my hands out of the way, I totter on the step and clutch his thick biceps to steady myself. I smile my thanks for him not mentioning my klutziness, too.

The locker room door bangs open, but with Riley this close to me, I don't look to see who it is. Riley is my best friend. I feel more for him, but I can never tell him that. He doesn't have the time for a girlfriend even if he were interested. And he certainly isn't interested in me.

Someone whistles. "Told you he was gettin' some!"

Riley's posture straightens as instantly as all humor drains from his features. He's turning into *Frozen Silk* right before my eyes. The chin strap swings, smacking into the top of my shoulder as he shrugs my hands off his arms, turning to his teammate.

Definitely *not* interested.

"Alex, leave it!" I recognize Jimmy from my study hall, his red hair, pasty white skin and bright freckles that cover his skin is pretty hard to miss. He's shushing the other boy and trying to drag him away. I know the kid, he's on the team, but I can't remember his name.

"Well, since no one else can have her, he might as well hit it once in a while," the boy defends himself.

My brows furrow. Is this really what they talk about? Who can have me and who can't? That's more disgusting than what I originally thought they talked about in the locker room.

Riley takes two steps towards Alex and Jimmy.

Jimmy's fear grows and shines on his face as he tugs Alex harder.

"Ri, let it go," I whisper and touch his shoulder lightly. He doesn't scare me when he's like this. I know he won't turn it on me and mean it, but he doesn't need this kind of thing to come between him and his teammates. These guys will likely have spots along side of him next year, and something like this might damage the on-ice relationship.

He shrugs my hand from shoulder and takes another step toward the guys.

I can't let him do something stupid.

"Riley! Just let it go."

"Tomorrow," Riley growls to Jimmy and Alex.

Surprisingly, both of them gulp before running out of the building.

Riley rolls his shoulders and cracks his neck before turning to me.

I grimly stare at him.

"What?" He snaps.

My mouth forms a thin line. I don't know what to say. So, I take his helmet off and check the insides, praying dirt didn't rub off. Luckily, none did, so I re-clip it on his stick and step around him.

"Look, I'm sorry. I'm planning on talking to Alex tomorrow. That's what I was pissed about when I came out," he explains.

He was pissed because Alex thought he's with me when he's not?

I shrug a shoulder, but I don't stop to talk to him. I don't like that anyone would think those things about me, let alone shout them when I'm standing right there.

But I'm almost glad that people think Riley and me are more than what we are. And for that reason, I can't say anything even more. If I tell him not to say anything, he'll think that I don't care if someone disrespects me or that I don't mind it when it's in reference to us. And that could damage our friendship.

But when people think me and Riley are a secret item, I don't have to pretend to like hanging around some loser that's only trying to round the bases with me. I wouldn't let them get to first, but Riley tends to scare anyone off before they get close enough for me to shut them down.

I slam the door open, much like Riley had done with the locker room door, and feel him hot on my heels.

"Are you okay?" he whispers as we enter the darkness.

I wrap my arms around myself, fending off the chill of the autumn night. "I'm fine, Ri."

"I don't believe you."

I unlock his door first, and walk around to the driver side to unlock my door. "I know."

Chapter 4
Riley

I couldn't feel like a bigger jerk than I do right now.

We should've left as soon as I came out, but she looked so cute sitting there digging the dirt out from under her nails. It was a rare moment that she seemed to actually care she was still muddy. Not that she's a slob, she's just Audrey. When it rains, she's hyped up like me on game day. Her sport is muddin'. Mine is my life and a ticket to getting out of the hellhole house I call home.

I look over to her for the hundredth time in the last five minutes. Her lips are still in a thin line, and I'd bet that she's replaying everything over in her head. Alex is an ignorant, cocky jerk. He just says things without thinking that maybe he'll hurt someone's feelings.

What I feel the worst about is what I said after she pouted. I implied that her being pretty is a lie. That's the furthest thing from the truth, and it's something that I always find myself doing. But at the same time, it's been a bit of a blessing.

Two years.

We graduate in two years. When I'm away from this place, and my mother, I'll be able to tell her the truth. But for now, as long as she believes the lie, she's safe.

"Usual spot?" she whispers.

"Yeah," I respond.

We go through the drive-thru at McDonalds, getting our shakes and head to the empty lot at the bottom of the hill from the park. When she parks, she immediately gets out and hops on to the trunk of her car facing the graveyard, milkshake in hand.

I slowly get out, feeling the adrenaline from the game seeping out and the soreness creeping in to replace it. "This or that?" I ask, climbing up to sit beside her.

"Near or far?" She asks before taking a sip of her shake.

"Far," I answer automatically. "You? Near or far?"

Her face tilts skyward and glows softly, like a porcelain doll, from the white light of the moon. She's beautiful as always. "I'll always stay close to home." Her fingers tap against her cup. "Wherever it goes, I go." She probably won't leave this place. My hope and heart sink. "Snowed in or froze out?"

"Snowed in, as long as *in* wasn't my house," I answer. That'd be a living nightmare.

"Jocks or nerds?" I ask.

She cracks a smile. "Jock if it's you, nerd for anyone

else."

"That makes me feel special, sort of," I admit. I'm not really sure what she means by this.

She glances my way, a sad smile on her face. "How's your mom?"

I shake my head and pick at the plastic lid on my cup. "She believes Ted is her soul mate, even after the hell he's put her through, put us all through."

Her hand delicately touches my forearm, a friendly gesture that I wish she wouldn't do. "She let him back in?"

I nod. "He promised not to drink anymore, but when I took the trash out yesterday there were fresh empties in there again."

"Why does she let this happen?" she whispers. It's one of the questions I've been asking, too. So I don't answer. "Have you tried getting a hold of your dad?"

My lips thin but I still don't answer her.

"Ri?"

I can't hear anymore. Not everyone has a happily ever after. And not every couple stays together. "Chocolate of Vanilla?" I ask, knowing that her answer will be vanilla, but I can't talk about my miserable home life anymore.

I feel her eyes roam over my face more than I can see the action. "Vanilla," she whispers tenderly.

"Does your taste ever change? That answer has been vanilla for as long as I can remember," I muse.

She half-smiles at me. "I like vanilla."

An engine revs, likely trying to make it up the giant hill to the park or development just behind it. Headlights bounce off the stop sign a few feet away, illuminating her light brown hair in a halo of white gold for a second. And in that second, I notice the dirt in her hair and remember she hasn't told me about it yet.

"So what's up with the extra dirt?"

She starts laughing and tells me about Greg getting stuck, again. When we're done talking and drinking our shakes, she takes me home. Not that I want to be here as it isn't even curfew yet, but it's where I need to be in case things get out of hand, again.

I walk through the front door, heading straight for the laundry room.

"Why you so late?" Ted hollers from his perch on the couch.

"Game day," I answer flatly.

His footsteps clunk on the hardwood floor behind me. "Post your schedule. I'd like to come to a game or two."

I'm taken aback by his admission. He's never shown interest in my life before.

"I can get a copy tomorrow after practice," I finally say, keeping my back to him as I put the clean clothes from the dryer into an empty basket.

"Look twerp, I'm tryin' to make things right this time." His tongue clucks loudly. "I didn't know what it meant, or took, to be a step-parent before. I'm really gonna try this time."

My hand stills on the damp clothes in the washer. This is new, too.

"I can't be your dad," he adds quietly.

"I don't want you to be," I say, working hard to not let the attitude fill my voice.

"Can I try being your friend?"

I nod. I can't say anything to this. I don't respect him, trust him, or like him, and I'm not sure I can forgive him from what happened almost a year ago.

Ted doesn't say anything, and after a few moments of silence, he walks away. His work boots giving away that he's heading to the garage and not to the living room.

I chew on the inside of my cheek and go back to putting the load in the washer into the dryer. It's the same load I put in this morning.

After I drop my practice clothes in the wash and wipe down my gear with Lysol, I check the hall table for today's mail. The electric bill sitting on top of mom's checkbook is still unopened. I stifle my groan and open it, checking the amount due before opening mom's checkbook. I write in the amount and pray she hasn't blown through her paycheck yet. Forging her signature like I've done since I was twelve, I place it and the slip from the bill inside the envelope and lick it closed before digging the side drawer for a stamp.

With chores and bills taken care of, I head upstairs, stopping outside of my sister's door and crack it open just to check on her. She's six, but she's so small that I worry about her. The only thing visible is her dingy, blonde curls. Even in this light, I can tell that Mom hasn't washed her hair.

I'll have to wake her up and have her take a quick bath in the morning before I leave for practice.

I resume chewing on my cheek as I quietly reclose her door and head to my room.

R

I lean against the door one hour before practice starts, waiting for Coach. My breath fogs around me for a second before disappearing in the air.

My mind isn't on hockey or today's practice. I can't stop thinking that I need to check the garage and get rid of any alcohol I find. That's what led to bad things before. Mom promised she was done with it and swore Ted was done, too. I know one of them is drinking again, I just need to figure out which one.

Maybe it's not Ted this time. He wanted my schedule, which in itself is more than Mom ever asked.

A diesel engine rumbles into the parking lot and distracts me from my thoughts. Coach is here.

"Riley!" Coach hollers from the other side of his truck. A moment later I see his smiling face, eyes crinkling with wrinkles from aging. "You're early, son."

"Yeah," I say with a small nod. "Figured I'd talk to you now since I didn't stick around last night."

"Well good. You can help me get drills sorted for today while we chat." He taps his folder under his arm and flips through his key ring for the key that opens the rink. "I know you've been off more than you've been on, care to share what's goin' on?"

I groan. Last time I talked to him, I told him about

my mom getting a second job again and all the worries with Hannah that that brings up. “As you know, my mom is working a second job at Strev-,”

“At the Tavern. I saw her car there three nights ago.”

“What? She told me she picked up the evening shift at Strever’s Grocery.”

He shrugs and holds the door open for me. “She might not have been working, just popping in for a drink. My wife stops in there and has a glass of wine sometimes when things get stressful at the hospital.”

I frown. “Miss Gen is nothing like my mom. One for her is a twelve pack.”

He nods. “As a nurse, Genevieve can’t drink much or she’ll lose her license, and she’s seen what can happen.”

“Do you think she lied about the second job so she can drink 4 nights a week?”

He looks at me, really looks me over as if he’s seeing me for the first. “I don’t know, Riley. Your mother is not someone I can predict or even guess at. She’s full of surprises, I can say that much. Are bills being paid?”

I nod but don’t tell him that I’ve been forging her handwriting on checks again.

“My guess is that she does have a second job, maybe she only stopped in at the Tavern. I didn’t go in so I’m not sure, but maybe she thought you wouldn’t understand if she worked at the Tavern versus the grocery store.”

I shrug a shoulder like it doesn't bother me. But it does. I know I need to ask her about this. I just don't know how it won't be a fight.

"How is Hannah these days?" He asks as we head for the locker room.

I smile. "She's good. She told me to tell you hi this morning."

He laughs. "Why does she always wake up so early?"

"I had to wake her up for bath and breakfast today." I follow him into the locker room.

He glances at me over his shoulder with his eyebrow raised.

"Mom worked last evening and was in bed by the time I got home from the game, and she was gone this morning before I woke up."

"Where is Hannah?" He asks in a panic.

I chew on my cheek and stare at the floor.

"Riley. You did not leave her home alone."

I shake my head. "Ted's home with her."

"Are you-,"

"Mom swears he's her soul mate. I don't trust him at all, but I'm not Hannah's dad so I have no say!"

He drops his folder on the bench and stares at me. "I am so sorry, Riley."

"Don't be sorry. None of this is your fault."

He shakes his head and smiles sadly. “No, not my fault, but as a parent, my heart breaks for you. You shouldn’t be going through this kind of thing. It’s not fair to you or Hannah.”

I shrug. “It’s all I know really.”

“No. It wasn’t always like this.”

“What happened back then doesn’t matter. It was fake. It was a lie. He left and took my chance of anything resembling normal growing up with him.”

“Riley, it wasn’t-,”

“Just stop. Please? I didn’t come here to fight with you. I just thought you should know what’s goin’ on.”

“Is Hannah okay with Ted?”

I swallow roughly. “Not really. She doesn’t like him at all. She stays in her room when it’s just the two of them, but when we’re all there she will try to play a game with him or something.”

He nods and straddles the bench, flipping open his folder. “Todd requested a shooting drill for today. Think you got a couple slap shots in ya?”

I breathe a sigh of relief that we’re done with the heavy and tackling practice. “I think I can manage.”

“I’ve got a few tricks up my sleeve for this practice to prepare us for next week’s game.” He winks and smiles in a way that I know I’ll be in pain later on, but I grin and nod as if I’m excited.

It's three on three. I have Rob and Andrew on my team with Todd as my goalie. Andrew is a second-string who needs to get more practice before he's ready for any lengthy ice time. Hump, Alex, and Scott are trying to score on Todd. Normally Scott is defenseman but he does well in the scrimmages at practice.

Coach blows the whistle and drops the puck between Scott and I. Scott's faster this time and tips the puck to Alex. Rob is blocking Alex, but I don't care. I rocket around Scott and check Alex, knocking him flat on his back. I swipe the puck and send it sailing down the ice.

The whistle shrills.

"Silk! What are you doing?"

"I saw an opening to get the puck," I answer.

He raises a brow at me. "You know the rules better than anyone else on this team. Laps. Twenty. Now."

I nod once and push off, gliding, gaining speed. Checking is used in caution while in practice because the practice gear is older. There's also placement of the shoulder and elbow. If this was the NHL, that move would've been acceptable, but I'm not pro.

I don't care that coach is unhappy. Alex deserved the hit and he knows it. I cross center ice again, one lap down, nineteen to go.

Normally practice is hard, but today was harder and I didn't make it easy for myself either. I did a total of sixty extra laps. By the time we head out, I'm ready for a nap. I didn't sleep well last night, staying up to make sure all the laundry got done and then finishing the dishes Mom didn't get to.

Todd's mom dropped him off this morning for practice, but I'm not sure what's going on with his car. I guess I'll find out after our trainer is finished checking his wrist, so I wait by my beat up Toyota for him.

Alex bursts out the door, running to catch up to Jimmy who came out a few minutes before him.

"Alex," I yell.

Alex freezes and slowly turns.

I jerk my head back, silently telling him to come here.

He jogs over to me. "Yeah, Captain?"

"Do me a favor," I start. He smiles. "From now on, don't talk about Audrey like she's trash." His smile slips. "Don't ever treat a woman how you were talking last night. That's not being a man, that's being a dead man." The hold I have on my anger begins to crack. I'll do anything I can to stop him from becoming another Ted.

"Yes, sir," he says quietly.

"Go," as soon as the word escapes my mouth, he darts across the lot to Jimmy's car. If he'd use that speed on the ice all the time, maybe he'd get more time.

Todd sidles up beside me. "Ready now, boss?"

"Shut up, someone's gotta teach that kid."

"Think you can stop him from being a horn dog for Audrey?"

I take a deep breath and try forcing my anger back down. "Maybe not, but at least he won't do it within earshot of me."

I unlock my door and pull the creaky thing open to unlock Todd's door and pop the trunk.

"Can I ask you something?"

I chuckle and look at him sideways. "You're asking this time? Dude, just spit it out."

"It's not an easy thing to ask," he mutters, and swallows hard.

"You've got my full attention," I promise him, not moving from the edge of the driver's seat.

He shifts his weight from foot to foot. "Well, there's this girl," he starts. Aw, shit. Don't tell me he knocked Libby up, because I've got nothing to say to help him out of that. That's his own mess and his responsibility. "I really like her, and I think she likes me too."

My brows furrow in confusion. "Aren't you still with Libby?"

His mouth pops open a little and his eyes widen. "We broke it off last month. Remember? We were practicing outback and you nearly took my head off with your stick 'cause I wasn't payin' attention?"

My brows furrow and rub my palms on the knees of my jeans. "Sorry, yeah, I remember that." This proves just how much I *don't* pay attention to anyone other than Audrey. I do remember throwing my stick at him one day because he let me score forty of sixty shots. But him and Libby breaking up doesn't ring a bell. I try thinking back to the last time I saw them together in the halls. How long has it been?

"Anyway," he says, pulling me from my thoughts. "This girl has an extremely overprotective friend...I want his blessing before I ask her out officially."

I grab my practice gear from the pavement and stand. "How protective we talkin'?" This could potentially be a problem. Guys protect what they love. If the friend sees her as more than just a friend, there could be some bad blood for Todd, and issues for all involved.

He runs a hand over his freshly buzzed hair as he puts some distance between us. "Like, he's been known to threaten people's lives just for lookin' at her."

I shake my head, dropping my bag in the trunk. "That's tough, man, especially if you're not friendly with this guy."

"Oh, I'm friendly with the guy," he admits as he meanders to the trunk with his stuff.

"Who?" I go through a list of all our friends, trying to pinpoint one being protective over a girl.

"The girl? Or the overprotective friend?"

"Both, I guess." I shrug a shoulder as I head back to my door.

"It's uh...you know what? Forget I said anything." He stuffs his bag in my trunk, slams it shut then hustles around to the passenger seat.

I shake my head at him. Why is he chickening out now? "Don't be wuss, just tell me," I say as I start the engine.

He covers his mouth with his hand and stares out the window. Whoever this guy is, it's really bothering him. Or maybe he's afraid to admit who it is that he likes.

I maneuver my car out of the mostly empty lot just when his knee begins to bounce.

"You're the overprotective friend, and Audrey is the girl," he blurts as I hit the main drag leaving the campus.

I laugh. "Audrey doesn't date jocks, Todd. And why would I stop anyone from dating her? She's had dates before!" Somehow, I keep every emotion raging through my veins locked up tight.

He clears his throat. "Yeah, and all those relationships stopped because of you."

I shake my head at him. "I didn't threaten any of them or tell any of them to dump the other."

"When those guys got *Frozen Silk,* they all headed for the hills," he says carefully.

"She deserves someone who isn't a pansy," I defend. "The girl is smart as a whip, loves goin' muddin', and has a meaner left hook than most guys I know. If her boyfriend dumps her because I intimidate him that just proves how much he wasn't worth it to begin with. So, how's it my fault for weedin' out losers? Keep in mind, if I didn't scare them away, I'd likely be expelled for fighting long before now," I say, feeling winded from my rant. I do feel a bit better, but we're still talking about him wanting to date my Audrey.

Two more years. Two more years.

I guess it's less than two years, that's a bonus.

"You've got me there," he admits. "Will you be

alright if I ask her out?"

I pull to a stop at the sign, knowing I have the right of way since I'm turning right. But I sit there and glare my death stare towards one of my best friends. He holds it, nervously, but not backing down like I was hoping he would. "You can ask out whoever you want. But I'm tellin' you now, Audrey doesn't date jocks."

I let my words hang between us, clenching my teeth and heavy footing the pedal as different images flash in my head.

Todd kissing Audrey.

Audrey kissing him.

Them holding hands in the hallway.

Going to prom together.

Her jumping into his arms after we graduate.

Where does this leave me? The annoying third wheel? The *Frozen Silk* glaring at both of them forever?

I pull in front of my house and shut off the engine.

Todd clears his throat and painfully slow, he unbuckles. "See you...tomorrow." His breath comes out in shallow bursts. I glance to him, confused. His eyes are wide and skin is pale. I shrug and pop my trunk. It's not like I have time to ask him what's wrong, and to be honest, I don't care anymore.

As I walk through the grass to the front door, tires squeal behind me causing me to pause. My mom's Hundai barrels into the driveway sporting a new dent in the front fender. I stifle my groan that she'll want me to try to pop it out.

"Riley!" She yells, rolling down her window.

I drop my practice gear and jog to the car. "What's up, Mom?"

She glares at me. "I left my wallet on the table. I need my license and insurance information."

I point to the fender. "That why?"

She nods. "It was a coworker so we didn't make any calls yet but she told me to grab my crap and get back there. I'm still on my ten minute break. Hustle."

I run into the house and grab her wallet from the side table in the hallway.

"The flag isn't up, should I grab the mail?" I ask, handing her the wallet.

"No. I'll get when I get off this afternoon. Don't think about it again." She grabs a cigarette from the pack in the cup holder and lights it as she back out of the driveway again.

My stomach growls, reminding me that I need to make lunch for me and Hannah because Ted probably hasn't. I grab my gear and head inside again.

Chapter 5
Audrey

"Finish the report, Audrey. Just catch those sneaky words that are floating around up above your head, and get this done," I mumble aloud to myself.

Mrs. Devers assigned a brutal analysis paper this term. It was fairly open, we were given topics to choose from, and in those topics were multiple examples. I chose a near Freudian topic, "Analyze the qualities of a good role model *(parent, guardian, teacher, coach…)*."

I chose my parents. Sure, they can be annoying but they take care of me, my brothers, and my friends. They help out in the community, offer their free time to family members or friends, and they're good people. This is also one of those assignments I probably won't show them. Knowing my dad, he'd let it go to his head and strut around the house because he and Mom are my role models. Teens are supposed to hate their parents and look up to celebrities. I'll just let him think that Lzzy Hale from the band Halestorm is my idol like I've told him for the last few years.

My head falls to the desk with a thump. Why can't I

find the words? It's due tomorrow! I shouldn't have procrastinated. Mom always said that she waits until the last minute because it helps her "creative juices," while mine have all but left the building.

My cell phone rings, breaking the small amount of concentration I had. "Hello?" I grumble as I press it to my ear.

"Hey Aud, you got a second?" Riley asks.

"Yeah, Ri, what's up?"

He clears his throat. "Would you be able to baby sit Hannah Tuesday after school?"

I look up to my calendar above my desk, checking my work schedule. "You got practice right?" I ask as I find the right week and day. I work Monday, Wednesday, and Saturday this week.

"Yes. I'm not sure what my mom and Ted are doing. They just told me I'd have to miss practice to watch Hannah," he explains.

I try my hardest to tamp down my anger over his mother and Ted. "Kim has me off Tuesday. So, I'll head to your house-,"

"No, I'll go and pick her up after school, just meet me at the rink. You guys can hang out for practice if you want. I've done it before, but Coach was annoyed. I figure if someone else is there with her, Coach won't be brutal."

I click the lead on my pencil a few times before pushing the tip against the paper, shoving it back inside, and starting over again. "Not a problem." I didn't know he's had to take Hannah to practice with him before. He should've told me, I would've helped.

"Thanks, Audrey."

"Any time, Ri. I mean it," I promise.

"I know," he whispers. "Look, I gotta go, but I'll talk to you tomorrow, yeah?"

"Of course," I whisper. "Tomorrow."

I lean back in my desk chair, staring at the words on my paper until they blur into a grey blob.

This isn't the first time Riley's mom has told him he would have to miss hockey practice or games in order to watch Hannah. It's also not uncommon for him to have to bring Hannah with him over here or to the café I work at in town. I can't remember the last time Riley and I hung out that we didn't have Hannah with us.

For me, one thing that defines a good parent is taking care of your children. In that sense, Riley is a parent to Hannah, but who is a parent to Riley?

I tap my pencil on the side of my phone, listening to the tap of plastic on plastic.

Riley is counting down to the day he can move out and move on with his life. We have two years until graduation. Two more years of taking care of Hannah and himself and working hard to be sure he passes all of his classes so he can play hockey. The unspoken plan is that I go where he goes. I'm not sure if he realizes that what once was a joke between us is actually a life plan. I'd follow him to the ends of the earth. I'll stay by him even if that means watching him fall in love.

But.

Hannah is the most important person to him. His baby sister. She'll only be eight and half when we graduate. I'm not sure if he has a plan for her. But either way, eight and a half isn't old enough to take care of yourself. Neither is sixteen.

I'm here for Riley, but who will be here for Hannah? All she has to depend on is Riley and me. If we both leave, she'll be left to handle the stresses of her mother and Ted, and an absent father, all on her own.

I can't let that happen. Not to Hannah.

In a snap decision, I shove my report to the side and start up my laptop. There has to be some decent courses in one of the local community colleges that would be beneficial. Something that I can plan for and stay close to Hannah at the same time.

I create a new file titled *Hannah* and begin researching anything and everything I can find that might help either her or me. I'll never have a leg to stand on to adopt her, but I can be her friend. I'll always be her friend.

I glance to the clock. It'll be a long night considering I still have a paper to write.

I zip out of my biology class, rushing to my locker for my energy drink. Mr. Blum seemed far too excited about DNA structure, or whatever he was droning about. I couldn't focus on him or I would've fallen asleep. Hopefully, Riley won't mind if I sleep through lunch. Twisting the combination on my locker, I unlock it and lift the trigger. My energy drink, a beacon of light, sits proudly on top of my English folder. I grab them both and trudge toward the cafeteria.

This school needs an autowalk like the airports

have. It might be slower, but it would save me precious energy.

After weaving through the crowd to get to our table, I collapse into my usual seat in the corner. I lean my heated cheek against the cool table as I hug my drink, folder, and book for next period.

The chair next to me scrapes against the floor. “You look as tired as I feel,” Riley says, sitting in said seat.

“Mmhmm,” I mutter without opening my eyes.

“Take you all night to finish your book report?”

I snort lightly. “Yes. It wouldn’t have taken so long if you didn’t distract me.”

“How did I do that?”

“You got me thinking about the future,” I explain vaguely. I open one eye to look at him.

His brows furrow as his blue eyes search my face. “How did asking you to watch Hannah make you think of the future?”

I yawn. “She’ll only be eight when we graduate, Riley. If one of us stays here, she’ll have a better shot at surviving.”

He closes his eyes and lowers his forehead to the table. “So let me guess, you’ve concocted a plan of sorts?”

I close my eyes again. “You can say that.” My breath starts evening out and pretty soon the buzz of chatter in the cafeteria seems nonexistent, peaceful even.

The warning bell shrieks, jolting me awake. I elbow Riley, and together, we stand. While he takes a minute to stretch, I chug my energy drink and watch him. I'm not sure why he's so tired today, but it doesn't look as if that nap helped him much. If he wasn't so against energy drinks, I'd offer half to him.

I turn away from our table, and he follows suit, closing the distance beside me. We lightly lean against each other for mutual support of energy. It's been a while since he's been this noticeably tired.

"Hey, Sleepy Heads!" Todd sings as we round the corner.

Riley yawns, nodding to Todd and gently rubs his hand on my elbow before he squeezes into the crowd. His locker is a few feet away and our class is just across the hall, so I wait for Riley to return. "Hey, Todd," I mutter, unsure if he heard me, but not really caring either. I lean against the wall, lightly pressing my head to someone's locker.

"Audrey?" Todd asks as he pokes my arm to get my attention.

"I'm awake. Promise."

He clears his throat. "Would you go to a movie with me this Saturday?"

Movie group night sounds good. I open my eyes and smile to him. "Who all is coming and what will we see?"

He rocks on his heels, giving me a crocked smile. "Um, just you and me, and it's a surprise."

My eyes widen. "I, uh," I stutter in shock. Riley's best friend is asking me on a date?

"It's okay. You don't have to answer right now." He leans down and kisses my cheek, centimeters from my lips.

I gasp, jerking my head away from him.

A locker slams, grabbing my attention from Todd. I see a small built boy brutally collapse into a cheerleader. As she screams, Riley roughly shoves past another group of classmates before turning down the hall.

I turn my attention back to Todd. His eyes trail after Riley, frowning. "I've gotta go," I say harshly.

His attention focuses on me again. "I..." he holds his breath as he searches my face for something. "Catch you later."

I glare after him as he hurries in the opposite direction from where Riley went. Taking a calming breath, I walk to class, slumping in my seat. I can only pray Riley comes to class. He can't afford to skip. Not with being the captain of the team. If he were second-string, he might be able to get away with, but even then, I doubt it, Coach Page is pretty strict.

Curiosity bites me. I slip my report out and place it on my desk. Grabbing my book and folder, I sneak out of the class as the last of the students enter.

He's got to be around here somewhere. I stop off at Riley's locker and toss my stuff inside.

I walk through the near empty halls, knowing I should be back in English class, but needing to find Riley.

If I were Riley, where would I be?

I chew on my thumbnail as I skip down the stairs. Turning down the left hall, I stop at the gymnasium. The school is remodeling the bleachers in there this semester, so classes aren't held there. I chose weight training, so I don't have to have class outside, luckily enough.

Peering into the small rectangle window on the door, I spot Riley. He has his back to me, slapping shots into a practice net with a bag full of pucks at his feet.

I take a deep breath and quietly open the door, leaning against it so it silently clicks shut.

I'll let him get through the bag then I'll help him clean up and make sure he gets back to class so Coach doesn't slaughter him tonight.

He nudges the bag with his toe, spilling a few plastic pucks onto the floor, pushing them into a line and then shoots them toward the net. His wild shots clank against the cement wall a few feet behind the net, and his grunts almost turn to yells with each slap of his stick.

I take a few steps forward. I don't want to disturb him, but I don't like seeing him this way. He's always calm, calculating, and near deadly with his accuracy of the puck. He's really messed up over… something.

Chapter 6
Riley

I didn't think Todd would have the balls to ask her out in front of me.

If she says yes, I'll have no choice but to sit back and let it happen. Let her fall in love with someone else.

I growl and force my anger into my next swing. The puck completely misses the net, bouncing off the cement wall.

Audrey's not leaving this town. Yeah, she's trying to care for Hannah, but she's leaving me.

My hopeful heart drops and I kick the bag again, using the blade of the plastic stick to set up the new line of victims. Each puck has a different face.

My father.

For leaving us the way he did for another woman.

He gets another.

He broke my mother's heart to the point that she's

not even the same woman she was five years ago.

He started this domino effect of bullshit, and for that, he gets a third.

My mother.

For letting a man break her down so badly that she can't function properly.

She gets another.

She's forgotten that she's a mother. I'm not old enough to care for my baby sister properly, not in the parental way she deserves. I still need a mom, but at least I'm old enough to figure things out on my own.

My mother gets another puck just for hurting my baby sister by ignoring her like she does. It smashes into the wall.

Another puck with her face, because it's her fault that Audrey wants to stay here. Audrey can see that Hannah needs a mother. So why can't Mom see it?

I kick the bag again, lining up another row.

She gets one more, for bringing another man into our house, causing a whole different world of shit for us.

I tap a puck forward, glaring at it.

This one's for Ted.

I purposefully miss the net this time. Smashing the puck into the wall so hard I hear it crack as it rattles across the floor.

One more for Ted.

His alcohol addiction nearly ended everything I know and love in one night with his drunken rage.

My mother gets another puck. This one's for bringing the man that beat her, almost to death, in front of my baby sister last year back into our home. I purposefully crash it into the wall again.

I smash yet another into the cement wall.

For bringing the man who hit my baby sister because she wouldn't stop crying, back into our lives.

Todd.

For asking my Audrey out and kissing her.

My stick hooks around the last puck.

It gets my face.

For being a coward and not asking my girl to be my girl, for not telling her how I've felt for years, for lying, and for hurting her feelings. This puck gets my face for not being a stronger man and calling the police to press charges against Ted.

The puck glances off the post and flies my way.

On instinct, I drop to my knees so I don't get hit, and hear a soft gasp followed by an echoing thud of a body hitting the floor.

I spin on one knee and see Audrey on the floor. I drop the stick and scramble to her side.

"I'm sorry, I'm so sorry," I repeat, tears in my eyes from everything going on in my head and knowing I've hurt her physically, something I swore that would never happen. "Aud?"

Her hand moves from her forehead and her big brown eyes look up to my face, worry etched clearly in her soft features.

"I'm sorry. I didn't know you were here," I whisper and lightly run a finger close to her hairline, checking for a bump. Her eyes flutter closed and her lips part. I lower my face over hers. Emotions clog my throat; relief, fear, and everything else. I graze my lips across hers, something I've wanted to do for years.

I freeze when she freezes.

Her hand comes up, gripping my bicep as she pushes her lips against mine.

I sigh and weave my fingers in her hair.

"I'm sorry," I whisper against her mouth. I'm not sure whether I'm apologizing for hitting her with a puck or for not kissing her sooner.

Her eyes pop open, scanning mine. "Why do you keep apologizing?"

I sit back on my knees and help her up. "Lots of reasons. First, I just pucked you."

She smiles and sits up, crossing her legs. "Pucked or not, I'm not sorry I came to find you."

I smile. "Me too."

We both stare at the floor. The longer the silence stretches, the tighter my chest squeezes my lungs feeling like something akin to confusion and panic.

"What are you doing in here?" She asks. "Besides missing the net?"

I swallow roughly and shrug a shoulder in answer.

Picking herself up off the floor, she walks over to the puck that hit her. "Who is this?" she asks, holding the puck out for me to see. Somehow, she knew *exactly* what I was doing.

"Me," I answer.

She nods, pointing to the far wall. "Them?"

I glare at all of them, every single puck, broken or not, they still bare the faces of those intended. This time, they seem to be laughing at me.

"Class?"

I shrug. "I'll catch up tomorrow and do extra laps when Coach catches wind."

"Feel better?"

"I guess," I say, standing to pick up the mess I've made. Quietly, she helps round up the pucks.

I should talk to her about this, about why those pucks got faces.

What's her answer to Todd? Does she really like him? Did me kissing her mess things up between us or between them?

I peek over my shoulder at her. She's spinning the puck that hit her in her left hand while using her right to toss the pucks in the net. Her brows are pinched together and her lips are shaped into a thin line. It makes me wonder what she's thinking about.

I walk my handful over to the bag and start grabbing the ones she tossed into the net, too.

Two years.

They'll be the longest years of my life. No matter how much distance gets put between us, I'll fight for her.

She kicks a puck my way before sliding down the hideaway bleacher wall. Sitting directly across from me, she spins the stupid puck that hit her in the head.

I'll do anything for her. Even if it means letting her fall in love with my best friend until it's right, until it's our time.

Things have to remain normal between us, somehow.

She deserves more than I can give her now. Hell, I can't even promise Prom.

R

I push through the door, heading straight for the laundry room. "Hannah!" I yell as I pass the stairs.

A thump followed but feet slapping the hallway floor echo through the silent house. "Ri!" She squeals as she runs down the stairs.

"Hey Han, how was kindergarten today?" I ask as I swap the last load of laundry into the dryer. It's a relief, but I'll need to start doing a load a day so we don't get backed up again.

"Mommy said today was a lazy day," she yawns.

I freeze, hand on the knob. "What?"

"Yeah, Mommy said every girl is allowed lazy days.

That's why she's still in bed."

"Are you hungry?" I ask her, quickly changing the subject so I don't lose my cool in front of her. She doesn't need to witness anymore anger than she already has.

"Umm," she drawls as she twirls around the room. "Can I have ice cream?" she pauses and stares at me. Laying the cute on extra thick, slightly pouting and batting her eye lashes. I have no idea where she ever picked up that pleading face, but dammit, it's hard to say no to her enough as it is.

"What have you eaten today?" I ask, praying she had something decent.

The sweet smile on her face slips. "An oaty bar for breakfast and candy from the bag I hid from Mommy."

"Did Mom make you anything for lunch?"

She shakes her head and resumes twirling. "You don't cook on lazy girl days, Ri!"

I walk into the kitchen, following Hannah, who is now singing about today being her favorite day. Her giggles and sing-song voice reverberate in my mind. I pull the salad mix out of the fridge and a bowl from the cupboard. She needs some healthy food to counter the junk, or she won't sleep tonight. And that'll start drama that nobody wants.

"Hey, Han?" I ask, turning around with her salad in hand. "Wanna pick out a fork?"

She skips over to the drawer. "I think...today I'll use the yellow. Yellow means happy and lazy, isn't that right Ri? It's Mommy's favorite color."

I chew on my cheek, trying to smile at her cheeriness.

Audrey's right. Hannah needs one of us. She's so blinded with her innocence that she doesn't see how awful life actually can be. I don't want her to become jaded, and that'll happen if she has no one to save her.

"Ri, can you paint my toes yellow, too?"

I glance at her with my brow raised, and she lets the cute loose again. This is going to be a long night.

Chapter 7
Audrey

Riley kissed me.

As much as that makes me want to walk around with a stupid smile plastered on my face, it also confuses the heck out of me.

I push through the front door, hanging my keys on the hook by the door. "I'm ho-," I walk right into Billy. "Ugh, Billy! What are you doing?" His arm is raised, hand behind his head like he's sniffing his pit.

"Smell it!" He shouts, confirming my fears. I sidestep him, and back my way out of the living room. "No, I'm being serious!" The utter confusion and innocence on his face makes me want to stop. But it's his armpit, and I can tell by his clothes that he has yet to visit a shower. "I swear your brother gave me chick deodorant this mornin'! Smell like roses to you?"

I run for the hallway. "I am *not* smelling your pit, flowery or not, you sick hog!"

"I need a second opinion, Dahling!" He whines, following me.

I cut into my room and slam the door. “You smell Mahvelous!” I tease. Hoping he catches the Billy Crystal reference.

“I told you I smelled like a chick, Greg!” He thunders. “You expect me to pick up Sarah smellin’ like this?”

I giggle. Greg must have given him Mom’s deodorant.

I drop my bag onto the floor and flop on my bed. The puck in my pocket digs into my hip. I roll to my other side and dig it out. Rolling it between my fingers, I stare at it in fascination. This little plastic disc gave me my first kiss with Riley. I don’t have loads of experience, but it’s the best kiss I’ve ever had.

I just wish I knew if it meant something to Riley.

Why did he kiss me? Was it because he thought he hurt me? I spin the puck between my fingers, rubbing my thumbnail over the scratches on the sides. This hollow, plastic puck stung, but I think it’s mostly from the force of Riley’s shot.

I rub my forehead, feeling the still tender spot. I may end up with a bruise, but luckily it wasn’t a real puck.

Did Riley kiss me because Todd asked me out in front of him? Does he even care about that?

I could talk to Sarah about this, but she’d likely tell Billy and that would give him more ammo to tease me. Alice enjoys gossiping too much, I can’t talk to her about this. Half the school would know before school starts.

Glancing to my clock, I check how much time I have

before I have to head to the café. I've got about half an hour before I need to leave. I wish I could just sleep all evening.

If Candy wasn't away on vacation, I'd call her and talk to her about this. She's been my friend since fourth grade when she moved here, she's like Alice and likes to gossip, but she keeps secrets for me. And if it's anything to do with Riley, she won't breathe a word to anyone. She's terrified of him and thinks he's a brute. She'd probably tell me he meant to knock me out with a puck and that the kiss was just a hallucination.

I roll over and put the puck next to my Pittsburgh Penguins puck that the team signed two years ago, and the puck Riley, Todd, Rob, and Derrick signed as a joke.

It wasn't too long after the joke puck that the worst night of my life happened. Riley's team won that night. It was the one win that we didn't do our milkshake tradition. We went to Todd's party instead. Everything started off normal, fun even. Riley was enjoying himself with the team.

My mom had given me photos from the county game to give to Sue, Riley's mom, so I told Riley that I was going to pop over and give her the photos.

When I walked into that house, I thought death was circling like a vulture. I've never seen that much blood before in my life. And Hannah's little body...

I dropped the photos and screamed at the top of my lungs. I was rooted to the spot just inside the doorway. We still don't know how I ended up with blood on me.

I know Riley feels guilty, that he should've been there to protect them, should've pressed charges for his sister's sake. But it fell on Sue. She wouldn't push it, and told the doctors and police she didn't know who it was.

A shiver runs down my spine, resting in my lower back. I snatch my phone from my back pocket and send a quick text to Riley. A lone question mark. It's our code to see if the other is okay.

We came up with this when we each got our phones a few years ago, after his dad left and when my brothers were leaving for college. If he responds with a smiley face, he's good. Anything else would mean that I stop in after work and sneak around to the back yard, so we can talk behind the shed. If it were reversed, he would come over and meet me in the garage. Before we had our cars, it was more difficult to accomplish, but luckily we don't live too far apart.

Griping my phone in my hand, I get up and grab my work clothes from my drawer. I try to ignore the ache and tightness in my chest.

My phone beeps. *:) ? Riley*. I smile, thankful he's good. On a normal day, I'd probably send a frown, I feel like I need him. But we kissed today and I don't think I'm ready to talk about it yet. I'm not ready to hear about how he doesn't think I'm pretty or the kiss was a joke or sympathy. I'd rather pretend that it meant as much to him as it did to me. I respond with a smiley face and begin changing for work.

Work last night was easy, not many people showed up, and the ones who did were mostly there to work. That's one thing I like about working at Cuppa. People come in for coffee or tea and a muffin, but they stay to use the wifi or even read a book we have on the shelf.

"Mom, I'm gonna be late tonight," I say, grabbing

my key from the hook.

"Why?" She asks suspiciously.

I yawn. "Riley needs me to watch Hannah while he's at practice."

She spins around in her chair, fishing in her purse. "Here, get her something to eat. Wait, how about all of you come here after practice for dinner?"

"I'll ask Riley, but I'm not sure if they have to head home after practice or not."

She purses her lips and gives me the mean mama look, too. "I don't care what excuse Riley gives you, you make sure he and Hannah get here for dinner."

"Okay, I promise. I'll get them here for dinner," I say in shock. She smiles and turns back around to the papers on the table. I'm not sure what the big deal is, but I don't argue with Mom when she gives me that look. No one wins. "I'm headed out, love you!" I don't give her time to respond. I just pull the door shut behind me and hustle to my car.

A cool wind slaps me in the face when I step off the porch. I flip my hood over my head and pull the strings tight.

On my drive to school, I think about how I'm going to ask Riley to dinner. The kiss we shared shouldn't change anything between us. It's not a mistake, never a mistake, it's just...I don't know what to call it. I can't let things be awkward between us.

What if he tries to freeze me out? What if he doesn't? What if he didn't like the kiss?

The traffic light at the intersection turns to red, I

stomp my foot on the break pedal, screeching to a stop and holding my breath. I close my eyes for a second and breathe.

I really need to stop thinking while I drive.

When the light switches to green, I carefully make my way to school and park in my assigned spot. I grab my book bag and hustle to the doors so I'm not late.

I weave through the swarm of half asleep students to reach my locker. When I round the corner, Todd is leaning against it waiting for me. My steps falter and my brows furrow, but I walk to my locker anyway.

"Good morning," he greets me cheerfully.

"Morning, Todd," I smile politely.

He slides to the right so I can get in my locker. "Audrey, I know I said you didn't have to answer right away, but I was just wondering if you've given our date any thought..."

I swallow and hide my face behind the door to my locker, pretending to be busy switching books out. I might as well tell him the truth, at least the part I can tell him. "I'm sorry, Todd. I actually haven't thought about it."

His hand touches the small of my back, causing me to freeze, hand hanging in the air inches away from notebook.

"I hope you think about it today, I'll see you later on." He leans closer and his lips graze my neck.

I cringe and raise my shoulder as I jerk away from him and his overexcited lips.

"Hey Riley!" He says before I can respond. Those words stir two reactions inside of me: running far away, and jumping for joy. But instead, I turn in place and freeze when I see him.

"Morning guys," he says around a yawn, eyeing the two of us with his beautiful blue eyes. Todd is still standing too close for my comfort and his hand is still on my back. "You guys a thing?" he asks and nods to himself. "You look good together."

My heart sinks and tears begin to form in my eyes. I can practically feel Todd's glee by that statement. I don't even have to look at him to know that he's smiling. Spinning away from them both, I busy myself in my locker again and try to regain my composure.

This isn't Riley. He has never said that I look good with anyone, or at all. My eyes form slits. He doesn't get to kiss me and then *give me away* to his best friend. Not me. Not him. I turn away from my locker, fully preparing to lay into Riley.

"We do, don't we?" Todd states.

"Mmm," I hum through my tightly pursed lips.

Riley eyes me, gauging my reaction, finally. Whatever he sees, it makes him look away. "Aud, you still gonna watch Hannah tonight?"

I take a deep breath through my nose. "Yeah. My mom is demanding your and Hannah's presence for dinner tonight. You can't get out of it."

He swallows hard and nods. "We'll be there."

"See ya, Aud, I don't wanna be late," Todd whispers and kisses my cheek, the same way he did yesterday; so close to my lips and nose that I can smell his spearmint toothpaste.

I smile to him, tight lipped, silently saying *goodbye* and *go away* at the same time. One problematic boy at a time, I repeat to myself. My eyes float back to Riley. His hands stuffed in his pocket and he's rocking heel to toe. I have so much I *want* to say to him, but they're things I can't say.

If I could say anything, I'd say, "Yesterday I had the most amazing kiss of my life, because it was from you," or, "Why are you practically giving me to your best friend when I only want you?" But, these are things I can't say. We're friends, best friends.

"I'm sorry about yesterday," he says quietly, taking two steps closer to me. I look into his blue eyes, feeling like I'm sinking, drowning in the deep blue waters of his eyes. "You belong with...Todd. I'm sorry if I confused you."

My heart silently shatters into a thousand pieces. Something he'll never know. Because standing before him is his best friend; quiet, simple, and caring Audrey. The friend he's had for years.

"I'm glad someone is good enough for me," I whisper through my internal pain. "I was beginning to think you wanted me to be the next crazy, cat lady."

He smiles gently. "Never, you deserve more than cats. Maybe a ferret, they'd keep you on your toes by hiding your keys."

I force a short laugh and scrunch my nose. "But they smell worse than cats. How about chinchillas?"

And just like that, we're out of the high tide. Wading through calm waves, and I'm careful not to kick sand in his direction.

I'll add this wet sand to my mud as I wait for the next cleansing rain. I've got to rebuild my crumbling mask so I will welcome it when the time comes.

Chapter 8
Riley

I drop my head on my desk. *Really Riley? You had to tell her she should be with Todd?* Yeah sure, she should be happy. But, at least now things can't be any more awkward.

Being friends is one thing, a thing that I can handle. And I almost messed everything up yesterday. The fine line I've been walking along vanished and I let my emotions drive me.

I raise my head just an inch and drop it back down.

"Beating yourself up?" A small whisper comes from beside me.

I tilt my head to the side and crack an eye. Libby, Todd's ex-girlfriend is leaning towards me from her desk beside me. "Um. Actually I kind of am and you're interrupting me."

She purses her lips. "Wouldn't have anything to do with what Jenny told me happened in the hallway this morning, would it?"

I raise a brow. "What happened?"

Her mouth pops open. "Really?" she glances around the room and taps her long fingernails on her desk. "Jenny said you were *right* there and they were making out."

I roll my eyes. "No one was making out with anyone."

Her eyes form slits. "Jenny is so gonna get it after this class." Her cheeks puff out and her breath blows in my face, cinnamon toothpaste. My stomach turns. I hate cinnamon. "So, they weren't kissing," she shrugs, "why are you so bent out of shape then?"

Ignoring her, I shift my head so I'm looking at my desk again and close my eyes. Going over coach's drill systems in my head, I weakly pray it's enough to keep me calm throughout the day.

Reverse breakout, puck dumping, and back checking zip through my head. Slowly, I feel myself falling back into normalcy. Nothing matters. Just the game. Just the ice. Just hockey. And that's a feeling I can live with. I can focus on my classes now, because doing well in classes means I'll have open availability for time on the ice.

That's what matters.

When I walk into the cafeteria, Todd is sitting in my seat next to Audrey. Instantly, all the anger, annoyance, and pain returns with enough force to shatter my thinly veiled peace.

Hockey.

Ice.

Wide lateral crossovers, left - right - left - slide...

Audrey smiles at Todd. Not just any smile, one of her real smiles, my favorite smile. It's the kind of smile that exposes her teeth and dimple, and ignites her brown eyes in a blaze of happiness. Todd's hands are going a mile a minute, probably as fast as his mouth. But what stops me dead in my tracks is her laugh. I hear the joyous sound over the chatter of everyone complaining about the quality of food or gossiping about anything and everything. Her laugh fills my heart with happiness and disappointment at the same time.

Someone bumps into my shoulder, jostling me. I turn my attention to them and glare.

"Sorry Silk," the kid mutters.

"Yo, Silk!" Todd yells.

Swallowing my emotions, I cross the cafeteria.

"Hey Ri," Audrey says with a smile when I drop into the empty seat across from her.

I take in her smile, allowing it to thaw me out some. "Hey, Aud."

She frowns. Apparently I didn't thaw enough to speak yet.

Todd smacks his hands on the table. "Don't let up on me tonight, Silk. I need to make the crazy saves, we play Tornados this week."

"I know who we play," I snarl at him. "Don't worry. I have no plans of lettin' up on you at all."

Todd's jaw ticks before he looks back over to Audrey. "We're away this week, you coming?"

She looks over to me, almost as if she's asking for

permission with the pleading in her eyes. "I wouldn't miss it."

Todd puts his arm around her and smiles to her. "My good luck charm," he says quiet enough that I barely heard it over the chatter echoing in the cafeteria.

I crack my fingers and count to twenty in my head, just to keep myself from ripping his arm out of socket.

This is what's best for her.

I grind my teeth and curse my father, his new wife, my mother, Ted, and myself. Closing my eyes, I run through the systems again. It worked earlier. I can only hope it works again.

Audrey clears her throat. "I always come to Riley's games."

My eyes fly open.

"Yeah, but I'm hoping that pretty soon you'll celebrate with me after a win," Todd says, hopeful.

"Out of the question," she argues with him, but locks eyes with mine. A second of silence passes between us. I thank her with my eyes, and she tells me I'm stupid to think otherwise.

"I'm gonna go grab some food," I say quickly. I don't want anything else to be said. I don't want to see any more of them together. Space will help me bring my calm back.

Hockey, I repeat on my way to the line. Hockey is the most important thing. Hockey is my life, hockey won't let me down. The ice is my only friend.

But even as the thought passes, I know it's a lie.

Audrey is my friend. And I keep messing up. I should be happy she's giving Todd a chance. That's what needs to happen. My feelings don't matter.

The ice matters.

The puck matters.

The game matters.

But dammit, Audrey matters, too.

A flash of pink and blue grabs my attention on the other side of the cafeteria. Libby waves and smiles at me as she heads my way. Apparently I look like I need company. Someone lets out a loud whistle toward the back, and Libby freezes about three feet away from me. Her face is stricken, almost with pain. I follow her gaze, back to my table.

Todd has his meaty paw resting on Audrey's cheek. Audrey's eyes are closed, lips puckered and parted. Her eyes pop open, and an instant blush creeps over her cheeks.

I see red.

Not thinking, I react. I shove a body out of my way, step on an empty chair, launching myself over a table. Weaving through chairs and people, I make my way back to the table. Me and Audrey's table.

Not his.

"I can't believe you'd be that moronic to kiss a girl who is barely interested in you!" Audrey shouts. I slow down a fraction but don't stop. "Todd, please just leave me alone."

"You're joking," he accuses.

“If I was joking I’d say, ‘A wrestler, a hockey player, and a quarterback walk into a bog. Which one comes out first? Obviously the wrestler because the quarterback is looking for a ball and the hockey player lost his stick....’ But I’m not joking, Todd. And that was not okay.”

I clear my throat, gaining a glare from Todd. His is no match for mine, I ice him out. “Leave her alone.”

A muffled sob breaks the silence, and slowly, everyone around us begins chatting again.

Todd stands. “This is your fault,” he seethes, pointing at me. “She can’t see anyone ‘cept you. And you don’t have a big enough stick to keep her in your net.” He storms around the table, walking straight at me.

My vision fogs as rage reignites. “She’s not a puck, Todd.” He slams his shoulder into mine as stalks passed me. I wobble and spin, ready to go after him. But a soft hand lands on my arm, keeping me from going after him.

“Riley, don’t,” Audrey says quietly. “Just...let it go.”

I won’t let it go. I make that promise to Todd’s retreating form. I won’t let this go, he’ll find out at practice. “You okay?” I ask her.

She nods and turns around, walking back to the table. “I’m fine, Riley. Not the first time I’ve defended these lips.”

“So that’s not the first time you’ve followed a kiss with a bad joke?”

She laughs. Actually laughs. “I’m sure I’ve got enough bad jokes to cover the rest of the bad kisses.”

I let her laugh soak into my pores. That's what I was missing earlier. The easy friendship with her not this complicated and awkward stuff. Hockey is my life, but so is Audrey and Hannah. So, that's what it'll be from now on. No messing this up. It can't happen.

R

I slip my key into the lock and throw the door open. "Hannah! Let's go!"

Silence greets me.

"Hannah!?" I shout louder, praying our mom didn't forget to pick her up again.

"She's coming!" Mom yells from somewhere upstairs. "We'll be late, fend for yourselves for dinner, Baby Boy."

"Not a problem, Mom," I say with as little annoyance as possible.

Hannah's footsteps barrel down the hallway, easing my worry. "Riley!" She sings as she skips down the stairs, blonde curls bouncing with her momentum. "Can I sit with Mister Page again?"

I smile and lift her in fragile little body into my arms and shift her to my hip so I can relock the door. "Nope." Her smile falls.

"I made him mad with all my questions didn't I?" she pouts.

I chuckle. "Maybe, but you're sitting with Audrey."

She squeals and hugs my neck. "I love Audrey!"

"Well, you'll be happier to know, we're having dinner with her, Miss Denise, and Mister Paul tonight, too."

Her squeals turn into high pitch shrills. Thankfully, I reach my car and let her hop into the backseat. "Is it my birthday? This is the best day ever! I should've worn my new dress Mommy got me," she rambles on and on from the time we leave the driveway and the whole way to the rink.

Audrey is going to have fun with her this afternoon. I think Mom let her have too much sugar, too. I can barely keep up with her words. Something about shopping at Mom's work and some girl teasing her and Mister Paul promising checkers. But it's all jumbled and doesn't make much sense to me.

Audrey waits for us at the doors, and Hannah starts running, dragging me along by my hand. Rambling about how much fun her and Audrey are going to have. Audrey's eyes grow a bit wide, taking in all of Hannah's excitement.

"Sorry. I have no idea how you're going to get her to listen," I whisper into her ear.

She winks. "It's a girl's secret. Have fun out there."

She has no idea just how much fun I'm about to have. I grin at her. "It'll be a blast."

She raises a single eyebrow at me, while tugging Hannah towards the seats. "You're actin' kinda creepy, Ri."

I laugh. It's all I can do. She has no idea that I'm about to give Todd what he deserves after the stunt he pulled in lunch. Things are about to get *fun*.

Chapter 9
Audrey

My mommy says that brown eyed people are full of a bad word that I can't say," Hannah says mid-ramble.

I chuckle. "Well, in some cases that can be true. I've heard that blondes are airheads, but not all people with blonde hair are airheads are they?"

She giggles. "I don't have any air in my head! How can you get in air in there?"

I hand her a crayon. "That's right, you're a smart girl. Want to help me draw a picture for Mister Paul?"

She begins to squeal again, but this time I clamp my hand over her mouth to muffle it. Coach Page keeps glaring our way. She looks up at me with her big blue eyes, and I remove my hand. "Sorry, I'll do better."

I wink. I don't believe her, she's a squealer. But she's cute as a button.

As she's preoccupied with drawing a picture for my dad, I pull out my notebook and begin studying for tomorrow's math test.

Guys start filtering out of the locker room, gracefully taking to the ice and gliding through stretches. My eyes find Riley's tell-tale blonde locks that peek out from under his helmet. He lifts his stick with both hands and pushes it behind his neck as he breezes along the ice on one foot.

Even from all the way up here, I can see his smile. He's a different person when he's on the ice. He's at peace there.

Sure he has his scary look, quick on his feet, and a wicked shot record, but he's happy on the ice. It's where he's meant to be.

He follows the boards, skating with the curve, round behind Todd and another guy who are setting up the net. Todd freezes and from here it looks like he's saying something. But he's not loud enough or I'm not close enough. Riley's stick connects with Todd's face as quick as lightning. The clap echoes through the arena.

My mouth drops.

Riley tosses his stick and gloves and launches himself over the net, fists connecting with Todd's face. Both scream with rage.

I shield Hannah's eyes. She doesn't need to see her big brother beating the crap out of their neighbor.

"What's going on?" Hannah complains.

"Nothing," I whisper and shush her. The last thing I need is for her to be on the other side of the emotion spectrum.

A whistle shrills. "What do you think you two are doing?" Coach screams, jogging across the ice in his sneakers. "Riley, locker room. Now. Todd, go clean up."

Riley flips the chin strap off and yanks his helmet off, smacking it off the boards as he gets close to the gate.

Todd moves slower, and when he turns around to head to the gate, I spot blood on his face. He glances up to me. I quickly look away, back down to my notes.

Thankfully, Hannah doesn't ask any questions about what happened.

"Do you have a green?" She requests, delighted. "Mister Paul says green is his favorite color. I want to make everything green!"

I smile and hand her the small pack of crayons. Focusing on her should be easy, it's what I'm supposed to do.

I can't ignore the nagging feeling in the pit of my stomach. Riley attacked Todd. He'll likely be pulled from this week's game. Not to mention in trouble with the school.

He's an idiot.

My anger skyrockets.

Violence? He's against it. He doesn't solve problems with his fists. He solves them with his words. Always has.

But things change.

I drop my head to my hands.

"Does Bonkey's have green colored strawberry snow cones?"

"I'm not sure honey, maybe."

What's going through his head right now?

Is he worried about Hannah seeing him attack Todd? Is he worried about the game? Me? Is he even thinking?

Hannah giggles. "My unicorn has two horns."

I tilt my head to look at her. She's completely oblivious to the violence her brother displayed. Perfectly content with coloring a picture for my dad. A green unicorn eating green snow cones, while sitting on a green bench. She signs her name at the bottom, missing an n, but perfectly clear and legible.

"Can I make one for Miss Denise, too?" She asks, batting her long lashes.

"You're too cute for your own good, Han," I say as I tear another page out of my notebook. "Do you remember Miss Denise's favorite color?"

She looks out to the ice, twirling the green crayon in the air like a wand. "Orange. But not during hockey season!"

"That's right," I say and lightly clap my hands. "Now, do you remember what it is when it *is* hockey season?"

"Hmm..." she putters, twirling the crayon in the other direction now. "Yellow?"

I nod. "Good job!"

"Yeah, I knew that," she says sassily, giving me her "duh" look. "It's my mom's favorite color, too."

"What are you going to color for Miss Denise?"

She looks down at the blank page. “Me of course, I have yellow hair! But I’ll have to use other colors for her picture too.” She pouts. “Will she still like it?”

“I’m sure she’ll love it,” I promise. And she would, she displays all of Hannah’s artwork on the fridge, just like she used to do for me and my brothers. Even when Hannah’s given her crafts from preschool and so far this year from kindergarten. My mom keeps them all. She said she’ll save them for when she’s old enough to appreciate them. I think my mom just doesn’t want to end up with empty nest syndrome. I’ll be graduating in two years.

At least I won’t be leaving home. I’m staying.

Hannah starts singing quietly about rainbows and farting, flying unicorns.

I’m staying for her.

A

“Come on, let’s get this over with,” Riley shouts as he climbs the stairs two by two.

I scramble, trying to collect the crayons and my math notes. “How’d it go?”

He makes a noise in the back of his throat. “You saw what happened. How do you think it went?”

I clamp my lips together and help Hannah get her coat back on. “You wanna ride with me Han?”

“Can I Ri?” She pleads, yanking on the bottom of his hoodie.

“I don’t care, Han. Come on, let’s get goin’,” he

says, ushering her out the door.

I follow Riley, Hannah gripping my hand, out to his car for her booster.

He doesn't have to be a jerk to me, I didn't do this.

He did.

He slips his key in the lock, leans down and pops the trunk. "Back doors are unlocked, just set the booster on the seat and she can buckle herself."

"I know, Riley. This isn't the first time I've had Hannah in my car," I snap, rolling my eyes. I reach in the backseat and grab the booster. "Come on Hannah, I'm parked over this way."

She glances between us quickly before running back to my side. With her gripping my hand, and me lugging her booster, I storm, as quickly as Hannah's little legs will allow me to go, to my car.

Jerk. That's what he is. A big, hairy jerk!

I grumble unintelligibly as we hustle to my car.

Dish me attitude for something I wasn't a part of, I'll show him. Dinner will be a nightmare; pepper on everything and salt in his tea!

I don't even care that it's juvenile and will only piss him off. He deserves it.

Yanking the back door open, I drop the booster in.

"Audrey?" Hannah whispers as she climbs in.

"Just buckle up, we'll be at my house before you know it." When she's sitting on her booster and buckling, I shut the door and get in behind the wheel.

"Are you and Riley going to break things like Mom and Ted?" She asks as I turn the key in the ignition.

I glance in the rearview mirror. She's frowning out the window.

"No sweetie. Breaking things isn't the way to handle disagreements." The words are out of my mouth before I even think. I've basically just said her mother and Ted don't handle disagreements well. It's the truth, but she's six. She doesn't need to see how wrong her mother is or have anyone tell her those things.

"I know. Riley says they communic-ate wrong."

Riley's car zooms out of the lot, and I follow him at a slower speed. I turn on the radio so I don't think too hard and miss a light.

Hannah sings happily to every country song that comes on. She doesn't know all the words, but she tries.

We pull onto my street and park in the grass. Riley slams his driver side door, harder than necessary. My anger towards him simmers.

"Ready to get some grub, Han?" I ask her, ignoring Riley.

"Do you have my pictures?" she whispers.

I nod and pat my bag. "Safe and sound."

She sprints to the front door and pushes it open. "I'm here!" she yells.

I can't help but smile after her.

"Hey, Punkin!" My dad coos and lifts her up for a monster hug.

“Hey guys!” My mom sings from the kitchen.

Riley walks over and kisses her cheek. “Thanks for inviting us for dinner, Miss Denise.”

She smacks at him with her wooden spoon while sporting a cheesy grin. “Enough suckin’ up. Sit and tell me about your day.” She then glances to my dad who is tickling Hannah. “Did you see that Paul? Riley is a gentleman, and kissed me when he walked through the door.”

My dad sighs dramatically and hoists Hannah to his shoulders, eliciting squeals and giggles. “I’m sorry, baby,” he tells my mom and pecks her lips.

She pecks him back a few times.

“Gross,” I mutter.

“Young lady, you don’t know how happy that makes me. Kisses still gross you out!” My dad bounces, jostling Hannah, and she death clutches over his eyes.

“I’ll be right back,” I say, exiting the kitchen, heading for my room.

“How was practice, Riley?” my mom asks.

I close my door before he responds. Digging in my bag, I pull out Hannah’s drawings before chucking it to my bed. The weight of my books hitting the mattress causes the bag to bounce and rattle my headboard and a puck rolls to the floor.

Using my foot, I stop its momentum and pick it up. It’s the puck Riley hit me with.

He kissed me.

Todd kissed me.

He beat the snot out of Todd.

No wonder he doesn't want to talk to me about this.

I place the puck next to my others and change my shirt like I originally planned to. I am talking to Riley tonight. Either here or I'll sneak out later to talk to him. This...whatever it was or could be, we need to talk about it. There's no other option I'm willing to consider at this point.

Closing my eyes and taking a deep breath, I exit my room.

Chapter 10
Riley

I watch Audrey walk out of the kitchen, her hips sway gently, and I close my eyes against the image. Why am I looking at her hips? She's leaving me with her happily married parents. I should focus on that. A small part of me hates her for having happy parents.

But that's not right either. I could never hate Audrey. And I'd never wish Denise and Paul to split.

"How was practice, Riley?" Denise asks me, brushing her soft brown hair away from her eyes.

"It wasn't terrible," I offer. "Worked over the goalie pretty good." It's not a lie. I just don't say *how* I worked him over.

"Well, that's always good. Todd needs a good work out," she says, stirring the noodles in the pot. "Paul? Can you set the table please? And find out if Greg is coming home for dinner?"

"I'll get the table," I offer, standing to reach for the cabinet with the plates.

"Thank you, hon," she says to me. "Paul? Call Greg?"

"On it!" He hollers back from the living room.

I pull out six plates just in case Greg shows up. Spinning around to go back to the table, I freeze. Audrey's walking back in, wearing an almost see through pale yellow Pittsburgh Penguins tee. I clear my throat and work to remember what I'm doing with plates in my hands.

"I'll get the parm and drinks," she says quietly as she passes me. "Tea good for everyone?"

"I'll pour myself some wine, love," her mom answers.

"I'll just have water," I say without looking at her.

I set the plates in a stack in front of me and begin placing one on each mat. Warmth brushes my shoulder as Audrey sets a wine glass at her mother's seat and the parmesan cheese in the center of the table. I hurriedly place the rest of the plates so I'm not in her way any more.

Before I kissed her, the attraction was easier to ignore. It was just a kiss, that's all.

That's all it can be.

I pull the forks from the drawer and wait until Audrey's done with the drinks before setting them out.

"Mom? How much longer?" She asks.

"Probably have another fifteen minutes or so."

"I'm going out to the garage. I'll be back in time for

dinner." She rushes out the backdoor.

"Can't keep that girl away from the garage," Denise mutters. "You can go out, too. Hannah will be fine with Paul."

I nod. I know they can take good care of Hannah. But I don't know if Audrey will want company.

As I sluggishly reach the backdoor, Hannah comes barreling in.

"Miss Denise! I made this for you!" she squeals in delight.

"Oh, baby girl! That's beautiful! I'm going to put it right here with the others," Miss Denise carries on with her.

I pull the door shut and waltz into their mudroom. Blue floors and tan walls between the windows. The door to the garage closes as I open the screen door, and wind whips around, blasting me in the face, reminding me that winter snow is on the horizon. I pull my hood up over my damp head and shove my hands in the pocket of my sweatshirt.

The light flicks on in the garage, giving the grass a golden hue and shadowing the side of the garage.

I pause just outside the door and look in through the hazy window and sheer curtain.

Audrey's sitting reverse on her ATV with her head in her hands. I don't know what she's thinking. I wish I did.

Suddenly, she hops off and shoves the socket kit off the workbench. Cracks and clangs muffle her angry shout, but I still hear it. I hear the hurt and anger in her yell.

She grabs a wrench off the hook in front of her and sends it sailing to the back, towards the cement wall.

If she doesn't stop now, she's gonna get hurt or break something. I push the door open. It creaks louder than I remember.

Audrey's hands grip the edge of the workbench and she hangs her head as her back heaves with her heavy breath.

"You okay?" I ask quietly.

Her breath leaves her sharply, almost sounding like a snort, as one shoulder rises in a half shrug.

"I'll take that as a no. Wanna talk about it?" I sit sideways on the seat of her ATV.

She sniffles and shakes her head.

"Okay, I'll start," I say with a tired sigh. "I'm sorry for being a dickhead after practice. Coach is letting it go for now and put Todd and I on watch. One slip up and we're pulled from the game. We also have to complete these insane partnering exercises during the next practice. It means I have to get along with Todd when right now all I want to do is rip his head off." I stop myself there, cracking my knuckles to release some of my anger.

"Do you know what Hannah asked me?"

My brows furrow. "No, I was in my car and you two were in yours."

"She asked if you and I were going to break things like your mom and Ted." She sniffles again.

"I-I'm sorry," I say, stunned. Why would Hannah ask such a thing?

"We aren't those people," she whispers, finally turning to face me. Her cheeks are red, darkening her freckles and her eyes are filled with tears that I know she's working hard to not let them fall. "You and I aren't the kind of people that fight, with nasty words or our hands."

I swallow. "I know."

"Riley, what is going on with us? One kiss and it's too much for either of us to handle..." Her chin begins to quiver. "I'm trying to pretend it didn't happen, but I can't forget it."

"I don't want you to," I say stupidly.

"That doesn't help."

I stand and gently place my hands on either side of her face. "Audrey, I just need to get through high school-,"

"Stop it." She bats my hands away. "Riley, you are my best friend." She glances around the garage, focusing on something I don't care to see. "We need to talk about this."

My heart rate rises. I can feel it and hear it. The beats echo in my ears as my breath quickens. "Talk. Why?"

"Why did you kiss me in the first place?" she whispers.

My vision blurs.

Lie.

Lie to her.

My brain begs me to lie to her.

My stomach churns and twists.

We don't talk about this stuff. Why is she making me do this now?

Every texture, scent, sight, and taste fogs over, becoming duller than it was moments ago.

Everything is gray.

"Because...I don't know," I manage to say through heavy breaths.

Better than nothing, but still a dirty lie.

Her outline moves further away. Or maybe I'm moving further away.

"Riley, what do you need?"

"You."

R

"I think he'll be okay, Aud. You did the right thing," Miss Denise says softly.

"He probably didn't eat enough today or-,"

"That has to be what happened!" Audrey interrupts her dad. "He skipped lunch today."

"Why on Earth would he do that? He knows how important sustenance is to athletes," Mister Paul scolds.

"He was...angry," Audrey answers in my defense.

"What happened?"

"Well, it's nothing really. It's completely stupid," she rambles.

"Out with it," Miss Denise interferes.

"I'm awake," I interrupt her, so she doesn't have to rehash anything yet. "What'd I miss?" I try for humor.

Audrey's eyes close as she sags into the chair.

"You fainted," Miss Denise says.

"Blacked out, Denni. He's a guy. Guys don't faint," Mister Paul corrects her.

She rolls her eyes at him. "Fine. Riley, you *blacked out*. Audrey made sure you didn't hit your head. Are you feeling okay now?"

The tightness in my chest returns. I nod, indicating I'm fine, regardless. "We can eat if it's ready, I'm starving," I say, going with Mister Paul's theory. I'll talk about anything, just not feelings. "Where's Hannah?"

"With Greg in the kitchen, they're eating already," Mister Paul replies. "Be thankful Denni makes enough to feed an army or you'd be out of luck for grub."

I smile. "Thank you for having us over."

"Go eat," Miss Denise orders.

As we eat, Greg tells us about his day and then tells us about his evening with Billy and Sarah. Apparently Sarah is trying to set Greg up on a blind date. But Greg thinks it's payback for the deodorant swap, that's a story I've yet to hear about.

"Where's the sponge?" I ask, standing in front of

the sink, ready to wash dishes.

Miss Denise stares at me blankly. "You don't have to do the dishes here. It's Greg's turn tonight. Why don't you get Hannah ready? I'll get a bag together for both of you."

I raise a questioning brow, but she says nothing, just busies herself around the kitchen.

I walk into the living room and find her curled up on Mister Paul's lap as he's catching up on sports highlights.

"What's the Ravens?" She asks.

"A football team. We don't like them," he answers, only half paying attention.

"Who do we like?"

"Steelers, but this week we're cheering for the Cardinals."

I smile. She's always trying to learn things about Audrey's parents. "Han, find your shoes."

She groans. "I'll do it. But I *really* don't want to leave."

"You'll be back before you know it," I offer.

"Tomorrow?" she asks, pulling her cute out in full force.

"Probably not, but soon," I promise.

She sighs dramatically and meanders to the front door to put her shoes on.

"Riley," Audrey says. "This bag is for you, and the

pink purse inside is for Hannah."

I take the bag from her and look into her eyes. "Thanks. For…everything."

"Ain't no thang," she teases with a wink. "Drive carefully, and I'll see you tomorrow."

"Careful's my middle name," I promise.

This easy conversation, I can handle.

We say our goodbyes, and I wrestle Hannah into the car.

The tightness in my chest lets up and I feel like I can breathe again. If Audrey ever figured out just how messed up I really am, she'd probably never talk to me again out of fear. I used to have a grip on myself. Somewhere along the line, I lost it.

I have two years to get it back in check. Two years to repair myself. Two years to repair things between Audrey and me. And two years until I can say goodbye to the people who caused it all to begin with.

As Hannah gets herself buckled, I peek in her bag from Miss Denise; granola bars, trail mix packets, two juice boxes, and a bracelet making kit. I smile, she'll love that. Inside of mine is Gatorade mix, granola bars, trail mix packets, and two tickets to a Pittsburgh Penguins game. I fish around in the bag and feel another piece of paper.

I've cleared it with your coach, you can miss practice the day of the Pens game. I just need you and Hannah to meet us here after school. Your mom and Ted are okay with you and Hannah joining us. I think you'll remember what the day is, it's Audrey's birthday. Your presence is the only present that would make our present of the game better. Keep this a secret. It's a surprise.

Denni & Paul

I'll have to check my stash from the summer to see if I have enough to get her something else.

I actually forgot about her birthday.

Dropping my head back into the headrest, I internally beat myself up. How could I forget about her birthday?

The tightness in my chest returns as I pull away from her house but it's dull enough to ignore this time.

Chapter 11
Audrey

I rush into Cuppa's, trying not to disturb anyone from whatever they're working on.

"You are one minute late Audrey Jacobs," Alice clucks.

I swipe my card into the register to clock in. "I know."

"That's one minute less we can pick out what you're wearing on your birthday."

"I keep telling you, I'm not doing anything special for my birthday."

"You're turning seventeen, Aud. You didn't have a party for your sixteenth, you wouldn't let me give you a makeover, *and* you refused to allow me to give you your present until *after* school was over." I roll my eyes. "Just let me pick out your outfit for the day this year. Please? I promise, if you let me choose your outfit, I'll go," she messes up her face and shakes her hands by her sides dramatically. "I'll go muddin' with you."

"Maybe."

Her mouth pops open. "I suggest something I think is disgusting for something you think is ridiculous, and I get a maybe?"

"Well, it would be amusing to watch you cry because of all the mud, but I'm not a fan of your taste in clothes," I counter.

"I'm not a fan of your taste in boys, but I let you have them without insulting you," she snaps.

I smirk. "That's only because your taste in boys have paper thin personalities and mine can hold their own out of a magazine."

"One more, Aud. One more jab and only because your birthday is coming up."

I smile, knowing I've won this round. She won't be thinking about ways to get me into whatever dress she's picked out for me. "Hmm...if I only get one, I'd better make it good one then."

She narrows her eyes and taps her fingers on the counter.

"Don't you have dishes to wash?" I ask, pointing to the mixing blades and carafes.

She huffs. "Don't think too hard, your head might explode."

I busy myself stocking the teas, straws, and lids, while I think of another way to tease her. Unfortunately, I keep thinking about how today Riley seemed so normal. For days we've had this awkward tension. But today, he came into school happy as a pig in mud, and joked with me like normal. It's hard to believe that just last night he had, what I thought was an anxiety attack that knocked him out.

One minute I'm having a nervous breakdown, fearing what else Hannah thinks or has seen, as well as the weirdness of Riley and me. And the next, he's barely breathing, telling me he needs me, and then crumpling to the floor.

But today he was normal.

A straw pegs me in the side of the head.

"Audrey?!"

"What?" I snap, picking up the straw.

"I've only been trying to get your attention for the last ten minutes," she informs me as I glance to the clock. "Okay. Two. Still. Wake up. We've got wardrobe planning to do."

I take a deep breath. "Fine. You come muddin' with me on a day of my choice *and* let me pick your outfit for that, and you can choose my birthday clothes."

She uses a cloth to dry a carafe and glances at me. "You have a deal."

I hold my right hand out and she grips it with hers.

"Sisters before misters," we say in unison, sealing our deal.

She won't have much time to come up with something hideous. I'm counting on that she can't find something ridiculous before Friday.

I glance to the magazines and store flyers she has spread out across the counter. Dresses and heels on every page exposed.

I'm in for it.

Clearly I've underestimated how hideous her taste is.

A

"Where's the call on that?!" I shriek, slamming my hand against the boards.

"Dude, you're embarrassing," Alice hushes me and grabs my arm to pull me back to my seat.

I glare at her. "Did you *see* that? It was tripping!"

She rolls her eyes. "For the love of all things *pink*, can you please, for two seconds, focus on me and not the ice?"

My top lip curls in disgust at her emphasis on "pink." "I told you, meeting me here was pointless, especially if we-, *Get the puck!* - win because Riley and I have a tradition." I tune her out, focusing on the player change. Riley and Allen hop over the wall as two second-stringers scoot through the door. *"Silk!"* I shout, starting a chant amongst the rest of the Warriors here.

He glides across the ice with deathly focus on the Tornado with the puck. His shoulder slams into the opponent's, who loses his stick from the force. Riley hooks his stick around the puck, pulling it into his control, and sailing down the ice.

"Go! Go! Now! Score!" I shout, hopping out of my seat for a better view.

"I honestly don't know why I bothered."

"No one's keeping you here," I remind her. Riley passes to Rob, Rob passes to Riley, Riley shifts around his opponent, gaining on the net. He fakes a shot that lurches my heart into my throat, the puck skids into Humphrey's stick, and he passes back to Rob.

"Take the shot!"

Rob circles back, shifting positions with Allen, before sending the puck to the back board behind the net. Riley receives the puck and barrels toward the net minder, dropping the puck in front of Allen.

My lungs fill with anxiety and my heart feels like it stopped.

Allen hooks the puck, pulls back his elbow, and flicks his wrist. The light flashes and the ref blasts his whistle.

I scream, jump, and slam the boards with both hands.

"Oh my god, Aud. You're the *loudest* one here!"

"I don't care! They scored!"

"Remind me to never watch the old guys on ice with-,"

"Old guys?"

"Yeah, you know...the old guys, in suits? You watch them all winter long on your TV?"

I burst out laughing. "You really have no idea do you?"

She rolls her eyes. "How about we talk about what color we're painting your nails when we get back to your house?"

I slant my eyes. "No. Hockey."

"Tomboy," she mutters.

I ignore her and look back to the ice. Todd's mask is facing me. That can't be right. If he's looking at me, he's not paying attention to the puck.

Tornado's win the face-off. Four on four formation with a Tornado in control of the puck.

And Todd is staring at me?

"Minder!" I scream, hoping Todd hears me.

Double-taking, he braces himself for the impact of the puck that's heading straight for his chest. Lucky for him, he blocks the shot, and smacks the puck away from the Tornado in front of him. Rob hooks his stick and passes to Troy, everyone on the ice shifts into overdrive, heading toward Tornado territory.

"Idiot!" I swear if he causes us the game, he won't have to worry about what Coach says. I'll kick his ass and then maybe even run him over with my four-wheeler.

"You realize none of that was silent, right?" Alice interrupts me.

I blink at her. "And I care?"

She laughs at me. But I tune her out again and glance to the clock.

"Go!" I yell.

Rob passes to Riley, Riley shoots from the hash mark and the lights flash. I launch out of my seat. "We won!" I scream and clap my hands on the boards. Since we aren't on home ice, I'm not in my regular spot.

Riley sails down the ice, heading for Todd, but falters when he sees me. He pops the chin strap off and his mouth guard pops out of the side of his mouth. With the grin plastered on his face, the mouth guard makes him look cartoonish. Alice laughs, I'm guessing at his face. He glides over to where I'm standing and slices his skates, spraying the boards with ice. I flinch, and he laughs.

He pulls off a glove and presses two fingers to the board. I press mine back, matching his.

"You with me or the bus?"

He winks. "You!"

"Hit the showers, Dirt Ball!" I yell with a laugh.

"On that note, I'm gonna head out, I'll meet you at your house."

"Alice, you could've just stayed there for the whole game instead of wasting your gas." Riley skates backwards to Todd, eyes on me and Alice. Probably trying to understand why she's here.

No one tags along for our tradition.

"I needed to see what the fuss was about. I made the right decision. Fashion is my thing. Not sports... Look at how gross they all look! And they're *swapping sweat!*" She nearly shrieks.

"Okay, Girly Girl. I'll meet you at home. Drive carefully," I say and push her to the doors. I should go warm up my car anyway. Riley doesn't need to sit in a cold snowy car right after a hot shower. He can't afford to get sick.

"You're walking me out, right?" she asks.

"Yes, I've gotta start my car."

"Okay, good."

"Why good?"

"Gives me time to ask you something..."

I roll my eyes. "No. I refuse pink. Hit me with a rainbow, but no solid pink. Or flowers. Or bo-,"

"No, no. Not that."

I give her a look. I'm no good at guessing games when it comes to her; we aren't alike in that way, or many ways actually.

"What's up with the shared peace sign at the end of the game?"

I snort. Peace signs? "It's just something we do," I say, avoiding a real answer. She doesn't need to know when we started counting down the years together. She wouldn't understand the meaning for Riley, or me.

"You two are so cute. Did you see that goofy grin he gave you?"

My brows pinch as I glare at her. "He was happy they won and his mouth guard was hanging out. That'd give anyone a lopsided grin." Again with the *cute* crap. When will I graduate from that? When I actually graduate high school?

I walk Alice to her car. Mainly to be sure she didn't fall. She's insane for wearing heels during a Pennsylvania winter. Once she's in her car, I hustle to mine and start the ignition, blasting the heat and ducking into my coat.

I really hope the early snow means an easy winter, and doesn't have a chilling effect on the frozen boy I'm waiting for.

Chapter 12

Riley

The brisk chill of winter smacks me in the face.

That explains Audrey's black scarf draped over her shoulders after the game.

I spot her car just behind the buses and jog to the passenger side. "No Alice?" I ask, glancing in the back as I toss my bag over the seat.

"Why would Alice come with us? She hated the game."

I laugh. "I didn't figure she'd like it, why was she here?"

She flips her turn signal on and goes around the bus. "That's the million dollar question."

"I'm afraid that's out of my price range," I say, shaking my head.

"It's all part of her torture she's planning for me," she grumbles.

"Do I wanna know?"

"No." She huffs. "I wouldn't tell you anyway. You're not a girl."

I laugh. "Thank god for that. We don't have a girl's hockey team, I'd be incredibly bored."

"This or that?"

I drum my fingers on the armrest as I think. "Music or movies?"

She glances at me sideways. "Music. Fiction or non-fiction."

"Fiction. Dancing or singing?"

She laughs. "Dancing in the rain. Dancing on ice or falling on ice?"

"I practically danced on the ice tonight!" I snort. "I don't fall...often."

"I don't mean that kind of dancing."

"Like? A slow dance or something?" She nods. "And shall I ask Rob to be my partner?"

"Well, you could do a crazy one armed, one legged, booty shakin' dance after a win," she offers.

I laugh, loudly. "Where do you come up with this?" She shrugs a shoulder as she merges with interstate traffic. "In that case, fall. High heels or bikini wax?"

"You say fall because you're a chicken. Do you even know what a bikini wax is?"

"If it's like the name...then yes, and I'm *not* a chicken."

"You are too, and I'd choose high heels. Feathers or snow?"

"You'd break your ankle! Snow. I'm still not a chicken," I argue.

"I'd likely break both, but you *are* a chicken."

"Will you stop calling me a chicken?"

The sound of her laughter centers me, I was meant to be right here with her. Just to hear her voice, her laugh...

"I will stop when you do a one armed, one legged, booty shakin' dance on ice for me." I hang my head. "Oh, and it has to be after a win, on home ice, and everyone has to see it."

"Not gonna happen, Aud."

"Same as usual, Chicken?" she asks as we pull into McDonalds drive-thru.

"Not a chicken, yes."

"Okay." She waits with the window cracked for an employee to take our order. A feminine voice comes through, asking what we'll have. "One chocolate shake for the chicken and one vanilla shake for the tomboy," she replies with a laugh.

"How many piece chicken nugget?"

Audrey laughs harder. "No chicken please, just the two shakes."

"See, a sign you should knock the chicken shit off."

"Not a chance, Chicken." She clucks for good measure.

"No electricity or no plumbing," I ask, hoping to pull her away from the teasing.

"No electricity, Chicken. One girl or all the girls?"

"One," I say, burning a hole in the side of her head.

"Aw, a romantic chicken. I don't think I've ever heard about one of those." She tilts her face toward mine. Both of us just staring at the other, with very little space between us. My eyes fall shut and I lean back further into my seat. *Way to make things awkward again, idiot. Chicken.*

"Pink or purple?" I ask.

She groans, passing me the milkshakes the guy in at the window handed her. "Purple. Doer or dreamer?"

I chew on the inside of my cheek as I work the straws out of their wrappers. "Doer." I'm too much of a dreamer. Or planner, but I don't follow through.

Hopefully, my dream of Audrey being mine isn't just a dream.

R

"You're home late," my mom greets me as I walk through the front door after milkshakes with Audrey.

"We won tonight, so Audrey and I stopped for milkshakes."

Mom purses her lips. "Must be nice."

I don't respond to her, I just walk to the laundry

room to start my cleanup routine.

"I saw your Coach's wife today at the store," she says, following me.

"She's a nice woman." I pull the Lysol wipes from the cabinet above the dryer.

"Yes. Except for that fact that she's snobby as all get out."

My lip curls in annoyance and confusion. "What do you mean?"

Mom leans against the doorframe and crosses her arms across her chest. "She acts like she's better than me. I don't much care for her hoity-toity pencil neck-,"

"Mom, she's not like tha-,"

"Right. I'm lying," she says in a huff. "I think you need to quit the team. You are obviously picking up this behavior from them."

"I'm not quitting hockey."

She rolls her eyes. "You think this hockey thing will bring you closer to your loser, dead beat dad? You're wrong. He left and never came back. Keep following in his footsteps, why don't you?"

I continue wiping my gear down, ignoring her.

"Riley, I love you to the moon, son. You're breaking my heart by just growing up. All you do is play hockey. I miss my boy. The little boy that used to hug me and tell me he loves me. What happened to that boy?"

"I'm still me, Mom. And I do love you."

"You have a funny way of showing it," she mutters

and walks away.

Guilt consumes me. I haven't been available to her, or sought her out for a while now. It's always Hannah and hockey. Autumn break is coming up soon, for Thanksgiving, maybe we can still do our traditional cookie baking. I eat more than I bake, and Hannah usually dumps a whole container of sprinkles on one sugar cookie, but it's something the three of us have done every year. When my father was still around, he'd go out and do the crazy Black Friday shopping while Mom and I baked and decorated cookies. It's usually just one batch of sugar cookies and one batch of special cookies; chocolate chip batter mixed with any candy in the pantry.

I drop my jersey in the washer and throw in a few whites from the basket and start a small load before turning off lights. On my way through the hallway, I notice an envelope on the floor, partially kicked under the runner on the floor. Kneeling, I pull it out and brush off the dust and dirt, revealing my mom's name in typewriter print.

Law Office of Seigman & Douglas

Family and Child Law

I frown and tap the envelope against my chin. Why would my mom be getting an envelope from a lawyer? I glance to the envelope again and see that the postage date was more than a month ago. Mom has forbidden me to open or check for mail. She opens all of my mail, which honestly isn't much; hockey league forms and signup flyers, fundraiser opportunities, and Christmas cards from a few people in town that I shovel snow for.

Placing the envelope on top of the bill pile, I flick the light switch and climb the stairs.

R

I jog down the stairs to finish getting ready. Things need to go smoothly.

"Your mom is pretty pissed," Ted announces as I walk into the kitchen.

My steps falter, he isn't usually here this late in the morning. "Yeah, she's never been too happy with me."

Ted chuckles as he rakes his fingers through his graying hair. "She's never been to a live hockey game-,"

"She could come to one of mine-,"

"Not the same thing and you know it. It doesn't stop you though, and here you are getting cozy with that girl's family and taking Hannah with you."

I swallow. "Don't-,"

"Now I've gotta come up with some extra cash to take her to a game," he mutters. "Do you know what it's like to live up to someone else's standards?"

I yawn and grab the cereal from the cabinet and set it on the table for Hannah. "You might not think so because of my age, but yeah, I get that."

He shakes his head. "Take whatever you're goin' through, and magnify it by about a hundred. That's what it's like living with a woman who has two children to another guy."

Grabbing a bowl and spoon for Hannah, I set them on the table next to the cereal and glance at Ted. "I don't think I'm the person to be talking to about this."

"I know you hate me, still, but I'm trying here. I don't understand why it's a big deal you and Hannah are goin' to a game tonight. But it is. I think it's cool you get to go, I would've liked to have gone too, but we weren't invited so it gives us a kid free night." He shrugs. "But your mom doesn't see it that way."

I nod. "I know." Not saying what I truly think. It's because we, her lowly children, are doing something that she didn't think of and she hasn't done.

"What does she like to do? I wanna distract her tonight."

I'm taken aback. Why is he asking me? "Um, I, well," I stutter. "She used to always tell my father that a good old fashioned dinner and a movie weren't out of style."

He chews on his cheek and looks away. "That's not what I was expecting."

"Sorry, that's the best I can do." I shrug. But I feel like dirt. I shoved her past in his face, not that it needed much shoving. I'm standing right here. "If it makes you feel any better, he never did the dinner and a movie dates with her," I whisper, remembering all her tears and whines and stories after he left her.

"Thanks, maybe."

"Good luck." I pick up my book bag and walk out the door.

The sad conversation Ted and I had, is just another reason I want nothing more than to leave the second I graduate.

Absentmindedly, I pat the front pocket of my bag as I drive closer to school. She'd kill me if I gave her a present during school hours, but at least I get to see her tonight. I park in my assigned space and head inside.

Various comments reach my ears as I pass through the halls to my locker. “I can't believe she's wearing a dress today.” “Did you see her legs?” “She's hot.” “I didn't think I'd ever see the day.” I don't know who they're-

My eyes widen and breath catches in my chest.

Audrey's smile is bright, as well as her cheeks. She's laughing with Alice and Candy.

I know what everyone's talking about.

Her.

Her hair is down and straight, framing her face and hugging her shoulders. The yellow dress she's wearing hugs her waist and only comes to her knees. She looks beautiful. Even down to the cowboy boots and the shine on her lips.

My hand rests on the combination to my locker. I need to get my things for first, but I can't take my eyes off of her.

Her eyes meet mine, only for a breath. She looks down and fidgets with her dress, smoothing it, pulling it down on her hips, but it emphasizes the swell on her chest, so she tugs it up a little. I'd be a fool if I didn't notice the blush creeping down her neck.

“Come on Candy, we should-,”

“Right,” Candy answers.

I don't see where they go.

I'm glued to the spot and I can only see Audrey.

She closes the few feet between us. "Stop it."

"Shto-," I clear my throat. "Stop what?"

"*That*. Stop staring at me like that." She crosses her arms over her chest, hugging herself. "I can't wait to make Alice pay for this."

"Alice?"

She glares at me. "Remember last night? I told you girly torture? This," she fans her hand in front of her, motioning head to toe, "is all Alice's fault."

I smile. "She did good."

She growls at me. "It's just a stupid dress and makeup. I'm still me. Quit lookin' at me like I'm some sort of escaped convict."

"That's not why I'm starin'," I mutter. I didn't mean to say that out loud. So to cover, "Have you gotten anything for your birthday yet?"

She brushes my hand from my combination and twirls the dial. "A million eyes on me, a gazillion, *"Lookin' goods,"* and some chocolate chip pancakes for breakfast from Mom." She pops open my locker and motions for me to grab my things.

"Sounds great so far."

"Shut up, Chicken."

I drop my book bag into the bottom of my locker. "Still on that?"

"Of course. You *are* a chicken. It only makes sense to acknowledge that fact when you're being a butt and when you're not."

I glance to her. Her eyes are sparkling right along with her laughter. I don't want it to ever end. "I suppose I should get used to hearing it."

"Duh."

On our way to homeroom, my arms ache dangerously. It's an ache so deep is hurts my chest. It's an ache I need to ignore and there's nothing to cure this kind of ache.

Two more years.

Two years, then I can hold her, kiss her, and love her openly.

Simply 17 Years
Audrey & Riley

Chapter 13

Audrey

I jet out the doors at the end of the day, not slowing until I get to my car. Alice is going to pay for this!

My phone buzzes as I flop, unladylike, into the driver's seat.

You look fantastic! I told you you would! Did you see how everyone looked at you? - A <3

I glare at my phone, willing it to explode, like everyone's memories of me today.

Yes. I saw how they all stared at me. You'd have to be blind not to. This day was horrible. Just wait. There's bound to be one more day of muddin' before everything freezes.

I chuck my phone into the passenger seat and start up the ignition.

"Couldn't even talk to my best friend without him staring all googly-eyed." I slam my palm on the steering wheel. I'm still me. Just because I wore a stupid dress that Alice made me wear shouldn't mean that I'm treated differently.

Blasting the volume, Easton Corbin's All Over The Road blares through the speakers. I grumble and press the button to my next saved station. I don't need some "she's so pretty" song right now. What Was I Thinkin' by Dierks Bentley, blasts my eardrums. "Yeah, what was I thinkin' wearin' this stupid dress?" I turn the radio off and fume the whole way home.

A peaceful evening with my mom, dad, and brother at Buffalo Wild Wings for tonight's game is the only thing I have to look forward to saving my birthday. Seventeen is just... Not what I thought it'd be yet. It's starting off horribly anyway.

When I park in front my house, my mom is bouncing on the porch, waiting for me.

Grabbing only my phone, I exit the car and slam the door as hard as I can.

"Bad day, Sugar?" My mom asks, smiling.

Her smile just annoys me further. "Yes," I snap but don't explain. "I'm going to change into my Pens gear and ignore the world until it's time to head out to BW3's."

"Well, you can change, but we're not goin' to BW3's tonight," she responds, opening the door for me.

I stop dead in my tracks and glare at her. "You and Dad promised that for my birthday-,"

"Correction," she interrupts. "I promised that as long as something better didn't surface, we would go-,"

"And you were to clear the "better" with me, since it's *my* birthday." I storm into the house, on the verge of tears. I just want to watch my guys play, and win, for my birthday. Is that too much to ask?

"Sit your pretty derrière on a chair and hold your tongue for two minutes!" She snaps.

I roll my eyes, but do as I'm told.

"You can change your clothes, but the reason we aren't goin' to the BW3's is because your older brothers all pitched in with us to get tickets for tonight's game."

"Wha-," I stop, then scream and leap from my chair. "You rescued my birthday!" I throw my arms around my mom's neck and squeeze her.

She laughs. "Don't thank me. It wasn't my idea."

"I have to call Luca!"

"Why do you have to call me?" My brother asks as he enters the kitchen.

I scream and run to him. "How di-, What?"

He laughs. "Have I ever missed your birthday?"

"But, you said, you're not-,"

"Chill, Sis. Now why are you thanking me?"

"Pens game!"

"That was Sean's idea. I went with it, but it was his idea."

This shocks me. Sean is a pretty cheap person. He doesn't like spending money.

"I'll take the credit where it's due," Sean shouts from the living room.

"Thank you, Sean!" I scream as I jog into the living room.

"We gotta leave soon if we wanna beat traffic, get out of that dress...Why are you wearin' a dress anyway?"

I glare at him. "Ask Alice."

He laughs. "I know that face! A dare gone wrong or you lost a bet!"

"I didn't lose. But payback's a bit-,"

"Language!" Mom yells.

I clear my throat. "Payback's a *female dog*, and I get to take her muddin'." Sean, Luca, and Dad laugh. "I'm gonna go change!" I squeal as I rush back to my room.

Grabbing my favorite jeans from the bottom drawer of my dresser, I quickly shimmy them on under the dress. I yank the dress over my head and toss it over my shoulder, not caring where the awful thing lands. Skipping to my closet, I flick through the shirts, looking for my favorite Penguins tee and sweatshirt. Lastly, I grab my Sidney Crosby jersey and throw it over my shoulder.

Pausing at my bed, I look on the shelf over my bed for my digital camera I got for Christmas. But it's not there.

I rush to my bedroom door. "Mom! Where's my camera?"

"I have it!" Dad yells. "Just hurry up!"

As I'm ready to grumble a response, someone

knocks on the door.

"Audrey, answer the door!" Mom barks.

With my jersey still draped over my shoulder, I rush through the living room to get to the door. With my permanent cheesy grin still plastered on my face, I yank open the door coming face to face with Riley.

My smile slips as I take in his attire; Penguins baseball hat and shirt. He's even holding a black gift bag with yellow tissue paper stuffed in it.

"Happy Birthday," he says calmly and not at all dreamy-like when I was wearing that stupid dress.

"Happy birfday!" Hannah shouts and shoves around me. "Mister Paul!"

I smile at her excitement of seeing my dad. "Thanks, come on in." I turn and let him follow me into the kitchen.

Greg looks at me with a wicked smirk on his face. "Got a thing for Captains I see." He nods to my jersey, or to Riley who's right behind me.

"You're such a jerk, Greg. Can't a girl have guy friends?"

"Greg, if you're smart, and I know you are, you will drop this conversation about your sister. Especially in front of your mother."

"I just, I mean-,"

"Shut it, Greg," I snap. "It's my birthday, don't crap on my friends."

"Audrey! He was-,"

"It's a figure of speech, Mom." Riley laughs, catching my attention. "What's so funny?"

He shakes his head. "Nothin' at all. You want this now? Or after the game?"

I purse my lips, taking an eyeful of the present, and then return my gaze to his blue eyes. "You know, after the way you treated me today, I think I'll wait. I'm not even sure I'd like whatever you have in that pretty bag." I sniff and turn away from him.

"Audrey," my mom whispers. "Be nice."

"He's the one who got all gooey over me wearing a dress today!" I forget to whisper.

Someone clears their throat.

"Are we ready to head out?" Dad asks.

"Can I ride with you Mister Paul? Can I Ri?"

"I'm riding with Luca!" I shout as I dart to the door. Why did I have to respond to Mom? He did get gooey, but I didn't want to rub it in his face. Why can't I make anyone go gooey when I'm dressed normal? I'm too *cute* for any guy to fawn over.

Happy Birthday, Audrey. You may not ever get the guy, but at least you get the game! I think sourly to myself as I rush out Luca's car, ignoring Riley completely.

The rain better hurry, I need to rebuild my mask. It's cracking along the edges and splitting down the middle.

“Thank you!” I launch myself at Sean and Luca, who are getting ready to leave. “Do you have to go now?”

Luca pats my back as Sean musses up my hair.

“Sorry, Squirt. Bossman says we gotta go if we want to make it back at a decent time.”

“Dude, I’m not the boss!” Sean shoves Luca, jostling me from their arms. “And you’re the one who drove to my apartment instead of here.”

“Boys!” Mom yells.

“We know!” They answer in unison. “We don’t have to fight over everything, we are blood, we are equals, we are friends…”

“Though I am smarter,” Sean grumbles.

“And I can kick your as-,”

“Really? You’ve gotta fight, even now?”

“Mom, it’s what we do. At least it’s out of love now,” Luca defends.

“I’m goin’ inside, I love you both!” I wrap my arms around myself, shielding me from the cold wind.

When I go inside, Mom is worrying over them about being alone in the car for another five hours without someone to run interference.

“So, was your birthday good?” Riley asks as I flop down on the couch.

“Yeah, it ended better than it started.”

He looks away from me and rubs the back of his

neck with his hand. "Yeah."

Ugh. There's that awkwardness again. Forget that. He's my best friend. "Where's that present? Or don't I get it since it's just after midnight?"

He smiles. The kind of smile that melts me. It reaches his eyes, and lights up his face. The kind of smile that reveals the one crooked, chipped tooth he got from a stick to the face playing Warrior's rivals two years ago. "It's yours, no reason you can't have it now." He stands up and goes to the kitchen, quietly, because my dad is cuddling with a sleeping Hannah at the kitchen table. I lean over the arm of the couch, watching my dad hold Hannah. He loves that little girl. Mom wanted him to lay her down, but he said it's been so long since he got to hold a sleeping rugrat so he's holding her and reminiscing, he says. He didn't like Greg's offer to hold him while he slept.

"Now, it's not anything really fancy, but I thought of you as soon as I saw it," he mutters, handing me the gift bag.

I smile at him. "You likely did wonderful, I'm not fancy." I set the bag on the coffee table, and tug the tissue paper out. Reaching in, my hand glides across a plastic box. I quirk an eyebrow at him as I lift the box out of the bag.

He leans forward, resting his elbows on his knees, and sucks his upper lip into his mouth.

Glancing down to the box in my hands, it's square shaped, with a little indent on one side. I press my fingers to the edge and pry it open.

Resting on a white tissue is a silver cuff bracelet, meant to look rugged. But what catches my breath are the words inscribed, *"She finds peace in the mud."*

"Ri," I whisper. Picking up the cuff, I slide it over my hand and stare at it resting on my wrist. "How did you...?"

He smiles. "Do you like it?"

I scoot closer to him on the couch. "I love it."

He stands and crosses the room. "I'm glad." He clears his throat. "I should get Hannah home before my mom comes here."

I'm not wearing a dress, no wonder he took off like that. I guess I can't hug him anymore. "Okay. Thank you for coming to the game, I had such a good time, and I'm glad you and Hannah had a blast as well." I stay glued to my seat.

"I wouldn't have missed this with you, for anything," he says nervously, but walks into the kitchen before I can respond.

Spinning the bracelet, I listen to Riley leave with a half awake Hannah.

Seventeen is something else.

Mom always said, sixteen is sweet and seventeen is simple.

It's definitely not starting out all that simple. Maybe it's simple for the parents.

"G'Night birthday girl," my dad whispers and kisses the top of my head.

"Night, Daddy."

I force myself off the couch and head to my room. I replay the game in my head, at least my team won.

That's the best birthday present I've ever gotten. Pittsburgh Penguins beat the Philadelphia Flyers on my birthday, and I saw it live.

Chapter 14

Riley

My phone buzzes in my pocket as I carefully cradle Hannah in one arm and unlock the door.

"This is serious!" Ted screams at my mom.

I run Hannah up to her room, hoping they don't wake her. Hopefully, whatever they're fighting about this time doesn't have the same end result as last time.

"I can't believe you hid that! For all these years. Who does that-,"

"Shut up! You don't know anything of what I've done!"

"I know you kept a man from his-,"

I turn Hannah's lullaby disc on, so long as that's playing, and the fight stays downstairs, she shouldn't wake up. Sighing, I quickly exit her room, to head to mine.

"But he's their *fa-*,"

"Shut your mouth, Ted."

"I think this will bite you in the ass sooner rather than later."

"I doubt that. They love *me*! They need *me*! Not him!"

I quietly maneuver the hall and stairs, not touching one creaky board, just as I've done every morning, trying to get more information to fill in the blanks in my head.

They fall silent for a moment, the only noise is the soft shuffling of paper and a tapping of something plastic.

"Sue, I don't know anything about kids, but I do know how it feels to have a parent lie to you your whole life. It hurts and messes you up, especially when those lies are about half of the person you are. I love you and I probably always will. So I hope that you'll do the right thing soon. Be honest for once."

I sit on the bottom step and try to wrap my head around what I'm hearing. Ted actually sounds sane tonight, like a person who I could trust. I know I can't trust him, everything that comes out of his mouth is bullshit. But this, this sounds different. Normal.

"Ted, I have been *protecting* my children all these years. I am not giving them false hope of something that may never be."

"Parents aren't perfect, Sue. Look at yourself."

"You're right. I'm not perfect. But at least they know who loves them best."

The envelope from last night comes to mind, especially since this sounds like it's a discussion about my father. But, I don't understand what exactly the issue is and why they are fighting about it now. Dad left years ago and hasn't tried to come back or contact me or Hannah. Why would this come up now?

Heavy footsteps pull me from my thoughts, and out of fear of being caught, I try to crabwalk up the stairs.

"I see you," Ted says quietly.

"I didn't hear much," I promise him.

He shakes his head. "I'm glad you heard some of it. Maybe things won't be so hard to hear later when your mom feels up to explaining."

"Thanks for the warning, I think."

"I don't know what to say."

I shrug. "What's there to say?"

"A lot. But none of it is my place to speak it."

"Are you leaving?" I ask curiously as my eyes fall to his bony fingers gripping the doorknob.

"Yeah," he says without emotion. "It's best for now. I'm going to my Dad's for the night. I'll be back tomorrow. Just need...some time."

I nod even though I don't understand. He and Mom fight a lot, but he doesn't always leave after they do.

"Go to bed, Riley!" My mom shouts somewhere I can't see. "Ted, get out before you ruin everything with your lies!"

"Woman, I'm not the one lyin'-,"

"Get out!" She screams carnally.

I cringe and rush up the stairs, fleeing from whatever else is about to happen.

"Be honest with your children! Tell them why they don't have a dad!"

"They know!" My mother screams at him.

I duck into my room and close the door.

"They know the lies you've created!" I hear Ted's muffled argument through my door.

What did she lie about?

My father left a little more than five years ago and he never came back. Not even once. Not for my big game two weeks after he left to begin with, not for birthdays, not for Hannah's Christmas recital, and not because he loves us.

My phone buzzes in my pocket so I slide it out. *?* from Audrey.

I set my phone on my nightstand, ignoring her text because I honestly don't know how to answer her.

Am I okay?

I throw open my bedroom window and sit out on the porch roof. A winter breeze cools my heated cheeks.

Betrayed. That's part of what I feel.

Do I want to know what she's been hiding from me? From Hannah?

Yes and no. Yes, I want her to be honest with me, but no I don't want to hear it all because things could change, again. I'm tired of everything changing all the time. I want something different, no more roadblocks or hurdles. I want smooth sailing.

Hannah doesn't remember our dad. She was barely one when he left. She stopped asking about him after a while and hasn't really asked why she doesn't have a dad yet. She's putting so much together though so I'm sure those questions are coming. Things that she shouldn't connect or pick up on, like when me and Aud were snipping at each other being similar to Mom and Ted when they argue. There isn't that connection. We aren't a doomed couple. We aren't a couple.

I drop my forehead to my knees.

Love gets in the way of everything. If I could kick my heart to the curb, I bet I could get through life easy.

When I think too much about Audrey, I can't focus. I need to focus on hockey.

I've got to get out of this place.

I'm going to have to find out what Mom's been hiding from me, I just don't know if it's a good idea to find out during season.

R

I slam my locker closed and shove off the bench. Practice was hard today. I couldn't control the puck to save my life, I made no good shots, and checks knocked me harder than ever before.

"Silk, you losin' your game, man?" Todd snickers.

I glare at him. "Like you've never missed a save."

His jaw ticks. "Look, I'm still your friend. Girls come

and go, but we've been friends for longer than I can remember. What's goin' on with you?"

My glare softens, but only for a second. *Girls come and go*, that just means he was planning on using Audrey until he was done with her. Just like he did to Libby.

"We're teammates. I don't think we can ever go back to being friends like we were before."

"Teammates are friends-,"

"On the ice." I grab my gear and head for the door.

Love gets in the way of life.

There's heartache involved with everything you love.

I loved my dad, he left. I loved my mom, she lied and kept secrets. She's made me parent my sister instead of her taking care of her son and daughter.

I toss my gear in the backseat and put the key in the ignition of my Toyota. It cranks a few times, I slam my fist on the steering wheel, and try one more time. It finally kicks over, sluggishly.

"That's just great," I mutter.

Everything around me is breaking. It's only right that my car falls into that theme, too. Praying that my car can make it home, I pull out of the parking spot.

Love is stupid.

I repeat those words the whole way home.

When I pull into my driveway, my car chugs to a stop and the hood begins to steam. I drop my head to the steering wheel.

Perfect. Just perfect.

There's a tap on my window. Raising my head I see Ted. My brows furrow.

I crack my door, and he backs up to let me exit.

"Want some help fixin' this thing?"

I jingle the keys in my palm. "Sure. Why'd you come back?"

"I love your mom." He shrugs a shoulder. "I may not always agree with everything that goes on, but I'm not perfect either."

"But love causes heartache. Everything that comes with love brings pain."

"Love doesn't bring pain. It brings joy and unknown blessings. It strengthens you."

My jaw ticks as I clench my teeth. He doesn't understand. How can he?

He's the type of person that shows his love through his fists, I remind myself.

"Pop the hood, let's have a look," he says, walking to the front of my car.

Without arguing, I reach in and pop the hood. A puff of smoke billows as he pushes the hood up.

"That can't be good," I mutter.

I pull a box of practice pucks from under my bed, my secret stash of cash. It's the money I've earned from working during off season and summer. I use this for every piece of equipment I need and gas, now that I have a car. The '95 Toyota Camry with more miles than I'd like to admit, it cost me eight hundred bucks from Mrs. Gerber. She even let me work part of it off by mowing and doing some odd jobs.

I've had this car for four months, and the radiator is shot. Ted called around and a new one will cost me eighty nine dollars through one of his buddy's that owes him a favor. I just need to make sure I can cover that eighty nine bucks, no way Mom will help. She hasn't in the past, and I'm definitely not asking her now.

Taking a deep breath, I open the near empty box, praying that there's enough cash and that I won't need to replace anything more. If I need to, I'll see if I can pick up a few hours on weekends at the restaurant.

I dump the remains of the box on my bedroom floor, pushing aside the coins and grabbing the bills. I breathe a sigh of relief that I have just over a hundred and fifty left, and stuff ninety in my pocket.

"Hey Riley!" Ted hollers up the stairs.

"I'm comin'!" I stuff the rest of my money back in the box and slide it behind some gear under my bed, before darting down the stairs. "Ready?"

"Whenever you are," he says.

We head out to his truck, the only working vehicle present at the time. It feels weird, being alone with him.

I'm still waiting for the darkness to cloud his eyes again. Waiting for him to snap. People don't change.

Once a cheater, always a cheater, but with Ted it's, *once a beater, always a beater.*

"Hey, I know you bust your ass to pay for your hockey stuff, so I'm taking care of your car," Ted says, cutting the silence.

"What's the catch?" My knee-jerk response tumbles out of my mouth before I can think twice about it.

"No catch. Just helping my soon to be stepson out."

My breath lodges somewhere in my chest as his words find meaning in my brain. He's proposed to my mom. He will be my stepfather.

"Don't tell your mom I told you, she's planning some dinner thing to announce to you and Hannah."

Everything about this conversation feels wrong, down to the announcement over dinner.

"What about what happened last night?"

"Things will be better after your mom and I marry, you'll see."

Empty promises.

"Well, don't jump for joy or anything."

I clear my throat. "No. It's great. You love each other."

Love causes pain again.

The relationship is doomed, it's been doomed. And now they're taking it to a whole new level of pain, involving me and Hannah in it now.

Audrey was right.

I'll need to stay back to protect Hannah.

"I didn't learn anything about relationships from my parents, I learned from my grandparents. I only stayed with them a few times when I was about your age, but they taught me as much as they could. Like, when you fight, it doesn't mean you break up. It means that you communicate and fight together for a common goal. That's what love is. You fight together for the same thing. The rest will fall into place. If I learned anything about relationships from my parents, it's that staying with someone because it looks right is the dumbest reason. If there's no love, it'll be more painful than stubbing your pinky toe in the middle of the night."

Love.

The darkness begins to seep into my mind like a disease. I can feel it creeping under my skin, hugging every part of me, and turning me to ice.

There is no room for love in life.

Chapter 15

Audrey

I stare out the window, ignoring the commotion in the cafeteria. It's a calm day. Not even a gentle breeze to rustle what's left of the leaves.

It's how life feels right now.

Eerily calm.

There's no fun, no excitement, not even a lick of drama.

Life is an empty, frozen wasteland since love no longer walks beside me.

I'm not sure what happened this time, but Riley is freezing everyone out again. He stopped answering texts, calls, and just keeps the glare plastered on his face.

"You should eat," Todd says, pausing on the other side of the table.

I tear my eyes away from the motionless trees, connecting with his concerned eyes. "I know. I will. I was just..."

"Staring off into space thinking about what's goin' on with Riley?" he finishes for me.

I shrug a shoulder. "You see him more than I do, what happened?"

He pulls out a chair and sits. "I'll tell you what I know, if you at least eat the apple."

I roll my eyes but pick up the apple and take large bite. I spin it around to show him, and motion with my other hand for him to continue while I chew.

He snorts. "Thanks." His fingers tap the tabletop a few times before he starts. "Practice has been hard on him lately. I think it started about two weeks ago though." My birthday weekend. "He was terrible at practice." He shakes his head. "You saw him those last three games."

I nod, remembering how long it took him to recover from a hit, nearly starting a fight on two different occasions, and lastly, how at the end of each game, he didn't stop by me.

"I think I know what triggered this," I mutter. My birthday was pretty much crap. He was acting funny even then. I hope it's not because of me, but either way, I need to make this right, if only for the team's sake.

"I don't know. He and Ted were workin' on his car for a few days, he might've had to dip into his gear money for that."

I raise my eyes to meet his, shocked. "I didn't know anyone else knew about that."

He shrugs. "It doesn't take a rocket scientist to figure out that he keeps money hidden from his mom."

I purse my lips. At least I'm not the only one who doesn't particularly care for that woman. She's nice enough, but that's a front for outsiders. A lot of people in town think she's mother of the year. I happen to know more than most of them.

"He doesn't talk to anyone at practice. Coach is getting' pissed." A solemn look masks his face. "After he benched him half through the first period last game, he started talkin' about pullin' his Captain title. He's not actin' like a captain, or even a teammate."

"He worked so hard for that though," I whisper.

"Eat." He points to the apple I abandoned on my tray.

I lift the apple and take a shallow bite, the sludge in my mouth tastes nothing like an apple, but if I want more on how Riley is, I'll have to stomach it.

"He doesn't talk to Coach anymore. But I think Coach has had enough of his attitude and silence."

I set the apple down again and lean forward a little. "I can't promise anything, but I will try talking to him." I glance to the windows again. "I have to try." I owe him that much.

Riley is my best friend and hockey is his dream. He has to do well if he wants to accomplish his goal of playing professionally. I know he can do it. Hockey is his blood.

A

I flop down on my desk chair, rolling it across the hardwood floor until stopping on a pile of dirty clothes. Candy and Alice sit cross-legged on my bed.

“Have you figured out what you’re gonna do for the Science project?” Alice asks.

I glance to Candy, my lab partner. “Did we settle on something?”

“No. Mr. Carmichael didn’t really give us strict rules for this.”

“Earth Science is weird,” Alice mutters. “And my partner has the I.Q. of Greg.” She grimaces and picks at a string on my comforter.

I snort. “Greg was good with science, though.”

She sighs heavily. “Fine, he knows as much about science as Greg knows about fashion.”

I laugh. “You’ve got me there.”

“What’s that?” Candy asks, staring at my headboard.

“Um, it’s called part of the bed frame?” I retort.

“Har, har, har funny girl. That,” she enunciates and points to the hockey pucks.

“They’re my-,”

“If you give me another snarky comment about what they are, without telling me what the new one is from, so help me, I will tag team with Alice and force you to wear a pink frilly dress in the next few days,” she snaps.

I purse my lips and glare at her. “Always threatening the wardrobes. One of these days I’ll wear a dress on my own just to mess with your heads.”

Alice laughs so hard she snorts. “I’m sorry!” she

fans her hands. “I’m just imagining you showing up to school wearing a blue dress from last year’s summer collection!”

Candy and I glance to each other then stare at Alice with confusion.

“Blue isn’t your color! You look better with autumn styles,” she explains flatly.

“Oh-kay,” I drawl.

“Tell me about the new puck. Now. It’s gotta mean something to you if you put with the Penguin’s thingy.”

I roll my eyes at her lack of knowledge of hockey. I’m a loner amongst my friends with my love of hockey. But Candy is more accepting than Alice.

“It’s just a puck-,”

“Don’t give me that load of -,”

“Fine! Riley hit me that puc-,”

“He what?!” Alice screams.

“Didn’t that hurt?”

I shrug and look away from both of them, trying to hide my blush. “Not so much, it’s hollow.”

“Why would he do that?”

“Because he was trying to kill her!” Candy argues. “Or give her a concussion.”

“He wouldn’t do that to Audrey,” Alice defends him.

I spin back to face them, staring intently at Alice.

"Why are you defending him?" She never defends him, she insults him.

Her left shoulder rises and falls gently. "I don't know. He's a lot of things, but he wouldn't intentionally hurt you. I can tell."

"Where is that coming from? You hate Riley!" Candy argues.

"I don't hate him." She ends Candy's argument immediately. "He's a brute to everyone, *except* Audrey. She's the only person who gets him and can get under his...*frozen* exterior." She shudders.

"That's Hannah you're describing," I mutter. "Not me. He's shut me out again."

"That's how you know he truly needs you. You need to go to him." Her eyes glass over slightly as she stares at nothing. "Wear the yellow dress, and he'll do anything you say."

"You're trying to thaw him out, not heat him to a boil. Do not ever wear that dress around Riley again!" Candy argues.

My eyes flit to the crumpled dress still balled up on my floor. "No worries there."

"Aud, you need to talk to him."

"Alice, what am I supposed to do? Climb the lattice to his bedroom and demand he talk to me?" I shout in frustration. "He won't even look at me! He doesn't answer texts or calls-,"

"Then yes. Be Jacob and climb to "Rachel's" window," she interrupts my rant with a country music quote from the song Jacob's Ladder by Mark Wills.

"Take this puck with you, hit *him* with it like he hit you. Wake him up."

I didn't tell them that when he hit me with the puck, he kissed me. I can hit him with his own puck. But I don't know what to say to him yet.

"So, that's it then?" Candy asks. "You'll climb to his bedroom window, all romantic like, and hit him with a puck? How does this plan solve *anything*?"

"Because then he'll listen!" Alice shouts.

"What if he doesn't?"

It's my turn to sigh heavily. "Then I leave the puck in his net and move on."

The girls both stare at me with a look of sadness crossed with confusion. Yeah, I'd have to agree with them. I never thought I would walk away from my best friend, but there's only so much I can do.

A

Patting the puck in my pocket one last time, I take deep breath and grip the flimsy wooden lattice nailed to the side of the Silk house.

"Please, don't break," I chant as I pull myself up to and reach for the next open slot.

The outside light to their backyard kicks on. I freeze and suck my body as close to the wall as I can. *Please don't break, please don't let whoever that is see me!*

"Ted! Where are you going?" Sue, Riley's mom, hollers.

"I thought I saw somethin' when I got a glass of water," he responds.

"Come on, *fiancé*, come back to bed. I wanna cuddle."

Fiancé?

"Yeah, it was probably just the neighbor's dog." The yard goes dark and their backdoor clicks.

I let out a sigh of relief and climb the last few feet to the porch roof. It's been years since I climbed this lattice, I'm surprised it's supporting my weight.

"What are you doin' here?" Riley asks, startling me.

"Don't ask stupid questions," I whisper harshly. "Help me up!"

He leans over and stretches his hand to reach mine on the edge, I grasp his hand, all the fear of falling off the lattice catching up to me, making me grip his hand harder than necessary. He easily pulls me up, something I'm impressed by, but not willing to focus on.

"Why are you here?" He asks again.

"I came to see you," I state the obvious.

"You've seen me, you can go now. But try the other side, the lattice is newer."

I glare at him, pulling the puck from my pocket and gripping it in my chilled hand. "What is going on with you?"

He doesn't answer, eyes focusing on the moon with that stupid icy glare still plastered on his face. I give the puck one last squeeze before launching it at the side of his face as hard as I can.

"What the crap, Aud?!" He shouts and catches the puck before it rolls off the roof.

We both hold our breath, listening for voices and hoping no one heard his outburst.

"You're shutting me out again," I whisper after a few moments of silence. I breathe deeply, ignoring my racing heart. "I hoped by coming here I'd be able to break through your ice wall." His eyes drill mine with a look resembling wonder and fear. "But I can't do this anymore. I can't keep worrying that one day you'll completely shut me out. I can't keep worrying that I'm-," I stop myself from saying that I'll never be good enough for him. "The rate I'm going, worrying about you, I'll have a head full of gray hair by the time we graduate."

His head falls back to the siding, eyes closing. "Yeah, I kinda figured that'd happen," he mutters.

"What?"

"Love causing pain all over again."

"What are you talking about?"

His eyes snap to mine, searching for something. "Nothing. Don't worry about it. Just go."

"Riley." I look to the puck clenched tightly in his hand before meeting his eyes one last time. "The puck is in your net. The play is yours to make. Don't fake, don't fail, and don't give up. Quit icing your team, on the ice and off." I hope he gets it.

I stand up and carefully step over him to reach the other side of the roof. My heart sinks to my stomach as he doesn't say a single word to stop me.

Climbing down the lattice, a silent tear rolls down my cheek as the chilled wind encases me in a bitter cold. It's a cold that I know I won't be able to shake. It's that cold when you lose all hope and the realization that everything is changing and it's not for the better. That cold chill when your best friend doesn't let you help and pushes you away so far that you have no choice but to let go. The empty space they captivated inside of you becomes a frigid, dank hole.

And all you can think about is how you'll never be warm again.

Chapter 16

Riley

Walking through the hall to get to my next class, Audrey's voice finds its way to my ears, stopping me in my tracks. I lean against the wall just before it cuts the corner to my locker, and Audrey's.

"We could follow the creak that runs through town and collect soil samples and photograph the banks," she says.

"Fine. You touch the dirt, I got the camera," Candy answers her. "Did you do it?" Her tone is different with that question. I wish I knew what she meant.

"Yeah." A locker slams shut.

"I take it that it didn't go as well as you'd like."

I see Candy first. She's staring intently at Audrey. Audrey is staring at me, with wide, sad eyes.

I want to ask her what's wrong.

I want to tell her that I'm sorry for being so cold.

But I stay silent.

She grabs Candy's arm, and I don't miss the white of her knuckles pressing against her skin before she scurries away, tugging Candy with her.

I figured she would've said hi, but I guess I hurt her last night. Things just aren't...good.

Anywhere.

I throw my stuff in my locker and head to the basement, to Coach's office. I'm pretty sure he's cutting me from the team, it's what I want. If I don't have hockey to fall back on, I won't have to leave and won't have any reason to leave Hannah.

The door is open, so I lean in. "You wanted to see me?"

Coach looks up from his paperwork on his desk, and half smiles at me. "Sit, close the door."

I push the door shut and sit in the metal chair opposite his desk. "What's up?"

He taps his pencil eraser on his desk as his jaw works, obviously thinking of how to word, presumably my cut speech.

"Riley, you're my best player. You know the rules, you know how to manage in stressful situations on ice, and you're quick with the puck."

Just cut me already. I don't need the compliments. "But..." I encourage him to continue so that I don't have to hear any more of how good I was on the ice, before...

Before everything went to shit.

Before love took over and pulled the happiness from my life.

"You're right. There is a but." He sighs, drops his pencil and loosens his tie. "Frankly, I want to know what happened to my team captain. A Sophomore beats out Seniors and Juniors for Captain. Then... turns into a worse player than a testosterone filled preteen. Explain that."

I clear my throat. I don't want to explain my method; the why's of what I've done. "I can't."

"Okay," he mutters, leaning forward on the desk. "I've known you since you first set foot on the ice rink. I've seen what you're capable of on and off the ice, and I know this kid sitting in front of me right now is hurting. I've seen it before. I'm waiting for you to tell me the missing piece. What don't I know, Riley?"

I chew on my cheek to stop from lashing out. "Nothing."

"Riley, don't lie to me."

"This is me!" I shout, jumping to my feet and slamming my fist against my chest, not able to contain my anger again. "I'm this kid. Right here. Just cut me from the team!"

"I can't do that."

I drop my fist to my side and grip the back of the metal chair with my other hand. "Why? That's why you've called me down here. To take my C and cut me."

He laughs. "No. I'm not doing that. Are you quitting?"

I stare at him. I hadn't thought about quitting.

"Didn't think so. What happened?"

I continue to stare at him in silence. Why didn't I think to quit?

"Okay, I fill in the blanks." Please don't get it right. "The girl." Audrey? "She got under your skin and broke your heart." Maybe. No. We aren't anything, never were. "I've se-,"

"No."

"No what?"

"No, I'm not quitting and no, it isn't Audrey."

"Is Hannah okay?"

Too close. "Yep." I look away.

"So it's at home then."

My eyes snap to his. "No."

"What's your mom up to these days?"

I do not want to talk about this.

"Did she finally tell you what's really been going on these last five years?" I swallow, but I don't answer. I know about it, but I don't know what *it* is. "How do you feel about what she did to your father? What she keeps doing?"

"I - uh," my throat becomes instantly dry. I don't know how to answer him. "She's marrying Ted," the lame truth whispers through my lips.

Coach's eyes widen slightly. "Well. That was bound to happen. So she didn't - ?" I shake my head. "I'm sorry, I was out of line. But when that's all out in the open, I'm here. And I have some things to share with you, but not until you know what's been going on."

"You're the one who brought it up. Just tel-,"

"I was out of line for assuming. Please, talk to your mother then come find me when that happens."

I roll my eyes and look to the blank, cream colored wall. "She's marrying Ted. I can't leave Hannah." The words escape my mouth without fail.

His brows furrow. "Why can't you?"

My chest tightens in that unwelcomed way it did in Audrey's garage. My vision loses color on the edges.

I can't do this.

I can't explain what could happen if I leave Hannah.

The aftermath of what happened before hits me hard and my chest tightens further.

"I gotta go." I jump to my feet and rush out into the cool hallway.

"Riley!" Coach shouts, but thankfully doesn't follow.

I have no room in my life for love.

I love hockey, I should quit it. I love Hannah, but she needs me more than I need to get away from here. She won't survive the damage of Ted and Mom. She needs me, and she doesn't know it.

I can't leave her behind.

I strap my pads on, preparing for practice. The chattering through the locker room reverberates through my head, pounding against my brain. I should be a part of it. It wasn't that long ago that I used to join in.

Things have changed.

"Listen up!" Coach shouts to get our attention. "No pads today. We're doing something different this evening."

I tug the strap with a sigh and toss the pads back into my bag.

"Put your practice jersey and sneakers on, and meet me outside in five."

I can't help but think this has something to do with me not acting as captain.

"What are we doin' outside?" Todd asks, lacing his shoes on the bench next to me.

"Does it look like I know?"

"Ohh, he talks today."

"Shut it, Van Luit," I snap.

He kicks his duffle bag across the short walkway, slamming it against the bottom locker.

I finish getting ready and wait at the door, seeing that everyone exits the locker room. When the last straggler leaves, I shut out the light and follow the team out.

For this, I should've rallied them together, leaving the locker room as one, being in the lead.

“You’ll be divided into four groups. Our captain, Riley, will decide which group you belong in.” Some grumbles and groans follow Coach’s words, including my own internal growl. I walk over to coach. “We’re drilling with these,” he says, pointing to a net sack of balls of different sizes. “You decide where everyone goes, including yourself, plus which group gets which ball and the tasks of each group.” Coach crosses his arms over his chest and takes a few steps back, indicating wordlessly that he’s not helping me decide anything.

I glance to the team. They’re looking at me with various forms of unrest and annoyance.

With a sigh, I grab the bag and pull out each ball. There’s a hacky sack, a foam ball the size of a softball, a kickball, and a soccer ball. Different sizes, different weight...the members of each group will have to reduce their amount of strength with their footwork and movements according to each ball.

“We’ll do this with soccer rules. Each person can use any body part, minus the hands, to pass the ball to another member. Add in volleyball rules, one person cannot touch the ball twice in a row. Sound good?” I catch a few smiles, nods, and Todd stands off to the side rubbing his hands. He’s up for the challenge. Which is good because I’m giving him the soccer ball. That should awaken his hand-eye coordination, I’ve noticed he’s been lacking. He hasn’t been making as many saves as before and he’ll be limited without his hands. “Todd,” I call him up and hand him the soccer ball. He laughs, but accepts the ball and stands a few feet away.

Next I grab the hacky sack. This one is the closest size to a puck, so I need guys who aren’t quick passers on this ball. “Hump!” I toss him the hacky sack when he’s close enough. With the kickball in hand, I yell for

Robbie, my center, and pass it to him. He'll need practice controlling his strength, not everyone can control the rocket he tends to pass.

I keep the foam ball then divide the rest of the team into our groups. Each group has five guys.

"My additional rule, ball doesn't touch the ground. You heard your captain. Your hands don't touch the ball and no double tapping. Go!" Coach follows up with his whistle and directs us in different directions.

I bounce the ball in my hand while I figure out how I want to start.

"So, we just like, kick it to another person in our group?" Dustin, a second-string asks. "Should we stand in a circle or something?"

"Actually, a circle would be good," I agree, pushing against Dan to get him to move to the left. "How about we try calling out who we're passing to?"

"Alright," Dan and Dustin agree. Jeremy and Brock shrug but don't argue with me.

With our loose circle formed, I start. "Jeremy," I call out, toeing the ball in his direction. The ball goes a bit higher than I intended.

He backs up, raising a knee to tap it. "Dust."

Dustin launches his foot to the left, trying to get under it. "Br-," he starts, but stops himself when he misses the ball completely.

Dan snickers. "You're supposed to hit it."

"He tried," Jeremy drills his short temper at Dan.

"Guys, it's not a competition, it's a tool. Practice." While Dustin scurries to catch the ball that's rolling just out of his reach, I see the kickball sail through the air towards Coach. My guess is that was Robbie's attempt.

"Riley," Dustin says tossing the ball in the air, bouncing it off his head. The ball goes the opposite direction, to Jeremy. Jeremy uses his elbow to knock it towards me.

I let it fall closer to my foot before snapping my ankle upwards, "Dan."

Dan uses his elbow, too. "Brock." But it sails toward Dustin.

Dustin taps it with his knee. "Maybe we should just say got it or something, instead of who we want it to go to?"

The ball comes back my way. I lurch forward, trying to get under it before it falls to the ground. "Got-," the ball smacks the pavement. "Don't got it."

We finally get it down, no hands, and a way to keep everyone paying attention when Coach blows his whistle.

"Water break!" He shouts to us, Dustin shoves the ball under his arm as we all wander to Coach and grab water bottles. "Okay. You guys started lookin' pretty good. But I'm going to raise the bar for you."

I squeeze the bottle, squirting more water into my mouth and hoping this isn't going to be as bad as I think it is.

"There will be two groups now. Two balls each. Same rules apply, and you can only pass to your original group. When you hear my next whistle, that means you switch balls with the group you merge with. Riley, what group is merging with you?"

I glance to my group, then the remaining groups, before looking back to Coach. "Allen's group," I say. This keeps the two lightest balls together and the two heaviest balls together. It shouldn't be too hard to grasp the change of ball. Hopefully.

"Get to it." He blows his whistle, sending us back out.

R

Yawning, I drop my jerseys and the rest of my uniforms into the washer.

"Hey," my mom says. I turn my head and glance to her. She's standing with her hip against the doorframe hugging a manila folder to her chest. Turning back, I begin wiping down my pads.

"Can we talk?" she asks

I ignore her and focus on wiping the insides of my pads down.

"I'm your mother, and I say we talk. I can't live like this anymore."

I snort. "Like what?"

"Like I'm walkin' on eggshells around my own son."

I set the Lysol wipe down on the edge of the washer and turn to her. "What do you want to talk about?"

Her cheeks puff with a breath. "Why are you so

angry?"

I roll my eyes. "Why wouldn't I be? You've been lying to me for how long now? And you've known I knew that you were lying and you still won't tell me what about. How would you feel if you were the teenager in this scenario?"

She narrows her eyes at me. "When I was a teenager, I wasn't allowed to play any sport because we couldn't afford it. I had to work at the local convenient store to help my parents with groceries-,"

"Like I'm working to pay for my own equipment, car, gas-"

"But not to feed the rest of us! I make sure we have food-,"

"But who makes sure Hannah eats the food she needs? Who makes her breakfast, packs her lunch, and ninety percent of the time makes her dinner? Who puts her to bed? Who bathes her? Who washes her clothes?"

"I get it!" She yells, but closes her eyes. "I'm not around much. So thank you for doing those things while I'm working-,"

"Or goin' out to the bar-,"

"Which is not your busine-,"

"Who cares? You tell me to not go to games or practices so you can go out! You don't care that I was trying to work towards something better so I can leave this hellhole when I graduate!"

Her face is stricken. "You're...leaving?"

"That was the plan."

She pulls her features back together and swipes a piece of hair from her face. The movement causes a white envelope and a printed photo to fall from the folder. "Your father wants to see you in a few weeks, and in two months I have to go to court." She says as she kneels to pick up the things she dropped. "Since you want to leave and be just like him..."

"Court?"

"Your father is taking me to court. Ted is paying for my lawyer and he's the reason I'm telling you anything now. You'll figure out soon enough that I've been doing what's best for you and Hannah. He's dangerous."

"What can I do?"

"Play along and call your sperm donor. Make nice with them, make nice with Ted."

"What have you been lying about? Ted said you should be honest, not that I like him or anything, but honesty would be helpful right now. Why is Jack all of a sudden taking you to court and wanting to talk to me now? Why now?"

"Ted talks too much and overreacts. I haven't been doing anything wrong at all. But when you love someone, their opinions and viewpoints become important to you as well. I understand his point of view on this particular subject. And you're sixteen, almost seventeen. You're old enough to make the right decision, no matter what I feel about anything."

I turn my back to her and continue cleaning my gear. I'll never get the truth from her.

"His cell phone number is on the freezer door,

when you're ready."

I'm not calling him.

He probably just wants to rub in how great his life is now that he doesn't have to deal with us anymore.

I don't need anything from him.

My eyes betray me and curiosity gets the better of me. I walk into the kitchen.

I won't use the number. I don't need it.

I'm definitely *not* calling him.

Chapter 17

Audrey

I pull my arms inside my sweatshirt and stare at the golden yellow walls of my bedroom, wishing they were black.

"Hey Dahling!" Billy sings, cracking my door open.

"What?"

"Aw, is coot wittle Audwey upset?"

I glare at him. "Go bug Sarah."

"That's actually why I'm here. She wants to know if you want to hit the mall with her in a few minutes, something about girly bits and shopping, and I don't wanna go. Ever." His face scrunches.

"Sure, why not?" I mutter.

"You okay?"

"Fine."

"Ri-ight, 'cause that's believable."

“Leave me alone, Billy.”

He backs out of my room, closing it softly behind him.

I glance down to my sweatpants. Sarah would kill me if I walk out of the house wearing sweats. Sniffing my sweatshirt, I scrunch my nose. I should probably change that too. It did smell faintly of Riley’s cologne. But, that’s been a month. This thing could probably walk itself to the washer. I only wear it at home, when I miss him and have no other distractions.

Billy was good at distracting me, but I lost interest in keeping up with the joking. I reminded him that Audrey Hepburn was a great role model and of all the good she’s done. He knows, but says he does it because he knows it bugs me. I’m glad he’s getting the hint that I dislike it, but I think he’ll always call me darling, he’s a weirdo.

I throw some deodorant on and change my clothes.

“Audrey! Sarah’s here!” Billy yells.

“Don’t make her beep!” Greg adds.

The front door lets out its usual creak. “I won’t beep this time. But maybe on my way out because I know how much you love it.”

I hear Sarah tease Greg, and smile. She had her dad put in an old horn, one that doesn’t sound like a normal beep. It sounds more like “Ah-OO-gah,” and Greg hates it. So she does it to irritate him.

“I’m ready,” I announce as I waltz into the living room.

Sarah spins to face me and her smile turns into a grimace. "That'll have to do, but you need some new clothes."

"Billy paying?" I grin.

"Heck no! Ask your dad...or your brother!" Billy shouts defensively.

"Relax, I'm not asking anyone for money."

"No need, I just got my first paycheck. So I'm buying you something."

"Sarah, please save your money for things you need for college," I argue.

"What have you learned about arguing with me?"

"There is no winner because even when you win, you're still pissed," Billy teases and kisses her cheek.

"He's half right," I add.

She grins at me before saying bye to the guys and rushing me out the door.

Getting in her Ford, I buckle up and try to relax. I focus on all the fun times I've had with Sarah in the past, like hiking at her grandpa's farm in the woods, putting slime on Greg and Billy's soda cans, and even our shopping trips, which tend to be more pigging out on mall food than shopping. Her horn shatters the memories and my relaxation.

"I saw this amazing pair of shoes at Velocity, I definitely want to stop there," she says excitedly. "Oh, and don't let me forget to pick up CO2 cartridges and tips for my arrows."

I chuckle. "Odd combination, but I think I can remember the last two."

"Eh, I like shoes."

"And dirt."

"Yes, that too." She turns and beams a toothy smile at me. "So, what's goin' on? Greg and Billy say you've been a pretty big downer for a while."

I shrug. "They're nosy old ladies who should stick to talking about the weather."

She laughs loudly. "I'll have to remember that the next time they're sitting in my kitchen clucking like hens."

"I'm okay," I say, but even I don't believe the lie. I'm not okay. But I'll get there. It's just hard losing a friend, especially one like Riley.

"C'mon, it's me you're lying to," she reminds me, gently.

"Fine. I'll *be* okay. I just gotta get through some stuff. I promise, if I need any help I'll ask someone. But I'll be just fine with some time."

"It's about a boy."

I roll my eyes. "No," I lie again. It's not the way she means it, but Riley is a boy.

"You're lying again, but I'll let it slide. For now."

"What else did you need at the mall?" I quickly change the subject.

"I'm not sure. I want your opinion on what to wear to a courthouse wedding that Billy claims he won't go to. I'll fix that. He'll go."

"I've only been to one wedding, when I was five, so I think my opinion would be invalid."

"You're not five anymore and you know what looks good on me and what doesn't. Your opinion is enough for me," she insists.

I drop my head to the headrest. "Let me text Alice, 'cause I suck at fashion and you know it." Pulling my phone out I type in, *courthouse wedding attire*, and click send.

A few seconds later I get, *clothes*, from Riley's number. "Oh crud!" I yell, quickly dropping my phone like it zapped me.

Sarah jumps a little. "Easy Tiger, what's wrong? Did she tell you leopard print, alligator, polar bear bras?"

Placing one hand on the dash, I lean down and fish for my phone with the other. "Is that even a thing?"

She snorts. "Ask Alice."

"I didn't ask Alice in the first place."

"What?"

"I sent the question to the wrong person. I never would've known except I got a response," I explain, snatching my phone from under the seat finally.

"Who'd you ask?"

I close my eyes. "Riley." I take a deep breath and realize that I didn't implode, shatter, or cry at the mention of his name. Progress is progress. Two weeks ago, I might have cried. Maybe snotted up my sleeves, but I'm getting over it. I think.

"What did he offer?"

"Clothes," I repeat.

She laughs. "Males. They always have the wittiest answers."

I quickly type a reply to him, *Sorry, that was actually for Alice.*

It's cool - Riley.

I'm so shocked he even answered in the first place but I'm more afraid to say anything else to him. If I say anything now, it'll be like my slip up was on purpose, or that I only thought to ask how he was because I accidentally texted him.

I text the question of clothes to Alice as my mind spins.

Audrey, you're acting weak and annoying, and if you can annoy yourself, you should probably just shut up.

Alice responds with a list of questions that provide an excellent distraction from my brain. I go through the list with Sarah and reply with her answers. No, she doesn't think there's a theme. The invite was purple paper with black words and no patterns. The date is set for two weeks after Christmas.

"Speaking of Christmas, what should I get Billy?" She asks as we walk into the mall.

"No clue, I'd get him a new hat. Actually, I think I did. Don't get him a new hat."

She groans and tugs me into Velocity. “Whatever. What are you getting Riley?”

I glance to the doors that leave the store full of high-heeled shoes. “Nothing.”

“What? You can’t! You’ve always gotten him something amazing!”

“I can. Hurry up. I want a cinnamon soft pretzel with icing.”

“Ooo, that sounds divine. But you have to get Riley something. Even if he isn’t getting you anything. It’s code. You just have to.”

“I’m not arguing about this and I didn’t bring a lot of cash with me.”

“I’ll cover it, you pay me back whenever.”

“No.”

“You can’t argue with me.”

“This isn’t up for negotiations, Sarah. No.”

She smiles, a bit evilly, but it’s still a smile. “Fine. I’ll get him something, put your name on it, and give it to him.”

“Yeah right.” I snort, walking toward the exit. I’m going to get the soft pretzel with or without her.

“If you take one more step, I will. And I’ll make sure it’s two stuffed animals kissing,” she threatens.

“He wouldn’t believe it’s from me.”

“They sell little wooden hockey sticks in one of these stores. I’ll just attach one to each stuffed animal.”

“Pick out your stupid shoes. We gotta hit Spratt’s Sports before getting me a soft pretzel.” I huff and flop back down onto the bench.

She laughs and tugs a box off the shelf. “Let’s go.”

“You’re not trying them on?”

“I did that last week, but didn’t have money then. I have money now, so I get them now.”

I nod lightly at her logic as I follow her to the cashier.

Would she pay attention to the gift so much that she’d notice I didn’t give it to Riley? Would she guess that I’m intending to buy a gift for him, but keep it for myself? Darn her and her freaky ability to spot fakes and lies.

Fine. I’ll get him the gift I intended to get him anyway. I’ll just not put my name on the “from” part and leave it by his window when I know he isn’t home.

With a loose plan set in my head, I lead the way to the escalators, ignoring the soft pretzel stand on the corner. “I’ll be right back for a gazillion cinnamon bites,” I whisper, longingly.

“You’re pathetic,” Sarah teases. “But they look amazing today. Let’s make this our fastest stop yet!”

I smile, my first genuine smile of the day, and run down the escalator steps with Sarah hot on my heels.

Chapter 18

Riley

I crack my knuckles for the tenth time in the last half hour. Audrey startled and distracted me, but it wasn't enough.

My eyes find my dark phone again. I really shouldn't call him.

I grab my phone and punch in the number, my thumb hovers over the send button. What am I supposed to say to him? *Hey, Dad. It's your son. You know, the one you've neglected for five years.* Or, *Good afternoon Mr. Silk, it's Riley.* This is something I should've asked Audrey a few minutes ago, instead of letting the conversation fall. I didn't even know she'd be invited to Mom and Ted's wedding. I roll my eyes at the thought, and bump the call button at the same time.

I stare at the screen, **Calling...**

That's not what I was trying to do.

"Hello?" A man says, clearing his throat.

I open my mouth, but I have no idea what to say.

Something shuffles on the other end. “Hello? Can you hear me?” He sounds exactly the same as I remember.

“Hi,” I lamely manage.

“Who is this?”

“It’s your…uh…it’s Riley.”

“You sound bigger,” he chokes.

I don’t really understand why he’s getting caught up. “Uh, yeah. I am bigger than I was five years ago.”

“I’m sorry,” he whispers.

He’s sorry? That’s all I get, is he’s sorry?

“I tried to come see your games this year, but I wasn’t allowed through the doors. I saw you play last year. I went to all of your games. I always have.” He was there? “Hannah looks so much like your grandma, you, and mom combined. You both have gotten so big.” Someone says something I can’t understand in the background, stopping his ramble. “I guess, but I’m fine,” he whispers.

“Do you think it’d be possible to meet for lunch, dinner, something? Can we catch up?” He pleads.

“I’m not sure what you’re really expecting from me. What’s there to catch up on?”

“There’s a whole five years that I wasn’t allowed to be present for, I’d like to see how those five years treated my boy.”

He wasn’t allowed?

“I’ve spent all five working, going to school, playing

hockey, and taking care of Hannah. I'm sure you can figure out the rest," I snap despite my confusion.

A female clears her throat. "Riley, you don't know me, and I'm sorry you don't. My name is Louise, your father's wife. I'd really like to meet you and I have some things for Hannah. We can meet at the little coffee shop in Dalesburg on Main Street. Say four o'clock tomorrow afternoon?"

"I, we-,"

"We'll see you then, Riley," she adds cheerily, with no room for argument.

I press END even though she's already hung up the phone, and chuck my phone.

This is ridiculous! Who does she think she is?

Who is she?

I look to the ceiling. There's gotta be an answer for this, a right way to handle this situation.

There's only one person I want to talk about this.

I launch myself to my feet and grab my phone again.

Taking a deep breath, I open the glass door on the entrance to the mall. Before I'm through the second set of doors, I hear the loud chattering and yelling from the food court. When I called Audrey, I didn't ask her to meet me anywhere in particular. I actually didn't explain myself either. I just asked where she was, and when she hesitantly responded that she was at the mall,

I just hung up and drove here as fast as I could.

I scan the sea of faces in the food court, looking for Audrey. I quickly run through the stores I know she'd want to hit, no matter who it is that drug her here. Not seeing her in the food court, I jog to the end of the walkway and turn left to stop at one of the clothing stores that sells sports clothing. She loves to go in there to look for her favorite team shirts and hoodies.

I jog in, and slip through the isles. Not seeing her in here, I hustle back out and hit the music store.

On my way out, I hear her laugh.

"I wish you would've taken a picture of you in a dress!" Sarah laughs with her.

"Uck, I'm sure there's one or two floating around somewhere," Audrey replies.

I turn around, nearly bumping right into her and Sarah.

"Riley," she whispers, startled. "What are you doing here?"

"Idiot, he's allowed to be here. It is the *mall*." Sarah snorts. "Hey Riley, doin' some Christmas shopping?"

I shake my head, no. "If it's alright with you, can I steal Aud?"

Audrey sputters.

"Go right ahead. I think I can handle the rest of what I need." She smiles at me before turning to Audrey, who is still sputtering and staring at me in confusion. Sarah whispers something to her, she nods and hands the two bags she was carrying to her.

"What's up?" She asks nervously.

"I-," I stop myself and sigh. "I need to talk to you."

She grimaces a bit, but nods. I lead the way out back to my car, occasionally glancing over my shoulder to be sure she's following me. Each time I look back, she's got one arm crossed over her gut and she's chewing on the thumbnail of her other hand while staring at my shoes.

This is awkward.

I haven't been much of a friend. I don't deserve her right now, but I need her. This is something I can't do alone.

I'm selfish.

Rushing through the parking lot, I unlock her door and open it for her to get in before unlocking my door. Glancing to her, I can see how nervous she really is. Her eyes are flying around everywhere but in my direction, the hand she's not chewing on is white knuckle gripping her cellphone, and her face is paler than normal. Maybe she's not nervous.

Maybe she's scared.

Shit.

Say something, idiot.

"Are you afraid of me?" I blurt like the idiot I am.

She jumps, like really jumps in her seat. "I'm, um, well no. I, it's just-,"

"Please, stop." Slowly, I reach over to her and pull

her hand away from her mouth. She tenses, visibly. "Aud, please relax. I'm not gonna hurt you, I'd never do that."

Her face hardens instantly and she snatches her hand away from mine. "Really?" she spits. "No, you'd *never* hurt me!" The sarcasm dripping in her tone tells me I am in trouble. "You'd just send me away and freeze me out only to kidnap me when I was finally starting to feel closer to normal again. Then I'd bet your next stupid plan is to freeze me out again tomorrow! Riley, I'm not a doormat!"

"I know-,"

"Oh, you know. But that doesn't stop you from doing just that. Look, you were my best friend. But things change, and apparently I wasn't able to fix anything, or even help you. But that's okay. I get it. I'm not good enough for you, it's cool. But now you need me? Just convenient-,"

"I never said any of that-,"

"Don't interrupt me!"

"Dammit, Aud!" I shout. She purses her lips and glares out the window. "I know I'm an idiot. I've been a jerk. I get that. But I'm reaching out now. I can't do what I'm about to do tomorrow without your help." She turns her head to me, her beautiful eyes still hold anger, but it's slowly fizzling out. "I'm not really kidnapping you, you're free to go whenever you'd like." I tap my fingers against the gearshift. "And I never once said you weren't good enough for me."

"What are you doing tomorrow?" Her words are like a breath of oxygen straight to my soul.

"Meeting my dad and his wife at your coffee shop,"

I whisper.

Her mouth pops open and her eyes widen further.

"Yeah, I've got so much to fill you in on."

"What do you need me for? You haven't needed me-,"

"I've been fighting the urge to text you," I tell her honestly, without looking at her. "I've been afraid to talk to you."

She laughs. "Same here."

I start up the car. "Thank you for agreeing to talk to an idiot like me."

"Chicken," she whispers as I back out.

"Looks like we both are," I agree with a short laugh.

R

"So, your mom has been lying to you for years and now going to court and suddenly you're talking to your dad?"

"That's the gist of it," I say before sucking down some milkshake.

"That's...not exactly what I had originally expected. But okay." She taps a finger against the cup in her hand. "And your mom's totally cool with you hanging out with your dad tomorrow?"

I shrug. "Her and Ted went away for the weekend and took Hannah with them. She doesn't know I'm meeting him tomorrow."

"Where'd they go?"

"Somewhere to get a dress for their wedding." I shrug.

"Why leave town for that?"

"I'm not sure. I'm not a woman. Dresses are weird."

She laughs. "I couldn't agree more."

"But you look good in dresses," I mutter, shocking myself.

She stares at me, a hint of hurt in her eyes. "How do you feel about seeing your dad?"

I guess I said the wrong thing, but I thought it was a compliment. "I'm...I don't know. I hate him but I miss him."

Her hand moves as if to comfort me, but stops short and returns back to her cup. "I'm sorry. I think you should listen to what he has to say. Bite your tongue, let him do the talking and only speak when you're ready to."

"I snapped at him on the phone today and his wife got on the line."

She laughs. "Women tend to do that when they fear for someone they love."

I shrug. "No reason to fear me. What am I gonna do over the phone?"

Her head tilts to the side as she stares at me. "The bond between parent and child is something not many understand." She takes a sip of her shake. "My mom told me, not too long after your dad left, that parents are people too. They make mistakes, just like kids and teens. No one is perfect. She also thought he'd be around you guys and support you, but she was wrong."

"He was really choked up on the phone and said he went to all my games until this year, he wasn't allowed to enter anymore and wasn't allowed to see me or Hannah since he left."

"What?" Her lip cocks with her eyebrow. "That doesn't... What exactly has your mom been lying about?"

I shake my head. "I have no idea. I haven't asked her for details and she hasn't offered much. She had some huge manila envelope a while back. She was very protective of it and screamed at Ted when he touched it. But I don't know where she keeps it."

"Would it be wrong to suggest trying to find it?"

I smirk. "We could."

"We? You want me to help you find it?"

"If you don't mind. I don't know what I'm getting myself into tomorrow."

She slides off the hood. "Let's go."

Chapter 19

Audrey

I open his mom's closet, feeling like a horrible sneak. "You're positive they won't come back early?"

"I guess it's possible. But I doubt it. Mom said she had a rush fitting with a seamstress tomorrow. Their wedding is a few weeks after Christmas."

"Oh yeah, Sarah told me about that," I mutter. Sarah told me. Not him. And Sarah didn't even know it was his mom's wedding. She's going because her mom is Ted's cousin.

"Sarah told you?"

"Yeah, she's related to Ted apparently."

"Really? I thought you and your parents were invited?"

I grab a few toddler sized shoe boxes and set them on the floor to reach a larger box on the floor of her closet. "Not that I'm aware of."

"Got it."

I pause, hand on the flap. "Got what?"

"The folder I told you about," he says. I turn and face him. He's just staring at the folder that contains information about why his life has been the way it's been for the last five years.

I hurriedly put the shoe boxes back and rush to his side. "Do you want to open it here?"

He glances to me and shakes his head, no. "My room."

He stalks out of the room, and I follow him down the hall to his room. He sits in the middle of the floor and drops the folder in front of him.

"Are you sure you want me here?" He nods, but doesn't take his eyes from the folder. "Want me to open it?"

He clears his throat and shoves it closer to me. "Please?"

I take a deep breath of courage as I sit on the floor, and open the folder.

Unopened envelopes from the court system are lying on top. I put each one in it's own pile off to the side.

"These are dated as far back as six months after Dad left," he muses.

"She petitioned the school... four times to make it so your dad couldn't get any information or set foot on school property."

"Explains why he wasn't able to come to any games this season."

"Your anger is shifting already," I note.

He pauses, hand hovering over the next paper in the pile. "I've had anger towards her for a long time."

"Not like this."

His shoulders sag. "You don't really understand. Both of your parents are amazing and together. Both of mine are shitty and divorced."

"They weren't always," I defend them. "I remember your parents when they were together. Sure they fought, but who doesn't?"

He shakes his head. "That's too long ago. People change. Love changes people and tears feelings to shreds."

My brows furrow. "Love is a positive, Riley. You can't live without love."

He glares at me. "What's next?"

I purse my lips and look back to the paper in my hand. "Email print outs." I scan the documents out of curiosity. Each one is from the same email address and each one basically says the same thing. "I will haul you to court if you don't allow me visitation with my children." And so on. He tried negotiating with her, threatening, guilting, pretty much everything.

I instantly feel terrible for him. He's tried seeing his kids. He's tried sending money to help the kids, but she apparently returned the envelopes, he's tried sending packages and letters.

"No wonder she'd never let me get the mail," Riley mutters.

Everything shifts to Riley and Hannah for me. They've had five years without knowing just how much their father loves them. He may not be perfect, but he wanted to be there. And he sort of was. Behind the scenes because Sue forced him there.

"She did what she thought was best," he says quietly. "She was protecting us."

"You can't be serious, Ri."

"What?"

"You're defending her?"

"No." His eyes fly to mine, a scowl strewn across his face. "That was her argument. She kept saying this to Ted in different words, but the same message applied each way."

"I don't think cutting out your dad was best for anyone, not even her."

"She didn't have to watch him marry the woman he cheated on her with."

"How do you even know that's the same woman? How do we even know your mom didn't lie about that, too?"

He stacks the emails back in a pile. "I don't." He shrugs a shoulder.

"I mean, they could've just separated because they argued so much and didn't know how to heal. Or they weren't in love anymore."

"Why would they stay together as long as they did if they weren't meant to be?"

I glance away from him, to his plain white walls. "I think that's a question for them."

He snorts. "Right. I haven't seen or talked to the man in five years and I'm just supposed to ask him why he and Mom split? And it's not like my mother would bother telling the truth, she obviously hasn't before."

"I think if you just listen, you'd hear the truth."

"My own mom lied. Why should I trust him?" He argues.

I tap my finger on the sole of my shoe for a moment while I think. "What does your dad have to lose? What would fuel him to lie? He wants a relationship with you and Hannah, I'd guess. So, he wants to form a foundation. Like, I haven't lied to you, and you haven't lied to me. I don't think he will now. He may leave some things out, but he wouldn't outright lie. Not if he's trying to create a bridge."

He stares at me for what feels like hours. So long that I blush and look away from him. I replay what I said and wonder if I said the wrong thing.

"This is why I needed you today."

I shrug. "I'm no expert and I don't know your dad anymore than you, but my theory makes sense. To me anyway. I've been doing a lot of research..." I stop talking right there. I don't really want to tell him what I have been researching and why.

"No, it makes perfect sense. I just..."

"You still don't want to see him?"

He sags. "Not really. But in a twisted way I do. Like I said, I hate him but I miss him."

I stay silent, letting him work out whatever he needs to work out. It's not like we're okay yet, either. There's still this barrier between us. He was able to cast me aside so easily, but wanted me back the minute things got tough.

This is going to cause a hurricane for me later.

Maybe I shouldn't have given in to him. I'm not good enough unless I'm wearing a dress or when he needs help with dealing with what stresses him out. I suppose I should get used to this treatment.

I'm his convenient friend.

A

"I should go," I whisper to him. We've been sitting in silence on his floor. The sun has gone down and my parents will likely start calling soon.

He swallows loudly. "Can you...can you stay?"

I roll my head against the edge of his bed to look at him. "I-,"

"I mean, I know I don't deserve your company, but can you just stay...for a little while longer?"

The longer I stay here with him, the more hurt I feel. But this isn't about me. It's about my friend who needs me. I chew on my cheek for a moment. "Let me make a phone call. I'll be right back." I push myself off his floor and slide my phone out of my pocket. I send a quick text to Candy, asking if she can cover for me for a few hours. When she responds with a yes, I call my dad.

"Hey sweetie, where you at?" He answers.

"I'm over at Candy's now. Is it alright if I stay here for dinner?"

"I don't see why not. Just be home by ten."

I smile. "Thanks Daddy."

After ending the call with my dad, I quietly push Riley's door back open. His head is buried in his hands, so I quietly take my seat on the floor next to him.

"I'm tired of hurting," he mumbles.

Tentatively, I place my hand on his shoulder. "What can I do?"

His hand slowly reaches for me, landing just above my knee. "Don't leave me."

His voice begs me to stay. But I can't stay here with him. I'd get in so much trouble. "I can't stay."

"Please," he whispers. He sits up and looks at me, tears in his eyes. "Everyone good leaves me. Don't leave me."

His chest heaves.

"I have to go home in a few hours," I argue lightly.

He takes a deep breath and glances to the ceiling. The storm inside of him seems to pass for the moment.

"I'm gonna be a jerk again."

I groan. "You don't have to be, you know."

"I'm gonna get angry, again."

"Happens to everyone."

"I'm gonna get scared, too."

"Because you're a chicken," I say, hoping to make him smile.

"I might take things out on you that you don't deserve."

I frown. "Riley, it's not okay that you shut me out. I get why. But it's not okay. Don't shut me out anymore."

He turns his head and stares into my eyes. "I might try, though."

"Idiot."

He laughs and lightly squeezes my leg. "Can you come with me tomorrow?"

My hand falls from his shoulder as I shift away from him. "Isn't that..." I clear my throat and shield my heart with my arms. "Isn't that something you should do privately?"

He reaches for me, but doesn't make contact. "You don't have to sit next to me or talk to him or his wife with me. I'd just feel better knowing you were there."

My eyes fly back to his, filled with hope. My heart takes off in a happy beat. But my brain doesn't agree. All of this today is bordering rocky terrain. The facts of feelings. Feelings undefined but full of meaning.

"I'll be there. You may not see me, but I'll be there."

His mouth opens as if to say something, but closes quickly.

Instead of focusing on him and his reaction, I focus on the spot on my leg where his hand was. It's cold where it was once warm. Much like our relationship.

The freeze creeps back in, and I shiver.

He clears his throat, and my eyes find his again. The blue of his eyes, the ice inside of me, it's all too much. I feel like I'm trapped in a soggy blizzard. So many things I want to say, want to ask, but so many responses and answers I don't want to hear.

I need to get out of the slush, so to speak. Shaking myself, I sit a bit straighter.

"Want to see what we can make for dinner?"

"What time do you need to go home?" He asks, standing and stretching.

"Ten."

He nods and helps me stand.

His touch is like a warm summer breeze, comforting, but the look in his eyes, is an arctic blast in winter. I glance to the cuff bracelet that I haven't taken off since he gave it to me. *She finds peace in the mud.* I could really use some mud right now. Peace, or even a stronger mask would be welcomed right about now.

Following him down the stairs, I stay silent. I can't think of anything to say. The awkwardness is back.

Does he know what he's doing to me?

Do I?

A growl of frustration escapes my mouth.

Instantly, I become hyperaware of him. Every

single move, the way his head is tilted to the side and his stride is quicker than it was a second ago. My pulse drums in my ear and my cheeks heat. He heard my growl and apparently thinks I'm so hungry that he's moving too slow for my liking.

"We can heat up a frozen pizza," he offers as he flicks the kitchen light on.

"Whatever works for you."

"There's a frozen pasta meal, too?"

"It's up to you."

He turns away from the freezer. "Pasta or pizza?" I open my mouth to tell him to choose, but he stops me. "Pasta. You'll like it better than the pizza."

"Okay," I whisper and take a seat.

Why is a conversation with him so much harder than it used to be? It wasn't so long ago that we could joke and talk about anything and everything.

I'm still waiting for the simplicity of seventeen like my mom said, but I fear I'm an anomaly and nothing will be simple ever again.

Chapter 20

Riley

I'm going to vomit, I think, as I pace the living room for the hundredth time. I shoot a quick text to Audrey, making sure she's meeting me at Cuppa's.

I don't want to see him.

He probably has nothing good to say.

His wife is going to make everything worse.

Maybe Mom was right to keep me away from him.

I'm five, staring at my dad in awe. "How'd you get this?"

He smiles, eyes crinkling the way they do when he's happy. "I bought this for you. I knew you had to have it as soon as I saw it."

I hug the jersey to my chest. "Will it ever fit me?"

He laughs, loudly. "Let's try it on." He takes the jersey from my hands and slips it over my head. My hands barely make it to the elbows and it almost touches my feet. "Well, you swim in it now, but you'll grow into it."

I look down at the jersey again. My favorite team. Pittsburgh Penguins. And this one has my last name on it.

"This is what I wanna be when I grow up, Dad."

"We can make that happen, Buddy. I have no doubt you'll be the most talented boy on the ice."

I'm nine. I had my first real injury on the ice. Another boy tripped in front of me and I landed on his skate. Cut my shin wide open.

I cried the whole way off the ice.

Dad met me at the edge, scooped me up and ran to the EMT on site. "Ri, you might need stitches, but one day, you'll show this scar off with pride."

I sniffle. "Am I gonna skate again?" I ask, trying to ignore the lady messing with my pant leg.

His lips twitch. "Do you think she's gonna cut it off?"

My eyes bug out. "No!" I yell.

The lady chuckles. "No amputations today, young man. Just a few stitches and you'll be as good as new."

My shoulders sag. "Good. I wanna skate. I like it."

He straightened and turned away for a moment.

In a panic I latched my hand on his arm. "Don't go anywhere."

"I'd never leave you, buddy."

I never felt the lady give me stitches. Dad joked the whole time, keeping me distracted.

But then he left.

And then he stayed away, or maybe Mom really did keep him away this whole time.

Glancing to the clock, I should leave now if I'm going to meet him.

I take two steps toward the door and my chest tightens like the way it did in Audrey's garage.

Ignoring the tightness, I take a deep breath, clenching my keys and phone, and continue walking to the door. My stomach churns and leaps to my throat.

I force myself to the door and exit the house. Audrey is waiting on my front porch. Holding up my pointer finger, I dart around the side of the house and upchuck in a bush.

Closing my eyes, I pray I'm done. I spit a few times, trying to get rid of the bile taste.

"Here," she whispers.

I open my eyes, she's handing me a piece of gum. "Thanks," I mutter and take the gum.

"You don't have to go through with this if you're sick."

I stand, wobbling a little as I'm unsure what I want. "I'm not sick." With my hands fisted, I walk to my car. This time, there's just the tightness in my chest. "Can you drive?" If what happened in her garage happens today, I do not want to be behind the wheel.

"Yeah, sure." She reaches for the keys, brushing her fingers against mine. My heart squeezes and thumps loudly in my chest. The urge to hold her hand is overwhelming.

But I can't.

Love brings emptiness and sorrow.

I don't need any more of that.

R

My leg bounces and my stomach churns again.

A man approaches the corner I'm sitting in. He's tall, thickly built, and dark blonde hair pulled back into a ponytail.

My father.

He stands about two feet away from me, blue eyes as blue as mine shine with tears and the smile on his face is reminiscent of every time I won growing up.

"You made it," he says quietly.

I nod. Not trusting my stomach yet. Glancing to the chair closest to the cash register, I find Audrey's eyes. The warmth shining through her and her sweet smile, gives me the comfort I need.

"I'm glad you made it, Riley," he says as he takes a

seat.

Again, I don't trust my stomach enough to say anything.

"I know you hate me, but if you'd give me-,"

"I don't hate you," I say, surprising myself.

"I'm glad to hear it."

Not trusting myself to respond, I don't. I continue to stare at him. The scar on his right index finger where he smashed it working on a car when I was eight is still there, and silver. There's a new scar on his right hand that I don't know how he got, but other than that, he seems the same, just older. The curious part of me wants to know what he's been doing these last five years, but most of me just wishes he'd leave and stay gone. Everything is so complicated.

"I never left you and Hannah," he says solemnly. "Your mother and I had our problems and I couldn't live that way anymore. I will always love her-,"

"Why love someone you aren't with? If you love her, you never should've left," I snap.

"Riley, one day you'll understand. It's okay to love people no matter if you're single or married. I love your mother in the way that friends have love between them. It goes a little deeper though, she was my first for everything." His shoulder rises and falls in a light shrug. "We made two amazing kids out of love-,"

My lip curls in disgust. "Gross-,"

He gives me a crooked smile that reminds me of myself. "We may not have stayed in love, but I do love her. She's your mother."

"How are you not pissed at her?"

"I never said I wasn't angry with her," he adds. "But, I've had time to deal with things, especially with the help of Louise. If it hadn't been for her, I probably wouldn't be sitting here to talk to you today."

Not wanting to understand what he's talking about or hear any more about love, I change the topic a small degree. A topic I can remain empty and not feel. "So, you married the homewrecker, then what?" My lungs squeeze inside my chest.

"Homewrecker?"

"Your wife, the woman you left us-Mom for?" I remind him, letting anger color my tone.

"I didn't leave your Mom for Louise." He looks at me in confusion.

"You didn't cheat on Mom with Louise?" My brows furrow.

With his lips pursed, he shakes his head no. "I never cheated on your mother."

I can't say I'm not completely surprised that that was a lie, too.

"O-kay. How'd you meet Louise then?" Trying to look uninterested, I add an eye roll for good measure.

For some unknown reason, I'd really like to know how he ended up with Louise, and if she's a good person or not. And that curiosity makes me want to run from this café and never look back, or tell him he's stupid for leaving Mom, maybe hit him. But those options make me feel worse.

It gets harder to breathe.

"Did your- never mind." He shakes his head. "Louise and I met at the courthouse."

"The courthouse?" This is a perfect distraction, they're criminals.

"Yeah, we were both their for hearings-,"

"Criminals?"

"Um, no. Neither of us. We both had family court hearings," he explains.

Things my mom said swirls in my head. "But Mom never showed up." Everything I know shifts again, for the hundredth time. I should ignore everything I thought I knew, nothing is the same and nothing was true.

His lips thin and he shakes his head, confirming my statement. "It was the third time she didn't show the first year after the divorce finalized. I thought it was a lost cause, that I'd lost my kids for good." He closes his eyes and takes a deep breath. "It was a bad moment for me. But Louise, she sat beside me on the bench and listened. She didn't know my name, or I hers at the time, I just needed someone to hear me and she needed someone to distract her." Tears pool in his eyes again. I swallow and try not to notice. "She loved me through the hardest time in my life. She never let me give up on you or Hannah. I don't know what happened this last time, but your mother finally contacted me."

"Ted," I say flatly. "Mom's fiancé. He grew up in a broken home."

He looks down to his hands clasped on his lap. "Does this Ted treat you right?"

Ted's alcohol use and previous abusive behavior instantly comes to mind. But he's been taking a different path recently.

"I mean, is he acting as a father?"

"Not really."

"Hannah?"

"No." Ted doesn't treat us like a father treats his children. "It's better now. But still not like...parental."

His eyes snap to mine, searching my face.

I won't tell him what happened. Should I?

I shift uncomfortably under his stare and quickly glance to Audrey. She locks eyes with me. I try to tell her to come here, without moving or speaking, just willpower alone. Panic begins to bubble, my chest tightens and my stomach drops to the floor.

My vision starts to fray along the edges and gray seeps in.

"Is that Audrey Jacobs?" He whispers, breaking my concentration and easing my panic a fraction. "I haven't seen her in-,"

"Since before you left," I finish for him.

He blanches at my abruptness. "Are you and her still friends?" I nod. "Would you like to invite her over? If it'll be more comfortable?"

I start to object, but then I think about it. I need Audrey. She's the one who's always pulled me from the darkness. The only one who truly knows me. "If you wouldn't mind."

He smiles. "Not at all. Would you like to meet Louise?"

I remind myself that Audrey will be by my side. And as nervous as I am, I nod despite myself before darting over to Audrey.

"What are you do-," she watches my dad leave. "Are you guys done already?"

"Not exactly." Her brows furrow. "Sit with me over there? He's bringing Louise in-,"

"I shouldn't, Ri. Really. It's okay. You're doing great."

"Aud, please? He asked if I'd invite you to join us."

She sucks her lips into her mouth but nods.

"Thank you." The words tumble from my mouth as my shoulders sag with relief.

R

I sit on the hood of my car and watch Audrey climb over and sit next to me.

"That was a bit unexpected," she mutters. "But your dad was very nice."

I nod.

"Louise seems like a cool person."

I nod again.

"You okay?"

Not knowing exactly how to answer, I don't. My

father has been in a non-existent spot for so long. It's weird to talk to him, to have his number in my phone, and to have agreed to meet him for lunch next week. The things I thought I knew, I didn't know. I don't hate him.

But I don't really know what to think of him either.

Louise is just...the way she made my father smile was weird. She didn't really have to say much, he just smiled because she was there.

Mom and Ted aren't like that.

Maybe something is wrong with my father or Louise.

"They're weird," I mutter.

"What do you mean? I thought they were very nice. And they even had stuff for you and Hannah."

I turn my head to her. "They were...I don't know. Just weird."

She snorts. "They were happy to see you."

I shrug. "Louise talked to me like she knew me. She doesn't."

"No, but she's trying."

"But why?"

She shrugs. "I don't know. Maybe because you're her husband's child?"

"Can't be it. There's something I'm missing."

"Riley, will you ever let anyone love you?"

I glare at her. "Why would either of them love me? What did I do to deserve their love? They don't know me." The anger I've been ignoring most of the day starts to consume me, and the tightness in my chest completely vanishes.

"That does-,"

"I mean, really, who loves me? My mother doesn't. Hannah doesn't know what love is, she's too little-,"

"Hannah knows love," she shouts, stopping my rant. "Hannah knows love can be warm, kind, and important. She has you! You care for her and make sure she has everything she needs. You are her world. She also has my parents, who love her-,"

"That's different," I protest. "And it's not love."

"I'm sure your mom loves you too, she just shows it differently."

"Or not at all."

"Riley, there is love all around you. Quit thinking about all the negatives and try looking for the positives."

I look away from her pleading eyes.

How can love be all around me? It's nowhere. It's nothing.

Love is pain.

Love is empty.

Love hurts.

Love isn't in my house. My house is a hellhole. This is the first time I've ever had the weekend to do whatever I want to without having to tiptoe. Love doesn't save my sister from their drunken fights and fits of rage. Where was love when Ted beat my mom? Where was love when my father left in the first place?

"You'll never understand," I spit.

"You'll never know the good in life if you don't let love in," she whispers. "I'm afraid for you, Riley. A life without love is a painful, lonely existence. Not just for you, but those who do love you." She hops off the hood of my car. "I'm sorry."

I watch her leave. She's leaving after she said she wouldn't leave me.

"Where's love now?" I mumble to myself. Rolling off the hood, I kick the tire before getting inside and punching the steering wheel. "Love is painful and pointless. A life without love is a damn blessing."

Chapter 21

Audrey

What is life without love?

Love is in every breath, every touch, and every movement. Love is beautiful, and beauty is everywhere. Would the night sky look the same without love? Would the feel of the mud be the same without love?

I drag my chucks along the gravel on the side of the road, my shadow stalking my every movement as I pass under a streetlight. The golden hue of light casts over everything, turning my white chucks yellow and my blue jeans to a rust color.

Headlights bounce along the road.

Each time I see headlights, I hope it's Riley.

For whatever reason, oh right - Love.

I snort and kick at a larger rock, sending it skittering across the road.

The car slows down and pulls over along the

shoulder across the street. It's a black, four-door car with the bass loud enough that I can hear it over here.

You always hear stories about kidnappings late at night in small towns. I swallow hard and my muscles tense instantly.

"Aud?" I hear Todd yell over the music that's just gotten louder.

My breath hitches as the silly fear leaves my muscles and mind. "What are you doin'?"

He jogs across the street. "What you doin' walkin' out here in the cold?"

My mouth pops open to respond, but I stop my first reaction. I hadn't even noticed how cold it was. "I'm walkin' home."

"Let me give you a ride, please."

The chill of the night seeps through my fleece hoodie, I nod.

His hand lightly presses on my back as we cross the street to his car. "Holy crap, you're frozen." He runs ahead of me and opens the passenger door. "Get in, the heat's cranked."

I sit down and as he shuts the door, I shove my hands in front of the vent. My eyes close with how good the heat feels.

"You look iced," Todd says, turning his music off, thankfully.

"I hadn't noticed until you pointed it out," I say through chattering teeth.

"What are you doin' on this end of town?"

I chew on my cheek, not really wanting to talk about it.

"Trying to talk to Riley again?" I nod, refusing to look at him. "How'd that go?"

I take a deep breath. "It was awkward, but I don't really want to talk about it. Please, just take me home." I shift my eyes to the window, watching the streetlights come to view and pass within seconds.

How can Riley be so adamant about how unimportant love is?

"Love is unimportant to... Did you-? Wait, I'm confused," Todd stammers.

"What?"

"You just said-,"

"No I didn't," I nearly shout at him. How could I have said that out loud? Crap!

He blows out a breath and taps his fingers on his steering wheel. "Did you tell Riley you love him?"

"What? Don't be ridiculous, Todd."

"Audrey, you..." he becomes silent, the only noise is him jingling his keychain dangling from the ignition.

I swallow roughly as he turns onto my street. "Todd, I said it was an awkward night with him, please don't make our relationship awkward, too. I kind of happen to like having this loose friendship with you. Ya know, since you're not being a jerk and all."

He snorts a laugh. "Hey, I apologized for that

already. But listen, I didn't mean to make it awkward. I'm just shocked and-,"

"Todd, it was a passing thought that escaped me. I didn't mean to say it out loud."

"In a way, it makes sense... Uh your thought about Riley, I mean. If you had his parents, would you think love was important?"

"I would want to fight harder for-,"

"That's you. Not Riley. He's hyperaware that people he cares about most, leave him. It's only a matter of time before Hannah does, and anyone else he cares about. You."

"I-,"

"I'm not saying what he's doin' is right. I'm just sayin' that's who he is. I thought you figured that out a long time ago."

I stare at the front of my house for a full minute before responding to him. "I guess I deluded myself into thinking that he'd never shut me out."

"I still don't think that was intentional," he admits.

I chew on my cheek again. He doesn't know about the kiss. No one does. But that's where the awkwardness started.

That stupid kiss.

That beautiful kiss.

It ruined us. We're no longer best friends. "I should get inside before my parents freak. Thank you for bringing me home."

His hand pats my arm, and I quickly glance to him, not expecting his touch. He flashes me his charming smile. "Anytime Aud, no one deserves to walk in the cold."

I nod and try to smile. It doesn't reach my eyes, but it'll do for now. Bracing myself against the chill of the night, I run to my porch and push open the door.

"You're late!" My mom yells. I close the door and turn around to face the music. "Where have you been?"

I swallow the building saliva in my mouth. "I-,"

"We tried calling your phone, and no answer!"

"I'm sorry!" I shout so she stops her rant. "Riley and I fought and I walked home until Todd picked me up."

Mom's face softens. "Could've answered your phone-,"

I pull it from my pocket to show her it's shut off. "I turned it off earlier when we were visiting his dad and stepmom."

"I take it things didn't go so well?"

"I thought they went alright, but Riley..." I shake my head, frowning.

She pats the cushion next to her on the couch, and I trudge my way to her. "Baby, these things take time. Things haven't been smooth for him. You know that."

I nod. "I know. But he sounds like he's given up on...everything."

She puts her arm around me. "Just give him time,

love." Love, something that Riley doesn't believe in. "Now, get to bed, it's still a school night. And we'll talk about your punishment tomorrow."

I nod and hug her before heading to my room. I don't bother changing. I drop on my bed and throw the covers over my body. Hugging my pillow, I try to ignore everything, the pain of the frozen feeling inside of me, the worry of my punishment, and the worry of what will happen tomorrow when I see Riley.

I empty my head.

At least, I try to. Even if sleep doesn't come easy, it won't be because I'm wallowing.

A

"I had the *best* weekend, ever!" Alice sighs dramatically.

I try to smile. "That's wonderful."

"Oh my gosh! I met the cutest boy at daddy's work. He was working off his debt to his dad-,"

"Lovely, a criminal," Candy teases.

"No, he borrowed money from his dad to repair his car."

I nod, trying my hardest to keep up with the conversation. But eyes keep scanning the hall, hoping to catch a glimpse of Riley. He's been back and forth so often lately, I probably shouldn't care anymore. He's made his choice.

"He's watching you," Candy whispers.

I snap my head in her direction. "What? Who?"

"Todd," she says pointing to where Todd's locker is.

Disappointment floods me, threatening to pull me under again. I hadn't realized how badly I wanted her to say Riley. I give Todd a half smile and he waves me over.

"I'll be back," I tell the girls and walk over to him. "Mornin'."

"You look like hell," he says with a sad smile.

I shrug. "Who cares?"

He shakes his head. "It'd be cheesy if I said that I care, wouldn't it?"

Snorting, I punch his shoulder. "Shut up. I'm fine. Just didn't sleep much-,"

"I know you're worried, but I think you should give him space. All he's doin' is hurtin' you." He wraps me in a hug.

For whatever reason, I let go. I let go of the pain, the worry, the fear, and more importantly, I let go of my tears. They flow freely into Todd's shoulder and I clutch his shirt.

I don't want to lose my best friend.

A locker slams, pulling me from my personal misery, and causing me to jump away from Todd.

"I knew you two had a thing," Libby spits. "Audrey, I thought we had an agreement."

I swipe at my eyes and glare at her. "Libby, we never had any sort of agreement. We don't talk. And excuse me for not discussing my friendships with you."

"I'll let you two be all cozy. I'm sure the tears will pass and in a moment, you'll be all over each other again."

"Lib. Stop," Todd pleads.

"Libby. I've never been all over Todd. Our friendship isn't like that. I'm having a bad enough morning, do you mind taking a hike with your attitude, maybe right off a cliff?"

Libby's eyes grow wide and a look of terror crosses her face.

"Libby, why do you care if Audrey seeks *comfort* from Todd, he's your ex. Not your property," Riley spits.

My back stiffens. "I didn't seek him. He was there. Unlike someone *else*." I don't even look at him. I want to, but I hold my resolve and keep walking.

Candy frowns and links her arm with mine. "You're doin' great."

My chin trembles. "No. No, I'm not."

Chapter 22

Riley

I'm numb inside.

There's nothing but an echo of my former self.

The old me, the one that made it a point to care about Audrey, never would've let this happen.

The old me never would've hurt her.

I

am

numb.

Love does this to people. The illusion of love lifts you up to your highest but as soon as the light dims you crash hard. People hold onto the illusion like a fragile vase, but as soon as it shatters, what do you have? Blood, tears, and broken pieces that never quite fit together.

Love

is

breakable.

R

"Who can tell me the lesson Romeo and Juliet teaches us?" the English teacher asks.

I tap the eraser of my pencil on the edge of the desk.

"Riley, what did you learn from Romeo and Juliet?" Annoyance colors her tone.

I raise my eyes to meet hers. "That love kills you."

A few gasps and snickers follow my words.

"Why do you say that? It wasn't love that killed them-,"

"They held the illusion of love higher than the physicality of living. Love killed them. Regardless of the torment each experienced, they both chose wrong. You can't live with love-,"

"Love isn't an illusion, it's a feeling from your heart and soul," Audrey interrupts me. I don't look at her. I refuse to allow that. "They faced their world without each other and couldn't stand to live without the light of love. They were doomed from the start-,"

"Holding love higher than life is for fools," I interrupt her. "What's the point of life or the "feeling" of love if it only breaks you or kills you? Life is meant to be lived."

"This, class..."

I tune out. I can't listen to anymore or participate. Succumbing to the numbness is easier than dealing with a discussion about love.

It's pointless.

R

I rush into the house after a hard practice. "I'm home!"

"Ri!" Hannah hollers and runs over to me, tears in her eyes. "Mom…"

Ice trickles through my veins. "Stay here," I command, pushing her back against the door and run into the kitchen.

Mom is curled in a ball on the floor.

"Mom," I ask, tentatively. "Where's Ted."

"Take Hannah up to bed," she whispers.

My brows furrow. "What happened?"

Slowly, she sits up. "Leave."

"Wha-,"

She spins on the floor, face red, tears drying. "Leave if you want to! I know what you did!"

My mouth drops open. "What did I do?"

Her eyes become hard and eyelids form slits, glaring at me. "You went to *him*! You're going to leave me just like he did! Well I'm beating you to it! *Leave!*" She screams at me. "All Silk men ever do is leave!"

"But you told me-,"

"I never thought you, of all people, would betray me the way you have!"

"I didn't betray anyone!"

"You are just like your father! Always taking the coward's way! Get out of my house!"

Confusion and anger cloud my mind.

Backing out of the kitchen, I turn to Hannah. She's hugging herself, confused and frightened tears streaming down her face.

What's left of my heart goes through a grater hidden in my chest, leaving it in a dirty pile on the floor to be swept up like trash.

I walk over to her. "Come on, let's get you to bed." Holding my arms out to her, she launches at me, trembling in my arms.

"Don't leave me," she whispers into my shoulder.

I swallow hard. "I won't be gone long. You'll see me tomorrow morning, promise."

"Mommy said th-things today."

"Mommy is just...angry and confused. It'll be okay, Han." Nodding, she squeezes my neck as I take her up to her room. When I reach her room, she sniffles as I set her on her bed.

"You'll be here to wake me up?"

I pull her flannel pajamas from her dresser drawer. "Yep. I wouldn't miss our mornings for anything."

She tugs her jammies out of my hand when I reach her again. "Okay. Can I have Fruity Pebbles?"

"Of course." I smile. "I'm going to run over to my room quick, I'll be right back to tuck you in, get your jammies on and put your dirty clothes in the hamper." I leave her room and throw some clothes into my spare duffel bag. Squatting down, I dig under my bed for my stash of cash and unplug my phone charger while I'm there.

With my bag packed, I head back out to the hallway. Mom glares at me from the bottom of the stairs. Dropping my bag, I quickly walk over to Hannah.

"Goodnight, Squirrel. I love you." I lift her blanket up to her chin and make sure she has her stuffy before kissing her forehead.

"I love you, Ri. See you in the morning," she whispers.

My heart feels like ground beef. My mother will not keep me from my sister. I will be back in the morning to get her up and give her breakfast. If I don't, Hannah would likely go without food.

"I promise, you'll never be without me," I swear to her, and our mother, as I close Hannah's door.

Picking up my bag, I stalk down the stairs. My mother points to the door, unflinching.

Without a word, I exit the house I hate, the house I call home, the place where my sister stays.

Mom slams the door, locking it and the deadbolt slides with a resounding thud. No return.

Love

hurts.

I grip the handle of my duffel bag and walk to my car, pulling the hood of my sweatshirt over my head. Where am I going to go? I throw my duffel bag in the backseat and drop into the driver's seat.

Everyone who's ever liked me doesn't like me anymore.

Because I pushed them away.

Glancing to my neighbor's house, I begin to think that, maybe, I have some hope. He's a teammate and we used to be friends for years.

Resigning to the fact I may have to grovel, I back out of my driveway and creep to a stop in front of Todd's house.

Tires screech to halt beside me. I turn away from Todd's house, looking straight into Todd's Jetta. He tilts his head to the side and purses his lips. I shrug a shoulder and he pulls into his driveway. I get out and walk towards him, slowly.

"Um... What's up?" Todd asks over the roof of his car.

I take a deep breath. "I need some help."

He snorts and shakes his head. "Yeah, you do. But I'm not the right person for that job."

"Look, I'm sorry alright?" I swallow a lump in my throat. "I've been treating everyone like..."

"Dirt? Scum? Crap?" he offers an answer for me.

I nod in a agreement and ignore the tightness in

my chest. “All of the above.”

“What do you want, Riley?” He rolls his eyes and looks skyward. “You should be apologizin’ to Audrey.”

“I need a place to crash, hopefully just for the night.”

His eyes fall to mine then travel to my house. “Let’s go talk to my parents quick.”

“Thank you.”

Without another word, I follow him into his house. It’s set up about the same as mine, Just reversed. Directly in front of the front door is the hallway and stairs to the second floor, but the hall is on the left side of the stairs instead of the right. And it smells strongly of potpourri instead of Clorox. Though, I’m almost positive Todd doesn’t clean everything every day so he doesn’t get sick as often. His mom probably does that for him.

“Ma!” Todd yells.

“Kitchen, sweetie!”

I kick my shoes off next to the door and follow Todd down the hall to the kitchen. Belatedly I notice Todd kept his shoes on, even though they’re wet with snow and road slush.

“Hi, baby. How was practice tonight? Was-,” she stops midsentence as she sees me follow behind him. A large smile blossoms across her face. “Riley! How are you, honey?” She reaches for me, giving me an awkward, one-armed hug while trying not to touch me with her hands. I glance around her and see that she’s cutting up strawberries.

"Hi, Mrs. Van Luit," I respond with the best smile I can manage. "I've been better."

"Yeah, Ma, about that. Can Riley crash here for the night, or maybe a few days-,"

"It's really no trouble, I don't want to impose-,"

"Don't be silly. You can stay here as long as you need." The sincerity in her tone takes me by surprise. "Is the couch okay for tonight? I haven't been able to change the bedding in Andy's room since his last stay." She frowns.

"The couch is completely fine," I say relieved that I have a warm place for the night. "It might only be for tonight. I'm sorry to intrude last minute like this." This time I frown, because I'm not sure how to explain what happened. Or what she knows.

"Not a problem. Why don't you go bring your stuff in from the cold? I assume you have your gear and book bag, right?"

"Yes, ma'am. I brought some clean clothes as well."

"Go ahead and grab them. Todd, set the table for us and Riley," she orders.

I nod and quickly rush out to my car. Opening my backdoor, I lean in and grab the strap to my gear and the tug it closer to me.

"Riley!" My mother screams. I jump, smacking my head on the hanger hook on the ceiling of my car. "Why are you home so late? And why are you not parked in the driveway?"

I rub the back of my head, more to try to wipe away the pain than in confusion, though I'm plenty confused. "I'm staying with Todd tonight. You kicked me out," I remind.

She crosses her arms over her chest and smiles at me. "Silly boy, I'd never do that! Get your stuff and come inside to help me with dinner before Teddy gets home!"

My mouth pops open and my brows furrow with my confusion. "Mom, are you okay?"

She snorts. "I'm fine, my sweet baby. It's too cold out here, I'll see you inside."

I'm frozen, and not from the temperature, not from the ice that I love and cling to, not from the game either, but from this huge mood swing that Mom doesn't seem to remember. I watch as the "good" mom walks back into the house.

Should I just go to Todd's as planned?

What happened to my mom? Is she on something? Is this a trap?

Would my mom really hurt me?

Chapter 23

Audrey

I stare at my phone at three o'clock in the morning.

I need help - Riley

Riley's texting me.

Asking *me* for help. At three something in the dammed morning.

On a school day.

Why in the world would Ri-

I sit straight up in bed.

Riley's asking for help. My mind races at warp speed, displaying all sorts of horrible images that fuel my fear and stir memories from the past.

Did Ted... No. He wouldn't.

He could've.

I scramble off my bed, but remembering that I'm still wearing what I wore last night, I tug off my sweatshirt and throw on my brother's Scooby shirt. To help against the cold, I pull a pair of orange polka dot sweats over my jeans and rush to my door. Skidding to a stop at the door, I turn and launch myself back to my bed, snatching my phone from my mattress as I bounce.

Coming! A, I respond quickly.

Digging in my bag, I grab my license and keys from the front pocket and run for the front door. At this point, I don't care that I'm breaking curfew. I don't care that I'm grounded. I don't care about anything except reaching Riley's and making sure that he and Hannah are okay.

The bone-chilling cold of winter is no match for the fear and dread I feel inside. The whole way to Riley's, I pray that he and Hannah are okay. I can't stop shaking as I drive and pray that his mom and Ted are not still fighting.

I don't care if Riley never speaks to me again, so long as he's safe.

I pull into his driveway, and notice I don't see his car.

Panic floods me.

Was I fast enough?

Did he have to rush Hannah to the hospital?

I throw my car into and park and shut off the ignition. Yanking the keys out, I throw the door open and nearly fall out. As I regain my balance, I see his car in front of Todd's.

I have no idea where he is now.

Riley's front door creaks. I spin around, nearly sliding in the snow. He's standing in the doorway, blonde hair an absolute mess, sticking up in all directions. His face is a bit red, but he looks completely unharmed. Running, I launch at him, throwing my arms around his neck.

"Hi," he whispers, gently patting my back. He tenses under my touch.

"Thank god you're okay! Where's Hannah? Is she okay? What happened?" The questions tumble from my lips in rapid succession.

"I need your help with my mom," he whispers.

I back away to look at him. "I'm not a doctor, or even a nurse-,"

"I just need you help me get her upstairs then I can clean up after her."

My eyebrows shoot up. "This doesn't sound good."

"She was drunk, or high on something, I can't tell. But she was weird since I got home from practice." He pushes the door open behind him and takes a step back. "Now, try not to freak, it looks worse than it is. She kind of went nuts." He turns around quick, but not fast enough that I didn't see the new pink tint creeping up his neck.

How ever this place looks, he's embarrassed.

Shutting the door behind me, I pause, staring at the destruction Sue inflicted on the house. I'm thankful it was objects, and not people.

The handrail is teetering on one bracket, the four pictures on the wall in the hallway are smashed on the floor, and there's sand or something similar strewn on the hardwood floor of the hall.

"Wow," I whisper.

"Just wait," he mumbles.

I follow him into the living room and stop short of the entrance. Riley steps over the coffee table that's on its side. The couch is crooked and missing a cushion, the TV is on the floor instead of the stand, and Sue's bookshelf is collapsed on the floor.

"Where's your mom?" I whisper.

He clears his throat, and I tear my eyes away from the wreckage and find his. He points behind the couch. I carefully make my way to him as he pushes the couch further from the wall.

I walk around Riley to see his mom. She's got her face pressed to the wall and a bloody hand shielding the side of her face.

"Oh, Riley," I whisper.

With Riley doing most of the heavy lifting, we get her off the floor and rest her on the couch. She snores loudly, but other than that, she makes no noise.

"Are you sure she's going to be okay? I mean, she's not gonna-,"

"I honestly don't know," he says. "I imagine she'll sleep off whatever it was and be just fine when she wakes up." He glances at her, eyes full of disdain. "Probably be sore, too."

Without speaking, we clear a path to the stairs and go back to his mom. Lifting her from the couch is much easier than from the floor. I have one calf in each hand, and he has his arms just under her chest with her head resting on his chest. She has an angry red scrape on her cheek and she's drooling. I don't know what happened tonight or what she took to act how ever she acted, I just hope it doesn't happen again.

Carefully, we rest her on her bed, and Riley covers her up.

"Where's Hannah? Is she okay?" I whisper as he closes his mom's door.

"She's in her safe place," he answers sadly, pausing in front Hannah's door.

"Go check on Hannah, I'll get started downstairs," I encourage him. He nods and pushes open her door. I take a step towards the stairs and hear him getting to Hannah.

"Hey, squirrel. It's over. We're okay," he tells her. She sniffles and mumbles something I can't make out. "I would never let that happen. I told you, you'll never be without me. I love you too much to let anything happen to you."

My heart cracks open right here in his dark hallway. He knows love. He sees love. He feels love.

"It's okay to sleep now Hannah, it's over," he whispers.

The beautiful relationship they have, one full of love, makes me wish he could see past whatever is blocking him from everyone else.

In a soft baritone voice, he sings to her. It's just

Twinkle Twinkle Little Star, but it's full of concern and love.

Feeling like an intruder, I quietly retreat down the stairs to let them have their moment.

Seeing the mess in front of me, my brain scrambles to figure out the first step. It's overwhelming. I take a deep breath and make my way to the kitchen. My gut trembles with what Riley must've seen and heard. Broken glass and ceramic mix in with crushed cereal, bananas, and various other food items, making each step I take scream through the silence in the house.

I step over a toppled chair and open the cabinet under the sink, hoping to find garbage bags, but instead I find cleaners and dust pan. Grabbing the dust pan and the Clorox, I set it on the counter and stand. Wishing I paid more attention to where they keep garbage bags and a broom, I start righting chairs as I make my way to a set of doors on the other side of the room.

"What are you doing?"

I startle and turn my attention to Riley. "Helping you. Where's your broom and garbage bags? I figure we can start in here and work our way out."

He shakes his head. "You don't-,"

"Stop pushing me away, Riley. I'm not leaving." I stare into his eyes, hoping to project all of my truth to him. Hoping he sees that I don't just mean to help him clean up this mess. And also hoping that he *sees* me.

He lowers his eyes to the floor before I can see if he's registered any meaning in my words. Swallowing roughly, his Adam's apple bobbing with the movement, he shifts his weight from foot to foot.

"Garbage bags are in the drawer next to the can and the broom is in the hall closet," he says quietly. "I'm going to grab a bucket to get the big pieces of glass."

I sigh as he walks away, bringing my attention back to the matter at hand.

If I don't get to work soon, we'll never make it to school on time.

A

My phone tweets, breaking my concentration of balancing a broken shelf on the bookcase in Riley's living room. I pull it from my pocket and answer quickly so the noise doesn't wake Hannah. "Hello?"

"Audrey. Where are you?" My father nearly screams into the phone.

I glance to Riley, panicked. He nods and waves me to go outside. "Umm," I mutter on my way to the door. "Well, it's a long story that I don't know much about-,"

"Where. Are. You?"

I hug myself as the bitter cold wraps around me like a glove. "I'm at Riley's house-,"

"You're already-,"

"Dad! I know. I'm sorry. But he needed my help! What was I supposed to do?" I defend.

He sighs and spits a curse. "I had to have a girl. Couldn't be another boy..." he mumbles and then relays the information of my whereabouts to my mom. She sounds angry in the background, but I can't make out what she's saying.

"I'm sorry," I whisper.

"What happened? What time did you leave?" He asks, his boss mentality coming out. It's that take-no-crap tone that scares me to my core.

"I'm not entirely sure on the details. But Riley texted me just after three telling me he needed my help." I finish telling him what I know, about how the house looked, what I saw, what little Riley said, and how Hannah was hiding in her safe place, crying.

"This would've been a lot easier if you would have woken us up, left a note, or hell, you could've called the police and ambulance. This isn't something for two teenagers to be cleaning up!" He shouts at me.

Tears threaten behind my eyes like tiny daggers of stupidity. "I'm sorry, Daddy-,"

"No. Don't you dare "Daddy" me! This is serious, Aud. Someone could've gotten hurt, fatally. Have either of you checked on Susan? On Hannah?"

I swallow a lump that feels like a boulder in my throat. "Riley checks on them both every half hour. They're both breathing, Susan is snoring, and Hannah was talking in her sleep ten minutes ago about a football playing bunny," I answer on autopilot.

"Good. Let me speak with Riley. Now."

Dread fills me. I fear what he'll say to Riley. That he'll turn him to a frozen statue of his formal self, the way he was yesterday and for the last few months.

"Yes, Dad-dy," I stutter, trying to swallow the last syllable but it slips out anyway.

Chapter 24

Riley

"Why didn't you call the cops, Riley?" Mister Paul asks me, sounding annoyed.

I clear my throat. "I won't part with my sister."

He falls silent a moment. And his silence makes me more nervous than I've ever felt around him.

"What happened?"

"I'd rather not, Sir."

"I'm not giving you an option."

I chew on my tongue a moment as I mull over my options. I could not answer him, but he'd likely lose any respect for me, it'd get Audrey in more trouble, and he'd probably come here and see what's left of the destruction.

Deciding on telling as much of the truth as I can, I start. "I don't know what happened. As soon as I got home from practice, she kicked me out. Twenty minutes later she acted like nothing happened and was as normal and nice as ever." I shiver at the memory of how nice she was. Hugging me every few minutes, telling me I look just like my father when she met him, and telling me that she can't wait to marry Ted so our family will be whole again. "Then she became violent." I flinch, remembering the punches and kicks. Absentmindedly, I rub my hand over my left ribs. "Then she passed out behind the couch, and I texted Audrey."

"So you call your best friend, my *only* daughter, to help you clean a trashed house and move an unstable body?"

I flinch at his words and tone. He's angry with me. I never wanted that. Never wanted to see or hear it from this man. "I apologize, sir. I wasn't thinking."

"Damn right you weren't thinkin'."

"It'll never happen again, sir. I can promise you that. I'd never hurt Audrey-,"

He laughs hollowly. "Too late for that."

"Sir?"

"Are you guys almost finished?"

"We are, sir. We have almost everything cleaned up."

There's a shuffling sound and then the slam of a door. I look at the phone and see the call time still rolling and quickly put the phone back to my ear and wait.

"Do I need to pick up Hannah this morning? I have vacation time-,"

"Oh, no sir, that won't be necessary-,"

"If your mother is on something, I don't think it's wise to leave Hannah with her unatten-,"

"Hannah will be fine, sir," I cut him off. "My mother is lots of things, but she wouldn't intentionally hurt Hannah."

"I didn't - I'm sor-,"

"It's fine, Mister Paul. This problem won't happen again. Don't punish Audrey for sneaking out, it was my fa-,"

"Riley, I know you're trying to protect Audrey. But it was her decision to handle things the way she did. I can't fault her for helping a friend in need, but sneaking around at three o'clock in the morning...that is a problem and she will be punished for it."

I swallow and smile sadly at Audrey. I'm not sure if she could hear her father, but she's looking at me awfully worried. She shrugs at my sympathetic smile. "Is that everything? I still have a few things to fix. I'll send Audrey back home."

"Thank you. And Riley?"

"Yes sir?"

"Denise and I are here for you and Hannah. For anything. Just call us or come straight over."

"I know, Sir." I nod, even though he can't see it. "I'm sorry about this morning, sir. Here's Audrey," I say and give her back her phone.

She takes a deep breath and puts the phone to her ear. "Yes, Daddy. I know."

I push open the front door and look around. I have to fix two of the shelves on the bookcase, fix the handrail, and run the vacuum cleaner to get any last bits of broken glass. That'd be the last thing Hannah needs. Or my mom for that matter.

Picking up where I left off, I grab my screwdriver and continue securing a screw into the wall of the case.

The door closes softly and light footsteps grow closer.

"Thanks for your help, Aud. Get home before you get in more trouble," I say, without turning around.

She clears her throat. "I just wanted to say... see ya later."

"Yep, I'll see you in school," I mumble and twist the screw in a little tighter.

"Well, uh..." she blows out a breath. "Ri, this is stupid. Everything between us-,"

"Aud, this isn't the time for a heart to heart." I set the screwdriver down and pick up the particleboard shelf. "We just-,"

"That. What you're doing right now, this is why we have issues. You're my best friend, Riley. I hate when you freeze me ou-,"

"Are you sure that's all we are, Aud?" I turn and look at her. "Because this thing between us... it has always been there, simmering." My chest tightens. What am I doing? Why am I saying this now? I try sucking in a deep breath, but it's useless.

She kneels down in front of me. "Ri, breathe," she whispers and places her frozen hand to my cheek. I close my eyes, refusing to get lost in her.

"Riley."

"Audrey," I rasp. "I can't."

"Just stop for a second." She taps my cheek. "Open your eyes."

I take a deep breath, and this time, the oxygen reaches my lungs. I open my eyes, and she smiles.

"Just hear me out. I've been wanting to say this for hours." I nod, letting her say her peace. "I'm sorry. For everything or anything I did to encourage this divide between us." She glances away from eyes to the bay window. "You're my go to. And I'm yours." Her eyes come back to mine. The depth of the earth seems to swim in her eyes. "I can't keep making it rain to rebuild my mask. Eventually, I'll need some ice to freeze it in place," she says, confusingly.

My brows furrow. "Wha-,"

She shakes her head. "It's...something I've been thinking about for a while now. The thing that's been missing." She shrugs. "Before this school year, I had a healthy dose of the seasons imbedded in me. I know, it sounds stupid," she rushes. "But, without our friendship, I don't have winter or summer. I'm stuck in spring and fall. I'm in limbo. We have balance together." Her brows furrow as she searches my face. "Does this make any sense?"

I smirk. "Not really. But I guess I can see your point. You feel like you're half the person you were before." She nods. "I can't promise to not freeze you out, Aud. I'm sorry I've hurt you, I never wanted that."

She sits back on her heels. "It's not okay, but it's a

start. Riley, don't forget this, if you shut me out again, fine. Whatever. I'll manage. But always remember that you define yourself, not your parents, not your teachers, and not your friends. You need to do what's right by you"

"Sometimes I don't have a choice," I mutter. "If I don't take matters into my hands, what happens to the house? My sister?"

She shrugs. "I don't know, Ri. Maybe this is something that your dad can help with?"

"He's the reason all of this is happening."

"Because he left?"

"And because Mom found out I met with him while she was shopping with Ted."

She purses her lips. "That shouldn't have caused a problem. It's not like it's illegal to speak with your father."

"It's my life." I shrug. "Alright, Audrey, I will see you before homeroom, get home and shower and change. Maybe matching shoes would help, too." I point to her feet as she stands. She glances down.

"Oh my word. How did I not realize I had Mom's slipper and my sneaker?" she smacks her forehead.

"Well, it was three in the morning," I offer. "And you're less observant with less sleep."

"See you later," she says through a quiet laugh and walks out.

I drop my forehead to the shelf in my hands and wait until I hear her pull away. With her departure, I quickly fix the shelves and replace the books.

Nothing is going the way it should be going. I shouldn't have had to do any of this. I should've just left it for Mom and Ted and gotten sleep. I'll be useless all day and at practice this evening.

What am I going to do about Audrey? Every time I see her, I want to hold her and do things friends shouldn't do. But if anything like that happens, we'll only hurt each other.

Love is an illusion that fools grasp.

I'm not a fool. I'm a captain.

With a sigh, I dig out three screws from the Fix - It kit I picked up a few months ago and begin re-securing the handrail.

R

"Hannah," I say, loud enough to wake my sleeping sister. "Hannah, wake up."

"No."

I chuckle. "Come on, it's time for breakfast."

She stirs a bit and rolls over to face me. "You didn't leave."

"Nope. I've been right here all night."

She smiles. "Okay. Can I have Fruity Pebbles?"

"Um, how about I make you some peanut butter toast?" I ask, hoping she'll agree since the cereal ended up on the floor in Mom's fit of rage last night.

She frowns. “Alright. I guess that’ll work.”

“Okay, you go to the bathroom, and I’ll get your clothes.”

She slides off her bed and walks slowly to the bathroom.

I let out the yawn I’ve been holding back and scrub my face. With a tired sigh, I shove off the corner of Hannah’s bed and meander to her dresser to find her a pair of pants.

“Hey,” my mom says from the doorway.

I jump and turn around. “Hi.”

“I need you to come straight home after schoo-,”

“I can’t. I have practice.”

“You’re gonna have to miss it. We have company tonight.” Her eyes form slits as she looks me over. “Because your father is a liar, we have some people coming tonight to ask you kids some questions.”

I glare at her in confusion. “What are you talking about?”

“Your father thinks I’m abusing you kids. You know I’d never do anything like that!” The lines in her forehead deepen as she goes on. “If they find there’s any issue here, they’ll take you both away and put you with a couple of strangers who will really beat-,”

“What?” Hannah shrieks. “I don’t want to leave!”

Mom kneels down beside Hannah. “It’s okay. As long as you tell the nice lady tonight how much you love your mommy and that mommy takes such good care of you, making sure you eat, get to school, and gives you baths, you'll be able to stay safe with Mommy forever and not with some mean strangers who will hit you every day."

Tears come Hannah's eyes. "I don't want to leave. Or be hit!"

Mom smiles and pulls her into a hug. "Then tell the lady I do all those things and work two jobs, that I'm your hero that never left."

I can't watch any more of this and go to Hannah's closet to find a long sleeved shirt for her today.

"Okay, Mommy," Hannah sniffs.

"Han, here's your clothes, come on. Get dressed, and I'll go make you some toast," I interrupt them. Mom is asking Hannah to lie for her. She doesn't do any of those things, except get groceries from a list I make.

Hannah shuffles over to me and takes her pants and shirt from my hands. "Extra peanut butter, please?"

I smile and ruffle her hair. "Of course, and a tall glass of milk to wash it down." I turn around and squeeze past our mom still leaning in the doorway.

"I'll get her breakfast, you go ahead and get ready for school," she says softly.

I shake my head. "Everything's ready. I just have to make her breakfast, like I do every morning," I remind her. "We're alright, Mom. Why don't you go shower and clean up your wounds from last night's temper tantr-," her hand comes across my face with a cold hard slap.

Hannah gasps behind her.

Last night swarms my vision again. Her hit out of nowhere, followed by a kick. I squeeze past her and rush to Hannah.

"Ri-,"

"It's okay. Go to your happy place!" I watch her for a second as her face drains of color and she runs away from the door. I pull it shut and stand to face the woman who brought me into this world. Hannah is protected now, I'm ready for whatever she plans on doing. I probably shouldn't have spoken out like that, but I couldn't help it.

Mom turns around, tears in her eyes. "Baby Boy," she whines. "I'm so sorry!" Her hand, the same one that slapped me, flies to her own mouth. "Can you forgive me? It'll never happen again. I'm sorry!"

My face softens, watching her melt this way. She's sober now. The mom that wouldn't hurt me or Hannah. "Yeah, Mom. Yeah," I whisper. But I don't go to her. I turn and open Hannah's door to fetch her from her safe place, and pull the door closed behind me, shutting Mom out.

"Hannah," I whisper as I close in on her closet. Cracking the door, I find her curled in a ball with her back towards me. "Hannah," I say again and rub her back. She spins and lunges for me. "It's okay now. Everything's okay."

"Why'd Mommy hit you?"

I shrug a shoulder as I squeeze her to me. "I said something mean by accident. I deserved it."

"You shouldn't be mean, Riley," she scolds me. I chuckle. "Why does Mommy want me to lie?"

Looking into her innocent blue eyes, I wish I could make all of this stop, and let her be a kid like she should be.

"I don't know."

"We aren't supposed to lie," she admits.

"No, we aren't."

She nods. "Will God love me if I lie this once?"

My brows furrow again. "I don't know that there is a God-,"

"There is, Riley. He loves us. He loves everyone. He's right there," she says, pointing her index finger into my chest.

There's that word again. But it only seems to mean something when I'm saying it to Hannah.

"I don't know about that. But I know I love you, no matter what. I'll love you if you lie and I'll love you if you tell the truth. You never have to worry about that. Or about me leaving you. I'll never let that happen either."

She squeezes my neck. "I know."

I carry her down to the kitchen and make her breakfast while she tells me about her crazy dream. She said that a man with blond hair and blue eyes that looked like me told her to try some crab. I was there and apparently talked her into trying the shell, not the meat, and then she turned into a giant crab. She said it was scary, but funny because she used her pincers to cut down trees.

After I made her breakfast and a sandwich for

lunch, I write a few more items on the grocery list and then leave for school.

One of these days, Hannah's tears will make me miss school. I wish I could get away with it today, but I do not want to be around our mother any longer than I have to be.

I jog out to my car, keys jingling in my hand.

"Remember, no practice today!" Mom yells from a second story window.

I wave instead of answering her. I guess, if it depends on her court crap against Dad, I'll have to miss practice. Not that I want to.

Coach will be pissed, but hopefully he won't sit me out of Thursday's game.

Chapter 25

Audrey

"This is for your own good, Audrey," my mom says quietly as I stare out of the passenger window. "If we don't punish you for this, you'll start sneaking out more. For reasons other than just to help a friend in need."

"Sure, Mom," I respond noncommittally. It wouldn't matter what I say at this point. This punishment is so stupid. I know I should have woken them up or left a note. But really, I wasn't thinking about that. I was thinking, 'Riley and Hannah needed me.' That they were in trouble, possibly hurt. So I left, and now my mom is driving me to school for the next week as punishment. That means I'll have to get rides to the ice rink for games and rides home. I'm surprised they're even allowing me to go to the games. But they said it's school spirit and a dollar a game so it's fine.

"Well, if you're not going to talk, I will. I'm sure Riley will tell you soon enough, but I talked to his father this morning. I filled him in on everything that happened. He said a mediator is coming to their house this afternoon, but he will bring this up to his lawyer."

I gasp. “You did not! Mom!”

“Audrey. I am a parent, too! Jack is and always was a good man. He loves and cares for his children. The best and only way he can do that, is giving us little things to give to them that we can pass off that it came from us and him paying the neighbors to let Riley do odd jobs. That’s the only way he has been allowed to be in his children’s lives. And let me tell you something, that’s heartbreaking! No, he isn’t perfect, but he loves his children and wants only the best for them. And Sue, their mother, can’t see past the past long enough to see the damage she alone has caused.”

I stare at my mother wide-eyed. “I, I-,”

“Yeah. It’s a lot to take it. But-,”

“You’ve hid this from me? From Riley?!” I shriek. “Mom! You played the game just like Sue!”

“I did not. I did what I could! If I told Riley or Hannah that something was from their father, what would’ve happened?”

“Riley wouldn’t think his father left him. He wouldn’t be loyal to his mother alone! He wouldn’t have to do everything in that house!”

“What do you mean, everything?”

I take a deep breath and resume looking out the window. “I think now is a good time for you to let me out. I’ll walk to the rest of the way to school.”

“Or, you can tell me what you’re talking about and then I’ll drop you off near the lot.”

“Why should I?”

"Because it can help save Hannah from going through half of what Riley's been through," she says quietly.

"Maybe tonight. Not right now." I need to ask Riley if it's okay. I need to tell him what my mother told me.

"Audrey. Just be careful, okay? Things like this aren't easy...it's very psychological. I think you should stay away from Riley for-,"

"I don't think so! I just got him back this morning! He needs me!"

She frowns. "I know honey. Just. Just be careful."

I glare at her. "Yeah. Mom. Thanks for this informative chat. Stop the car."

She nods and slows at the bottom of the driveway to school. I hop out and slam the door behind me.

I can't believe she even considered asking me to stay away from Riley. What is wrong with her? These last five years she's done nothing but lie. Riley's dad was there all along. Only he's been communicating with her and Dad and not Riley.

I growl and kick a rock, sending it sailing into a frozen tree.

This is so stupid.

A car horn breaks my thoughts that are leading me nowhere. I don't look to see who it is, I flip them off and keep walking.

"Ha, ha, very funny, Audrey," Riley says.

I turn to look at him, still reeling over my mother.

"Hi."

"Get in, Crabass," he says, leaning over and pushing the passenger door open.

I roll my eyes and take his offer. "Thanks," I mumble and flop in the seat.

"So, did you walk this whole way?"

I shove my fingertips into the heat vent, trying to warm them. "No. just from the bottom of the drive. That was my punishment for sneaking out this morning. They took my car for a week."

"Shit," he breathes. "I'm sorry, Aud."

I shrug. "No worries. It was worth it."

He snorts. "Really? Then why are you so jacked right now?"

He pulls into his parking spot, and I turn to look at him. His face is etched in worry, but I can't tell if it's because of why I'm angry, or something else.

"You know how my mom is," I mutter. "Lecturing me all morning long. It got old," I half lie.

He shakes his head. "Need a ride home tonight?"

I shrug. "I can probably get a ride from Candy, you have practice today."

"Actually, I can't go to practice to-,"

"What? Are you hurt?" I panic and look him over. No visible bandages, no scrapes, and no bruises. But he's wearing a jacket and long pants, so I can't really tell.

"Not injured. Promise. But, my mom needs me to come straight home after school..."

My brows furrow. "She always does this! I'll watch-,"

"No, it's not like that this time," he interrupts me. I stare at him expectantly. "Someone is coming to the house to talk to Hannah and me because there's been abuse claims or something."

I sit back in my seat and stare at the school. My mom warned me about this, but she said nothing about abuse claims. She said it was a mediator. They're different. Mediators seek to find the best possible outcomes for children going through divorces and child custody cases. They're especially beneficial when it is a high conflict case.

All of my research explodes in my brain, seeing possible outcomes for Riley and Hannah, big changes, and small, are coming their way.

"I guess my father has been trying to get my mom into court for years-,"

"What father wouldn't want to see his children?"

"A father that leaves," he snaps. "Anyway, my mom is finally going through with it. I guess they threatened jail time. That's the only thing I can think of."

"Your father may have left your mother, but he didn't want to leave you and Hannah. He wanted to maintain that-,"

"I know, Aud. It's whatever. What's been done is done. No changing that."

"But you know he tried. Are you still writing him off?"

He taps his finger on the steering wheel. "I don't know."

"Okay. Well, whatever the people say tonight, you know you have to be honest. Even if it means telling them about last night," I whisper.

Someone taps on my window, interrupting our conversation. Riley's eyes widen a little and he drops his head to his steering wheel. Turning my head, I see Todd. He smiles widely and waves at me. I wiggle my fingers at him in a quick wave and turn back to Riley.

"What's wrong?" I ask him.

He clears his throat. "He probably hates me. His mom is probably just as mad."

"Why on earth would you think that? Did you send a hockey puck through their living room?"

He snorts. "That would've had a better turn out than what transpired."

"I think you're overreacting," I say and open my door, stepping out. "What's up Todd?"

"What happened to your car?" He asks as I close the door and sling my backpack over my shoulder.

"Nothing, my keys have been confiscated for a week," I answer and turn to look through the windshield, waiting for Riley to finally exit his car.

"What could you have done? Put itch powder in your dad's briefs?"

I snort. “Don’t worry about it.” Growing impatient, I tap the hood until Riley looks up to me. I wave him to come out and he nods.

“I’m glad you two are talking again,” Todd says.

“Yeah, me too.”

“Things just keep getting weird.”

I turn my attention to him. “What do you mean?”

He shrugs. “I don’t know. Riley asked to crash at my place last night then I swear I saw your car at Riley’s house this morning, but when I looked again, I didn’t see anything different.”

Riley closes his door and clears his throat. “Sorry about last night, Todd. Somethin’ came up and I couldn’t stay.”

“It’s okay. Mom was disappointed, though.”

Riley swallows roughly. “I’ll stop in tomorrow and apologize to her.”

The bell rings from inside and the three of us swear and run inside.

“I gotta see Coach, I’ll catch up with you guys later,” Riley says and jogs to the stairwell.

“I wonder if Coach is tearing him a new one this early?” Todd muses.

I roll my eyes. “If anyone would need a rippin’ into, it’s you. What were you thinkin’ last game? Net minders stay put. They don’t get involved with fights or check out the crowd,” I snap at him, and keep my knowledge to myself.

He bumps my shoulder with his, knocking me off balance, but I catch myself. "Net minders *can* fight. We just try really hard not to."

"Yeah, because then another teammate has to take the penalty."

He laughs. "Your knowledge of the sport is impressive."

"Always. How long have you known me?"

"Kindergarten."

"Do you remember what I wore on my first day of school?"

His forehead creases. "No. I don't even remember what you wore yesterday."

I snort. "I wore a hockey jersey. I'm a hockey baby."

He shakes his head. "That's right. Carl Shultz used to call you a boy!" I growl. "I don't know Aud, it's just weird. You're a girl. You're supposed to not like hockey and mud."

"The girl gene skipped me." I shrug and pop open my locker. "Besides, you wouldn't want another Alice around here, would you?"

He shudders. "No! You stay in the mud! See ya, boy!" he teases and jogs to his homeroom.

I swap out my books and let out a big yawn. I have next to no energy. If I'm lucky, I'll be able to nap in science.

Chapter 26

Riley

Sitting in my bedroom, I pretend to do homework.

But I'm actually listening in on the woman who's talking to my sister.

"Oh, I like purple best," the woman says. When she got here, she said her name was Bonnie Carrington. She has thick, black-rimmed glasses, black hair piled on top of her head, and she was wearing bright colors.

Not at all what I was expecting. I don't really know what I was expecting, but this woman looks nice, fun even.

"I like red," Hannah says. I'm not sure what they're playing with. But they're making a lot of patting and scratching noises.

"Your dad told me that you have the prettiest blue eyes and you love horses."

The patting noise stops. "I don't have a dad. I have Ted. Did he tell you that?" There's a long pause. "He probably didn't. He doesn't play with me."

"Your mom likes how helpful you are when she works late, that you bring her a bowl of cereal in the morning."

"I do that when Riley leaves an extra bowl down for me. I can't reach the bowls yet. I'm *still* too short. But I am growing!"

I smile. She tries every day to reach the cabinet. It frustrates her when she can't do things on her own.

"Do you like your brother?"

"I love Riley, he's the best."

I smile.

"Is there anything you don't like about Mom?"

The patting gets louder.

"She works too much," Hannah answers quietly.

"How does that make you feel?"

"I don't know. I have Riley. He gets my clothes ready and plays with me in the tub. He makes me sing a silly song when I brush my teeth!"

"Sounds like you have an amazing big brother," the woman sounds like she's smiling. "Look! I made a horse!"

Hannah giggles. "It doesn't have ears!"

"What are you making?"

"Done! It's a sun!" Hannah shouts.

"It's so pretty. Does Mommy or Daddy make things with you?"

"Riley makes things with me. But he says play-doh stinks."

"That's nice of him. When was the last time you saw your daddy?"

The silence is deafening. I want to rescue Hannah from this talk. But I can't.

"Riley has a picture of a man that looks like him under his bed in a puck box. Sometimes I imagine he's my dad and he saves Riley and me from my secret spot. But we have Mom and Ted. Ted says I can't call him Dad."

I never realized she knew about my boxes under my bed. I guess, when she's got nothing better to do, she snoops around. I just hope she hasn't told Mom about my money stash.

Crossing the room, I kneel next to my bed and pull out all of the puck boxes. I know my extra money is in my duffel bag still out in my car.

There are other things in these boxes I want to keep.

A picture of me, Dad, and Hannah the day we brought her home from the hospital. Mom took it. Then Todd's mom took one of all of us. I also have a few little things in there that Hannah made, like her ceramic handprint from last Christmas. Mom was going to throw it away, but I couldn't stand seeing Hannah's handprint in the trash.

Dumping the box on the floor in front of me, I watch as physical memories spill and splatter. One item rolls over to my desk chair. Crawling over, I grab it. It's the plastic puck I hit Audrey with.

I smile at the memory. When I hit her with this puck, it was the first time I kissed her. Then it was...her way of trying to reach me.

But I shut her out anyway.

Putting everything else in the box, I sit in my desk chair and stare at the puck.

Laughter from Hannah's room grows louder. "Okay, Hannah, I'm going to speak to your brother. I promise I'll stop back in here and say bye. You work on making that unicorn for me?"

"Alright! I'll make it purple and red!" she shouts her excitement.

Great.

Now Bonnie is coming here, probably to play play-doh with me. I spin the puck on my desk, wishing I was at practice instead of here.

There's a tap on my doorframe. "Hi, Riley."

I don't look up. "Hey."

"Mind if I come in?" Bonnie asks.

I snort. "Would you leave if I said yes?"

"No. Probably not," she admits. "I'll tell you what, Riley. We can do this the easy way or the hard way."

"Oh, really? So I just have to talk and play nice or you'll... what? Build me a time-out box out of play-doh?"

She snorts. “I was thinking about taking your attitude outside and turning you into my net-minder.”

I look at her for the first time, shocked.

“Don’t think I don’t who you are, Captain.” She smiles.

I glance away from her, annoyed. “Fine. Let’s play hockey.”

“Alright. We’ll make a game of it. But since it’s raining, we’ll stay inside.” She digs in her oversized purse, revealing two small hockey sticks and hands me a black one, keeping the white one for herself. “Each time I score, you have to answer a question. Each time you score, you can choose to pass or ask a question yourself. Can we use that puck there?”

I glance down to the puck on my desk. “No. This one isn’t to play with,” I answer and shuffle back to my bed.

“Why not? It looks like it’d be perfect for what we’re doing.”

I chuckle. “You didn’t score yet, so I don’t have to answer.”

“Oh, fine. Throw my rules in my face.”

I open my nightstand drawer and dig out the foam puck that came with my old knee-hockey set. “It’s a few years old, but it should work.”

She sets her bag on the floor next to my chair. “Okay. If you make it past me, into the hallway, then you score. If I make it past you and it hits the wall next to your bed, I score. Got it?”

I grip the small stick in my hand and drop to my knees. “Sounds great.” We knee-walk to the middle, and I drop the puck just like a ref would. She hits the foam puck first, batting it away from me.

“I thought you’d be quicker.” She laughs, hitting the puck, directly behind me. The puck hits the wall with a soft thud.

I groan and sit on my heels. “What’s your question?”

She smiles. “Of course I have to ask this. Why couldn’t we play with that puck on your desk?”

“Because it’s cracked,” answer noncommittally.

She snorts. “I don’t think that’s it. But it is an answer, and I wasn’t cagey enough to specify you had to give an honest answer. Ready to go again?” She smiles a bit mischievously at me.

I nod and crawl to grab the puck. This time, she drops it, and taps it first. But I lunge and don’t let her score. I push the foam puck away from her but it rolls toward my closet. She gets to it first and sends into my wall, again.

“How much do you know about what’s going on?”

I cock an eyebrow. “What do you mean?”

“Well, your mom said that you are aware there is a court date set.”

I nod. “All that I know, which some of I found out without her knowing, is that my dad has been trying to get her into court for custody or visitation or something, for years. But we’re only now going through with it for a seemingly unknown reason.”

She nods. "Damn. And I can't ask another question can I?"

"Nope. And that is considered a question, too."

She snorts. "Let's get to it."

We play for a few more minutes. I got one pass, and she quit because the hard floor was tearing up her knees.

"So, what now?" I ask as she rubs her knees.

"I don't really know. I used to play this game with my big brother when I was little. I don't remember it hurting though," she admits with a laugh.

"How long have you been doing this? Coming to houses and stuff?" I ask curiously.

"Hmm," she mutters and looks up to my ceiling. "About fifteen years now. But I don't always go to houses. I have an office with a playroom for little ones. But when I took on this case, I felt that it'd be better to come to you."

I nod. Not really knowing what to say.

"Can I ask you a question now?"

I swallow. "Yeah, I guess." She does have a job to do, whether I want to answer or not.

"When was the last time you saw your dad?" She asks carefully.

"Not too long ago actually, but before that? The day he left," I answer quietly.

"Do you want to see him more?"

I shrug. “I do and I don’t.”

“Do you want Hannah to see him?”

I open my mouth but close it immediately. That’s hard to say. She deserves a father who will love her and not leave her. He left once. But Mom kept him away.

“What’s going through your head right now?” Bonnie asks carefully.

“She doesn’t know him. He doesn’t know her.” Among other things, but she’d be afraid with him at first.

“What if you were with her? Would you be okay with visitation then?”

I nod. “Yeah. When she’s scared...I-,”

“It’s okay. I know things get weird sometimes.” She smiles. “What sort of visitation would you expect with your father?”

“I can’t decide that!”

“I’m not asking you to. What are you expecting to happen and what would you like to happen?”

I swallow my panic and look at the wall, in the direction of my mother’s room. “What I expect will happen won’t be anything a judge can decide,” I mutter, glaring at the wall. “If he lived in this town, I guess I could see some sort of eventual fifty-fifty for Hannah. I’m eighteen in a little more than a year, so it really doesn’t matter what I do. But until Hannah is comfortable with him, I’d like only an hour or two.”

“That’s tough, Riley.”

"Yeah, well. He left five years ago and now it's all coming out. So, he'll have to take his time. I won't allow him to hurt Hannah again."

"She was a year old and doesn't remember-,"

"Everything that's happened to us since then can be blamed on my father's leaving. So, yeah, it's my dad's fault."

"And what's happened since then?"

Dread fills me.

I've said too much.

Chapter 27

Audrey

I pace in the hallway between the living room and my room, with my phone in my hand, waiting. Riley should be finishing up soon. We've been out of school for two hours now. That woman should've left by now so they can partake in a "family" meal.

"Squirt, you're buggin' the hell out of me," my brother whines.

I snort. "I'm not even talking to you."

"No, but you're cramping my relaxing aura with your impatient puttering."

"I'm not puttering, dweeb. I'm pacing."

"Go pace and putter somewhere else," he snaps and sticks his tongue out at me.

I roll my eyes at the back of his head as he turns back to the TV and stalk into the kitchen to grab a soda.

"Your son-,"

"He's your brother," my dad interrupts. "And he has a point. You're not really allowing anyone to relax. Panic is rolling off of you like cold from the snow." His nose scrunches.

I groan. "I'm worried, I can't help it. And I'm still mad at you!" Turning away from him quickly, I yank open the fridge and grab a can of pop.

"If you slam that door closed like you did earlier, you're cleaning the inside with your toothbrush and a bucket of bleach," my mother scolds from her stance in front of the stove.

I press it closed softly and stick my tongue out at the back of her head.

Dad snorts.

"I saw that young lady," mom snaps and whips a plastic serving spoon at me.

I duck and let it clatter to the floor. "Mom!"

She smiles. "My aim was off on purpose, but it got your attention, didn't it?"

I cross my arms and press my lips together.

"Do us all a favor. Sit down and breathe."

I roll my eyes and pull out the chair across from my dad.

"Before you sit, bring me that spoon please," she requests.

"You threw it," I gripe.

She puts her hand on her hip. "Child, pick up the spoon and bring it here."

Dutifully, I pick up the spoon and hand it to her. “Don’t use that on dinner,” I plead as I turn away from her.

She taps my butt with the spoon. “Enough with your attitude, and no, I wouldn’t use a dirty spoon on our dinner. Maybe to serve yours…”

“Mom!” I whine again. My phone beeps, halting any further response. I hurriedly check the message, nearly dropping it twice.

? - Riley

:/ - A

Yeah. Me too. - Riley

“Are you sure I can’t go to him?” I glance up to my mom, hoping that the worry on my face tells her everything.

“No. I’m sorry. You’re still punished.”

My dad clears his throat. “You can, however, go to the garage and call him if it’s that bad.”

Without checking Mom’s reaction, I run to the mudroom that’s just off the kitchen. Stepping into my boots, I dart out the door, not caring the laces aren’t tied and that I’m not wearing a coat.

My phone chirps again and I check it as I shove open the garage door.

You busy? - Riley

I press his number on my speed dial and turn the knob for the kerosene heater.

“Hey,” he answers.

"Hey yourself, how'd it go?"

"I messed up," he whispers.

I close my eyes. "What do you mean you messed up?"

He clears his throat. "I didn't lie and I didn't tell the truth."

"You stayed silent?"

"Well, no. Not exactly."

I groan. "Riley. Give me somethin' here. I'm graspin' at straws!"

"It'd just be easier if this was face to face."

"I'm grounded."

"I know," he says with a sigh. "I was vague with a few of my answers. They could be taken in many ways." He growls. "But I wouldn't answer with specifics or example."

My mouth drops open. "So you didn't tell the woman about last night?"

"No! God no. Why would I?" He nearly shouts.

"Um. Maybe because that's not normal. She kicked you out, pretended it didn't happen, went through each stage of grief and every emotion known to man before falling into a fit of rage that could've fatally injured you, Hannah, or herse-,"

"I know!" He interrupts my rant. "It could've been a lot worse than what it was. But it's okay. Nothing super bad happened-,"

"Riley, are kidding me? You're defending her? Again?"

"She's my mother. What am I supposed to say, Aud? I know she sucks. I know she shouldn't be this damn selfish. But I can't turn her in."

"What if someone else did?"

"Someone like you?"

I swallow. "No. Not me."

"It wouldn't matter. Not like it'd be my decision. But I'd hope that my best friend wouldn't do that to me-,"

"Do what? Potentially save your life or Hannah's?"

"It's not-,"

"Riley. Stop this," I beg. Tears slowly coming to my eyes. "I don't want to get a phone call in the middle of the night saying something bad happened to you or Hannah. 'Cause you know the Van Luit's would call me."

"Aud. If you'd listen, this entire argument would be pointless," he says, ice licking his tone. "While I didn't say anything specific, and neither did Hannah. It's made pretty clear that neither of us is happy with the current situation. Hannah basically told the woman that I take care of her and make sure she has everything she needs."

"So do you think you'll end up with you dad?"

"Anything's possible."

"But, how is your mom going to be until court in two months?"

I'm greeted with silence. It's a worrisome silence that promises unknown outcomes. Of course no one can predict the future. You can hope all you want, but the past enters my mind and creates an awful future for Riley and Hannah in my head.

"She isn't a violent person," he reminds me.

"But she was last night. If it's a drug she's taking... it could happen again, Riley. What if it happens when you're at a game?"

"I'm not even goin' there, Aud."

Hopefully, his dad can do something fast. I don't want anything to happen to him or Hannah. "Okay," I whisper.

He clears his throat. "Look, I'm gonna go. But, I just want you to know that...I'm back. I'm sorry for being dumb before. We won't always agree, like now, but I'm back."

"For now," I add to his statement. Something else will happen with his mom or his dad or a teacher, and I'll be frozen out again.

"See ya," he whispers and hangs up.

I pocket my phone and turn off the heater before exiting the garage. My boots clomp against the frozen ground, crunching snow as I make my way back into the house. At least things are moving and they won't be subjected to the things they've been subjected to.

I push the kitchen door open and see Mom putting dinner on the table, kissing Dad's cheek as she leans around him. Everyone should have parents who love each other and their children. Even if the biological parents separate, blended homes can be just as happy.

Candy is lucky enough in that sense; both sets of her parents love her and her sister unconditionally.

"Hi, Sweetie. How's Riley?" Mom asks with a grin.

I shrug. "I don't know. He's...Riley. He didn't give details but vaguely mentioned that stuff has happened since his dad left. Hannah told the woman that Riley takes care of her." With a long, tired sigh, I drop into my chair at the table. "He snapped at me but told me that he's back." I shake my head. "He'll freeze me out again," I mutter and glance to dinner. "I'm sorry, Mom. It looks great, but I'm not all that hungry and I'm still super tired."

I walk back to my room without another word. Could Riley really be done shutting me out? Is he really back to the old him? Is it possible to be the old us?

I just need to stick to the facts.

He's trying.

I'm trying.

Stuff happens and we're there for the other one.

He's amazing on the ice.

I'm amazing in the mud.

He's not freezing me out right now.

Chapter 28

Riley

I'm scared," Hannah whispers.

"Don't be," I tell her. We're on our way to see our father's new house. He wanted to move into the same school district so we would be able to stop by on school nights if allowed.

Hannah still hasn't met him. Mom wouldn't let me take her anywhere he would be. But, Hannah told me she was ready, and I told Mom we were going to the park.

"What if they don't like me?"

I smile and peek at her in the review mirror. "What's not to like?"

"Mommy said that no one will like me more than her," she explains.

"I like you a lot," I offer.

"You're my brother. You're not allowed to hate me."

I chuckle. "I think you'll be surprised. They're very excited to see you."

"Yeah?" she asks, her voice rising in pitch.

"They are. They decorated your room..." I taunt.

"How?" she squeals.

"The color of boogers," I deadpan.

"Eww!" she shrieks.

I laugh. "I'm kidding. I'm sure you'll love the room they picked for you." Jack and Louise painted her room pink with purple trim, her favorite colors, and put stick on ponies everywhere. It's very girly, just like Hannah.

Hannah bounces in her seat, looking out the window at every house we pass. I slow in front of a brick rancher at the top of the tallest hill in Dalesburg.

"Is this it?" she whispers.

"Well, the address Jack and Louise sent me was 228, is that the numbers on the door?" I ask her.

"Umm..." she unbuckles and presses her face to the window. "Yes."

"Then this is it, Squirrel."

She drops back into her seat. "I'm not ready."

The front door opens and a man pushes the screen door open. He looks just like me, but older and with longer hair.

Hannah gasps. "I've seen him before."

I nod, remembering how she told the mediator that the picture of the man with me is who she dreams of when she wants rescued.

Unbuckling my seatbelt, I open my door and smile at her over my shoulder. "Let's go say, Hi."

She doesn't move.

I get out and walk around my car, opening the back door and pick her up. She hides her face in my neck and squeezes me with her little arms. "It's okay, Han. You'll be fine. Nothing will hurt you here."

"Promise?"

"Would I lie to you?"

She takes a moment before shaking her head no and pulling back a little.

"Do you want to walk?"

She nods, blonde curls bouncing with the movement. I set her on her feet, and she grips my fingers as hard as she can.

Jack's smile widens the closer we get. "Hi," he says quietly.

"Dad?" Hannah whispers. He nods. "You'll rescue me?"

I watch as Jack's eyes fill with tears. He drops to his knees in front of us, looking into Hannah's eyes. "Always. I will always rescue you."

"Not my imagination this time?" Hannah looks up to me. I smile and shake my head. "Can I hug him?"

"If you want to."

She squeezes my fingers even tighter as she leans into him. Our father cries. I look away and movement from the doorway catches my attention. Louise stands behind the screen door, smiling at us. She mouths, "Thank you," to me. I nod in response but I don't know why she's thanking me.

"Come on in from the cold, guys," Jack says, standing up.

Hannah hugs my leg.

"Come on, Squirrel, let's go get warm," I say, picking her up.

"It's not a booger room, right?" she whispers.

I snort. "No."

"Okay."

When we walk in, there's still a few boxes flattened and leaning on the wall, but most everything looks unpacked now.

"Hi, Hannah. I'm Louise. Would you like to come with me to see something really pretty?"

Hannah nods and wiggles from my arms. I steady her on her feet and then watch cautiously as she creeps over to Louise.

Jack clears his throat and drops to a chair at the table in the kitchen. "I never thought I'd see either one of you again," he mutters and puts his hands over his face. I remain quiet, unsure of what to say to the man.

This is my fourth time talking to him, third time

seeing him in person. Each time I feel weird. Not a good weird and not bad weird, just weird. It's comfortable and uncomfortable at the same time.

Hannah shrieks from upstairs. *"Ponies!"*

Jack chuckles. "You were right about the ponies."

I nod. "She's obsessed."

His eyes find mine. "Riley, I gotta tell you something. Can you sit for a minute?"

I chew on the inside of my cheek, confused at what he could possibly tell me, but I sit anyway.

"When your heart belongs to someone, you do whatever you can do to see them smile, to see them happy, to protect them as much as you can." He rubs a circle into the table face as he falls silent. "A friend of mine told me I needed to tell you some things before you heard from anyone else." His eyes find mine again, and I shift uneasy. "I paid Mrs. Cramer to let you mow her lawn, clean her gutters, and do odd jobs. I paid her well, so that you could earn enough money for your hockey fees and equipment. I tried sending your mother checks for it, but she returned each one, unopened. She always said that hockey was too expensive of a sport for you to be in, not to mention the danger. I guessed, after I left and heard that you were trying to find jobs from the neighborhood, that she wouldn't help pay for any of it. So I did everything I could to get you the cash you needed-,"

"You didn't talk to me about it," I interrupt him.

He nods. "I wasn't able to. For a lot of reasons, but mostly, I was afraid. I was afraid of what your mother would do if she found out somehow. I never thought for a minute that she'd do half the things she did without me provoking her, but she was afraid I'd take you and Hannah from her. So she sabotaged every chance I had to communicate with you."

"Do we have to talk about this now?" I ask him. He left us. He has no right to talk about my mother.

He shakes his head, no. "I just wanted you to know that I never forgot about you guys."

"I didn't think you did. I just don't like talking about Mom like this."

"I'm sorry. I didn't want you to think I was attac ,"

"No, I don't think you're attacking her. I just-." How do I explain it? He's justifying what she did and blaming her. I blame her. But he has no right to say anything. He left, he doesn't know how it was after he left us. Her. Us.

"It's okay, Riley. I don't know a lot of what happened after I left. But I know it wasn't fair for you or Hannah to have to deal with-,"

"Jack," I say, cutting him off again. He winces. "I really don't want to talk about this."

Disappointment covers his face like a curtain closing on, not only topic, but me. My hope of a relationship with this man sinks like a cannon ball. I shove out of my chair, standing forcefully under my anger.

She did this.

She ruined

Love

Hope

Relationships

Futures

My mother killed it all in her selfishness of keeping Hannah and me under her thumbs.

"I can't," I mumble and head for the door. I pause, knowing I can't leave Hannah, but I can't stay here.

"Riley, what's wrong?"

My body shakes from the amount of anger coursing through my veins. I can't contain myself. I feel like I'm cracking in half. Slowly, I sink to the floor and stare at the odd pattern of blues and greens in the carpet.

Count.

I count each shade of green.

Eight different strains of one color.

I count the blues.

Four different strains of this color.

Plays.

In my head, I check my opponent, I backhand the shot, I pass, I fake, and I avoid the penalty box.

In my head, this is a play. It's a one on one with interference, I feel like the puck. I'm passed, I'm sliced, I'm shot, I'm backhanded, and I'm blocked from both nets. The net minders are in control.

To the point that I don't even know which side I'm

meant to be on.

"How can I choose?" I whisper to myself.

"You don't," Jack answers. "You love with your whole heart. Listen to it, lead with it, count on it."

"That's stupid. The heart makes fleeting decisions. My heart is confused anyway."

"It's taken me a long time to process all of what happened and process actions that led to painful things, like your mom keeping you and Hannah from me. But, Riley, there's room in your heart for all of your parents. You have a mother, love her. You have a stepfather, love him. You have a father and stepmother - can't you find a way to love us, too?"

I raise my eyes from the carpet in front of the front door, finding his as he kneels beside me. "I love Hannah. That's the only thing I know anymore. She's the only love that doesn't hurt. She's the only love that doesn't scare me."

"Why does love scare you or hurt you?" He asks, raising an eyebrow. "Love can be scary, try having a child." His lips turn up in a smile. "Love doesn't hurt you, people hurt you, but not because of love. It's because of fear, anger, confusion, jealousy."

My eyebrows furrow. "When people love people, they leave them. That hurts."

He looks to the floor. "I can never apologize enough for that. Riley, people fight for what they love. If love isn't there, there isn't any reason to fight except against each other. That's what your mother and I had. We fought against each other on every decision, every thought, every move, every moment... Neither one of us were happy. We both loved you and Hannah. I thought that by staying, by denying both of our happiness, it would tarnish your views on how relationships were meant to be. I wanted you and Hannah to grow up wanting to find pure happiness in a relationship with whomever you fall in love with. I hope that day for both of you is when I'm fifty or older, but I want for you to want what I finally found with Louise. Not to want or settle for what I had with your-,"

"How do you tell the difference? How can you tell if you're settling or loving?"

"Sometimes that's difficult," he admits, a sad look in his eye. "One day, you'll meet someone and not be able to picture your life without them. But that's only part of the key. You gotta trust her. That's the biggest tell, trust. If you can't trust her, you shouldn't even try to build a life with her. If you feel like you're not good enough for her, but she sticks around and shows you just how good you really are, that's a key. It's you who feels like you don't deserve her. It's not her making you feel that way. You constantly better yourself just because of the way she loves you"

Time stands still.

His words make sense in my fogged brain.

"Those things, is that what love is?"

He smiles. "Love is more than that. It's more than words can describe. But once you feel it, you won't be able to let it go, so long as it's the real deal."

"And if it's not?"

"You won't miss it."

"Does it only happen after a certain age?"

He smirks. "It happens when it happens. It can't be rushed or ignored. You'll know it when you feel it."

"What if I feel it now?"

He cocks his head to the side, eyes searching mine for something. "Embrace it."

R

After my near breakdown with Jack, I find myself in a near empty room near the living room. I think it's a den or an office. There's no furniture in here yet, but there is a stack of boxes by the wall with the only window in it.

I lean against the wall and slide down to sit next to a box.

I close my eyes and instantly an image of Audrey comes to mind.

Can I picture my life without her?

I want to say no, but five and a half years ago I never thought I'd be without my father for five years. I thought he was a constant, like Audrey is a constant now.

Is she a "for now" or a "for life?"

Light splashes across the carpet as the door pushes open. Louise enters and closes the door softly. She leans her back against the wall, and pressing her hand to her chest, she closes her eyes.

I watch her for moment, in silence, but feel like an intruder.

Hearing her sniffle, I stand up.

"I'm sorry," I say softly and shuffle across the room to the door.

Louise gasps and turns her back to me. "No apology needed. I didn't know anyone was in here."

Feeling awkward, I reach for the knob. "Just needed a minute of quiet."

She chuckles. "I did too." Turning toward me, she looks composed, as if the last few minutes didn't happen. "Hannah is a dear, full of energy."

I pull the door open, letting the light from the living room illuminate us. "She has too much energy sometimes, but I'm glad she seems to be comfortable here."

Louise smiles, but there's a sad glint in her eyes. "I didn't think it would be this hard to be around you two," she mutters, looking at the bare wall.

"Why would it be hard to be around us?" I ask confused.

"Would you mind sitting with me for a minute?" she asks, pointing to the carpeted floor and kneeling down.

As I sit, I look at the soft features of her round face. The sadness in her eyes seems almost permanent at this moment. I've never really paid much attention to her before, and it makes me wonder if her eyes have always held sadness.

She unclenches her fist and looks down to her open palm. "When I met your dad, I was just coming out of a hearing with my ex, Jeremy. I was married to him for four years before we divorced. Our relationship was wonderful at the beginning."

My face scrunches up in confusion. I don't understand why she's telling me any of this. Glancing down to her hand, I notice for the first time that there's something resting on her palm. A silver heart.

"I don't know what happened, but it was when our son turned three that started our downfall. The last year of our marriage was awful, I left Jeremy, even though he wouldn't let me take my baby." She looks back up to my face with tears shining in her eyes. "Jeremy kept Howie from me for years. He'd interfere every time I visited or called. He told Howie that he didn't trust me not to hurt him. Howie was six the last time I saw him. Jeremy moved them somewhere. I never knew where they went. It wasn't until Howie was thirteen that I heard anything from Jeremy or him. And, it was only because Howie took his own life."

She clenches her fist around the heart shaped item in her hand and holds it close to her again.

Looking at her now, I want to hug her and that reaction in my head startles me.

"I'm so sorry," I whisper, not knowing what else to say.

She sniffs and smiles sadly at me. "I didn't tell you this for you to feel sorry for me. I just want you to know… I know what it's like for your dad. I didn't want him to have to go through what I went through. Encouraging him to continue on this journey has helped me cope in my own way." She shrugs a shoulder and bites her lip. "And I know what can happen to kids going through their parent's struggles. I never wanted my boy put in the middle, but Jeremy's actions weren't in my control."

"It seems really wrong for that to have happened to you," I tell her honestly as I think about the way she's treated me, and so far Hannah, too. When she's with Jack, she's happy, at least on the surface. I can't imagine what it must feel like to lose someone in that manner, and then to lose them forever. "You seem to really care about Hannah."

She nods. "And you, too. Thank you for saying that, Riley, and for giving your dad a chance. You don't know how happy he truly is now compared to before."

This is where I shrug at her. I don't know anything of what he was between the time he left and when I met him at the coffee shop.

"Hannah loves the closet in her room," Louise muses. "My son always hated closets, swore that there were gremlins living in them."

I smile and want to tell her that Hannah's safe place is a closet, but I keep my mouth shut and just let Louise have silence.

I need silence and peace, ice.

Slowly, my brain turns around, reeling from the story Louise told me.

"I know you don't know me, but if you need to talk about anything, I will listen and try to help you." The silent plea behind her words doesn't go unnoticed. "I can't imagine having to go through missing my dad for five years and having my mom lie about his whereabouts or him in general. I'm here for anything. Please know that. Even if I seem..." she shrugs a shoulder. "Even if I seem sad or distant, know that I'm here." Her hand clutches my forearm with reassurance.

I nod. “Thanks, Louise. I think I’m okay, just need to process everything.” I can’t tell if I’m honest or if I’m lying. I don’t know what okay feels like.

My chest tightens again, and all I want is to be alone, away from everyone who makes me feel.

Chapter 29

Audrey

The ice and snow are almost melted, and with any luck, the rising temperatures mean spring is really here to stay.

It also happens to be one of my favorite times of years.

Muddin' season.

Mud is everywhere, and it's heavenly.

Over the last two months, not only has the temperatures slowly gone up to melt the gloom of winter, Riley has been attempting to thaw the resistance in our friendship. It's been a slow go of it. We aren't as close as were before, but he truly does have a lot on his plate. I think Jack being there, truly there, has helped with some of the problem. There's always the icy silence when his mom's visits approach. I don't know why, he doesn't talk about any of it.

"Aud!" my mom hollers from the kitchen as I shrug into my muddin' clothes.

“What?” I answer her without opening my door.

“Are you ready yet?”

“Almost!”

Today, the guys are all working and Mom has off. We decided to celebrate our girl time with some dirt therapy.

“Alright, Pokey. I’m gonna start the prep!” The back door slams shut as I open my bedroom door.

I run down the short hallway and through the kitchen, sliding to a stop at the door and yank it back open.

Mom looks up to me as she ties the laces of her boots. “Come on! We don’t have all day!”

I chuckle. “We kind of do, Dad and Greg won’t be home until four thirty.”

“That’s still not all day, I want to hit the mud before I have to start cooking.”

I step into my boots and quickly tie them. “Okay, let’s go.”

“Took you long enough,” she huffs and follows it up with a wink.

I step out the door behind her and take a deep breath of the fresh crisp air. It stirs everything in my soul and steers me to my ATV.

“I haven’t seen Riley since hockey ended, everything okay?” she asks as I grab the WD-40 off the workbench.

I shrug. “I guess. He’s been getting used to the new

routine."

"Louise seems nice, don't you think?"

Nodding, I finish up my checks and toss the can to Mom. "Hannah thinks the sun rises with Louise's Hannah Casserole."

"What's that?"

"Trail mix, candy bars, and dried fruit in a warmed dish."

Mom laughs. "That girl, she needs to be in some kind of sport or something for as much as she eats!"

"You finished?" I ask, pointing to her ATV.

She tosses me the can and jumps on the seat. "Let's get to it, Baby Girl."

I chuck the can onto the cluttered workbench and crank the key. She presses the garage door opener and we inch forward until we have enough room to clear to the outdoors.

The chilled air swirls around me, and the faster I go, the more my cheeks sting.

This is rebuilding.

My mask needs mending and mud and air will repair it.

The mask that says I'm alright, the mask that says that I can survive the rest of my days in this awful in between, it's the mask that hides my hurt, my needs, my wants.

This is the new mask I'll hide behind. Rebuilding is rejuvenating, it's replenishing every weak spot and crack within my soul.

I pass my mom and head straight for the mud puddle.

"Audrey! Don't you dare pull a Greg!"

I swerve to miss the dip and spray mud up my leg and towards my mom.

"I'll get you," she says dryly. "Just wait, Baby."

I smile. "Hit me with your best shot, Mama Bear."

She grins and the twinkle in her eye says I'm in for exactly what I want, what I need.

My healing is coming.

Revving her engine, she circles me and sprays mud right in my face.

"You could've dodged it," she taunts, revving her engine again.

I laugh and swipe my hand across my eyes. "I asked for it. I'm not gonna duck out or bog out like Greg."

Mom laughs. "Your brother enjoys the chase, you just enjoy the mud."

We lock eyes for a moment. "You're right."

"You're a lot more like me than you think."

I roll my eyes. "I'm nothing like you, Ma."

"Keep tellin' yourself that, maybe you'll believe it one day." She inches away. "Enjoy the mud."

I take in a breath of mud and let it work its magic

on me.

All the hurt, months of being pushed aside, years of not being good enough, and worry over my best friend leaves my mind like the slow leak of a faucet.

The confidence I need starts to build its faux wall again.

I take another circle around the bowl of the dip in the field before traveling the length of the field along the road side. The wind whips and cakes the mud to my face and hair. I take a sharp right and steer toward the treeline again. As I slow, I wipe off some of the mud from my face.

Smiling, I recite the words that ring true to my soul.

I feel peace in the mud.

A horn honks, breaking my peaceful mood. I grip the handle and glance toward the road.

My heart skips a beat.

Making me want to throw it high in the trees and let the birds tear it apart.

Frowning, I wave and steer toward the edge of the field.

The sun shines off blond, shaggy hair, and I secretly wish the mud would just swallow me whole.

I'm going to say something dumb to him again.

I swallow the saliva building up in my mouth and finally smile.

"Hey, Aud," he says and bounces from heel to toe.

"Hey, Ri. What's up?" I ask. Looking around him, I check the car for Hannah but his car is empty.

"Um, I just, uh..."

My eyes travel back to his blue ones; his deep, arctic sea, blue eyes that make me feel like I'm drowning in ice.

"I came to talk," he finally gets out.

I turn the key to my ATV, shutting the engine down and hop off the side. "I've got time."

Mom's engine revs as she zooms past us. "See ya later, kids!" she hollers as she rushes to the garage.

He waves to her, but his eyes stay on mine, and my stomach grazes the mud beneath my feet as my heart climbs up my throat. Something big had to have happened. He wants to talk to me.

Where is Hannah? My confusion and fear elevates, making me want to scream.

I take a deep, calming breath and find my voice somewhere to ask him the question that's burning my insides. "Where's Hannah?

"She's with Ja-, our dad." He nods.

My lungs take in a gulp of blessed oxygen.

Though I'm grateful Hannah is with Jack, his facial expression and the seriousness in his eyes and tone, do nothing to calm my worry.

"That day in the gym," he pauses, shaking his hair away from his eyes that seem to be searching my face.

I know exactly what day he means; the anger, the

blowing off steam, the puck, the…kiss.

If he takes a breath, I wouldn't know.

At this moment, thousands of people could be surrounding us and I wouldn't notice.

My eyes are glued to his and my mask reveals its weak spots all too soon.

He has the power to shatter my false calm, to wreck my whole world with a few words. I never should've given him that power.

"I can't stop thinking," he pauses again.

My brain rolls into itself, trying to figure out anything to say about that moment in our past to stop him from crumbling the walls I've just rebuilt.

What can't he stop thinking?

"Audrey," he whispers.

My name sounds like a plea in this moment. I finally take all of him in; his chest is heaving and his hands are reaching for me. Something inside of me says to make contact. I take a step forward and gingerly place my hands inside of his.

"I need…"

I swallow my panic and stand on my tippy toes, pressing my muddy lips to his soft ones.

On contact, his breathing stops and his hands fall from mine.

I step away from him as he stiffens under my touch.

This time the stupid didn't come out of my mouth, it was just me. I can't look at him. Spinning away from him, tears come to my eyes. My mask is destroyed, my pathetic walls are ruins, and that calm and peace I once felt feels like years ago already. I messed up and did the unforgiveable.

Our friendship will never be okay, and this time, it's my fault.

My chest tightens as I bottle my sob inside of my heart and slide past my ATV. I run, feet squishing and slipping in the mud.

A solid force slams into my back, knocking me off balance and sending me sailing into the mud. Somehow, I land on my back and not my face and Riley lands on top of me.

I stare at him as he stares at me. He's seeing me, behind my mask, and I hate it.

Shoving my hand into his chest, I try shoving him away as I turn my face away from him.

"Move," I rasp.

He doesn't need to see these idiotic tears. I hate me for exposing this to him.

Pity will spew from his mouth, and then I'll lie and say I'm okay.

I can't stand lying to him.

But the need to get away from these tears, from him, from myself, it's too much. I shove his chest again and using my feet, I try sliding away.

His arms frame my head and shoulders like a cage,

and my heart stops as the tears fall faster. My heart releases the sob and I can't stop it.

"Audrey," he whispers my name right into my ear, the same way he did before. The same way that made me kiss him.

It takes everything inside of me not to look at him.

Slick fingertips touch my cheek, and my breath freezes in my lungs under his touch.

"I'm sorry," he whispers. "Please, let me try again."

My chest heaves, expelling yet another sob, and I shove him again.

"Audrey," he whispers again, this time he uses his fingers to tilt my face toward him.

Looking into his icy eyes and seeing hope reflecting in them, I clamp my teeth on my bottom lip to try and slow the tears. I can't imagine what he sees. If it's anything like what I feel then it's weakness, tears, doubt, and fear.

He lowers his face closer to mine, and my eyes widen. His lips touch my top lip and his fingers cup my cheek as his thumb works to release my bottom lip from my teeth.

My eyes flutter closed as I press my lips against his. I reach one arm up and place it on his wrist.

My heart, the stupid organ I wanted to feed to the birds, explodes into a thousand dancing leprechauns inside my chest.

When my breathing returns to normal and my tears slow, he pulls his lips from mine and drops his forehead to mine.

"I'm not good with talking." The tone of his voice sounds like he's smiling and it stops my tears. "I've wanted to do that for a long time."

My mouth pops open. "What?" He pulls back and I can see the grin plastered on his face. I also notice the dirt on his lips, nose, and forehead. "You're dirty."

He chuckles. "If I'm dirty, what does that make you?"

"Confused."

He gets to his knees and holds a hand out to me. I ignore his hand and stand on my own.

"So," I start but then stop because I don't know how to approach anything that just happened. I look away from him and glare at the mud.

Riley glides a finger across my brow. "Audrey." My mouth opens, but I close it quick for fear that stupid will fall from it. "I just..." he sighs and lowers his hand.

From the corner of my eye I see his thin lips in a straight line, his furrowed brow, and flared nostrils. I soften immediately and lean against his chest. His arms come around me just as his lungs expel a heavy breath.

"Thank you," he whispers.

I don't say anything. There's nothing to say at the moment. All I know is that he needs comfort from me, not in the way of words, just us being here.

We're in uncharted territory. I'll need words from him eventually, but right now, words don't matter.

If I had the courage and knew he could answer with words, I'd ask him what this kiss meant. I'd ask him why he tackled me, why he can't vocalize what he feels, and then I'd ask him what he feels.

I pull away from him when his breathing feels normal.

The longer I stay in his arms, the more I want to stay there, the more my heart dances like a leprechaun, and the more I want to throw it to the birds circling the trees. He drops his hand and links our fingers together.

Glancing down, I can't help but wonder what this means for us; if we're friends, if we're more, if we're nothing. My curiosity burns through me, but the dread and fear of rejection has me using that curiosity to rebuild walls around my heart again.

He clears his throat. "Louise wanted to know if you and your family wanted to come over for a cookout this evening. They're celebrating their anniversary or something like that."

"Or something?"

"I don't know. I didn't really listen after they suggested I come over here. I was already planning on coming over, but it gave me an excuse to come sooner."

"So, you don't know if we'd have to bring anything?"

"Not at all. But, I can call and ask," he offers.

We slowly walk back to my ATV. "You may want to towel off first." I smirk.

He shrugs. "I'm glad I left my phone in the car."

I chuckle at him. "If not, it'd be your fault if it broke. I never told you to tackle me in the mud." My face freezes with shock of my words. I shouldn't have brought it up so soon. Quickening my stride, I slip in the mud at first but end up regaining my balance as I jog the rest of the way to my ATV.

"If you wouldn't have ran, I wouldn't have tackled you, so it's your fault."

His words come out so blatant and heavy that I stop in my tracks and turn to look at him.

"Why do you run from me?" His chest begins to move in a faster breathing pattern. "Do I ... scare you?" he chokes on his words.

My mouth drops open and I shake my head "no."

His rounded eyes drop to the ground as he nods.

"Riley, I don't-,"

"It's okay," he assures me as he cuts off my response.

It's really not okay. I don't want him to think I'm afraid of him. I'm more afraid of losing him than I am afraid of him. Frozen Silk doesn't scare me, never has.

"Think your brother would mind if I borrowed some clothes?"

I stare at him with my lips tightly sealed. He's doing it again; chest heaving, wild eyes, subject change...this odd way of getting to a safe topic. I blow out an annoyed breath wishing I had paid more attention in Intro to Psychology last year. I'm positive these actions are symptoms of something mental.

"Riley, I'm not afraid of you. You don't need to fear that of me. And I'm positive Greg will whine, but he'll get over it."

He swallows roughly and looks up from the ground, but not in my direction. "Alright, I'll meet you by the door." Rigidly, he walks away from me toward the house.

With a sigh, I start up my ATV. Standing up on it to help free it from where it sank in the mud, I wiggle my body and release the tires. Coasting to the grassy area between the house and the garage, I watch carefully as Riley waltzes to the mudroom door and make a mental note to glance over my old notebook for Psych. His panicked reactions to certain things start playing in my head. The time he fainted in my garage, it was when we talked about Hannah's reaction to our stupid fight. Any time our kiss gets brought up, emotions… he's always been better at speaking facts, so have I, that's one reason we get along so well. But sometimes things need to be talked about.

I jump off the seat and grab the hose nozzle before turning the metal crank, releasing more hose length.

I'm not that great with talking about how something makes me feel, or what I feel for that matter. That's part of the reason I didn't pay much attention to Ms. O'Donnell in Psych, it was too feely and deep for me.

I point the hose at the mud caked wheels and squeeze the nozzle. A stream of water starts blasting away at the mud. Brown drips and sludge fall from the wheel and it makes me think of what Riley does to me. The mask I wear, he blasts through it like a jet stream of water.

Glancing over my shoulder, I look for Riley. He's standing near the back wall of the house trying to wipe mud from his arm. The crisp look of concentration on his face makes his eyes icier than normal.

I snap my wrist in his direction, sending a spray of chilly water at him.

"What was that for?" He shrieks at me.

I laugh. "You can't rub the mud off, you're just smearing it."

He smirks. "Should I mention how covered you are?"

"I already know that, don't worry so much." I spray him again before aiming the hose back at the tire.

When I'm finished spraying down my four wheeler, I spin off the nozzle on the hose and start drenching myself to rinse the mud. It's what I do every time I go muddin' before I go inside to shower. I've just never done it with Riley watching me like a hawk.

"Can you rinse my shoes?" he asks gruffly.

I nod, looking at him through my wet lashes. His chest is heaving again and his eyes are wild. Pressing my thumb over the opening to give the water some pressure, I aim it at his feet.

"There's some towels on the bench in here for you guys," my mom hollers from the mudroom.

"Thanks, Mom."

"Miss Denise, I was just telling Audrey," he pauses and clears his throat. "Jack and Louise are having a cookout in a few hours and wanted to know if you guys wanted to come over."

"Should we bring anything?" she asks. Riley shrugs and opens his mouth to respond but she waves him off. "You guys finish up and dry off, I'll call Jack and see what needs brought." Before either of us can respond to her, she rushes back inside, presumably to make a phone call.

"So, we're spending the day together?"

"Audrey, I wouldn't have it any other way," he says in a way that makes my heart drip into the mud puddle I'm standing in.

Chapter 30

Riley

I pace my room at my father's house. The walls are white, but the trim is black and the curtains are red. My team colors. It feels strange being here for an extended period of time. I don't feel out of place, I'm comfy here. But then the comfier I feel, the guiltier it makes me. It feels like I'm betraying my mom, in a weird way, and I sort of see why she compares it to taking a vacation every other week. It almost feels like it, but it doesn't at the same time. It feels natural, but weird.

This house isn't "home," but neither is my mom's house. "Home" is supposed to be a place you feel comfortable, where you don't have to be anything but yourself, a place to call your own. I don't have that.

Grabbing my phone, I check the time again. Audrey should be here in twenty minutes.

Before slipping my phone back in my pocket, I decide to call my mom.

She answers on the second ring, "What do you

want?"

I swallow. She must be having a bad day. "I just wanted to see how you are, Mom."

"If you really cared about my wellbeing, you would be here and not *there*," she spits.

"Mom-,"

"No Riley, you don't get to care about me. You left, just like him and you made your choice without caring how it affected me."

"Mom!" I yell, trying to get a word in.

"Riley. I'm done here. I'm going to the fair with Ted, I need to get ready." The phone clicks silent before I can say bye.

Staring at my phone, the time blurs with my background picture, making Hannah's face seem to shadow.

There's a knock on my door, breaking me from my downward thoughts.

"Riley," Louise asks, knocking again.

I pocket my phone before tugging the door open.

"Are you okay? I heard yelling."

I nod slowly. "Yeah," I lie.

The lie burns my tongue. Squeezing my lips together, I stop myself from telling any more lies. She doesn't deserve the lie I told her.

More guilt mixes in my gut, churning the acids.

She smiles softly, accentuating the fine laugh lines around her mouth and eyes. “I hope you don’t mind, but I’ve invited your mom and Ted over for dinner, too.”

“It’s cool, but she said they’re going to the fair.” I shrug and pop my lips like it doesn’t bother me. She was offered to spend time with Hannah and me, on Jack’s time, and she didn’t choose us.

Her face falls slightly, and I feel bad for telling her they weren’t coming. “Just as well, then.” She nods. “Hannah is requesting your help on the deck.” Without another word, she walks down the hallway toward her and my father’s room.

If I were her, with how my mother treats her, I’d be jumping for joy. But I don’t think she is. She doesn’t react the way I’m used to, she seems like Mom’s opposite. An example, she invited Mom and Ted, Mom wouldn’t and Mom likes when I clean up and do dishes, in fact, half the time I’m the only one who does those things. But when I do them here, Louise gets upset, I can’t figure out why though.

I chew on my cheek as I take the stairs two at a time.

“Riley!” my father shouts.

“What?”

“Can you take these plates out to the table since you’re goin’ that way?”

I roll my eyes and silently take the plates from his hand.

Hannah is dropping ice cubes in the tumblers at each place setting.

"Whatcha need, Squirrel?"

"Louise won't let me pour the lemonade." She looks up at me and pouts.

I smile. "Tell ya what. I'll pour the first couple, and then I'll help you pour the last few. Sound good?"

"I can do it by myself! But she won't let me and said I'm too small! I'm not that small!" Her eyes well with tears as she whines.

"Hannah. I know you're getting bigger, but the pitcher is full. I side with Louise on this one. Let me pour a few, then it'll be your turn, and I'll only hold the glass steady. Promise."

She crosses her arms and glares at me. "I pour Mister Paul's!"

I raise my hands in the air. "It's all yours, but only if I can pour yours."

She glances around the table at all the cups before looking back at me. "Deal."

I pour Hannah's first, then move to the right as she instructs. After pouring the third glass, I glance around the table, counting the seats, nine of them.

"Who are the extra two chairs for?" I ask her.

The doorbell rings from inside the house, echoing through the screen door on the deck.

Hannah squeals. "Mommy's here!" she shouts and runs to the screen door.

Anger boils. "Mommy isn't coming!" She stops, one foot inside the door and one foot still on the deck.

"They're not coming tonight, Hannah."

She turns around, eyes filled with tears. "She promised me."

"Apparently, going to the fair is more important than we are!" I snap. "It's your turn to pour."

She sniffles. "You're lying!" I turn back to look at her and see she's already run into the house.

The realization of what I just said hits me.

I've hurt her. Just like Mom has countless times.

"Squirrel!" I yell, setting the pitcher down and running inside after her. "Wait a minute!"

Jack blocks my path from leaving the kitchen. "What happened, Riley?"

I shove around him. "It's between me and my sister. Butt out!"

"Hey, Ri-," Paul says, but stops himself from continuing.

I rush up the stairs and down the hall to Hannah's room. Her white and pink door is closed. I tap on it. "Han?"

She sniffles.

"I'm comin' in."

I push the door open and look for her at her bed. But she isn't there. Closing my eyes, I take a calming breath. When I open my eyes again, I look at her closed closet door.

"Hannah, I'm sorry." I walk over to her closet and

sit on the floor, back to her dresser. I crack the door so I can see her. She has her back to me, head buried under he favorite blanket. "Please, Squirrel. Look at me?"

She shakes her head.

I sigh. "I'm sorry for snapping at you. I'm not mad at you, I'm just mad."

"I love you," she says, words muffled by her blanket.

"I love you, too. Do you forgive me?"

She nods her head and rolls over, peaking one eye from behind the blanket. "Mom's really going to the fair?" she asks quietly. I nod. She covers her face again.

"Mister Paul, Miss Denise, and Audrey are here. You want to come down?"

"I bet Mister Paul would take me to the fair," she mutters.

"I think Louise and Jack would, too. If you asked them, but probably not tonight."

She wiggles away from the back wall, sliding closer to me. "Are all mommies like our mommy?"

I feel the frown on my face turn into a flat line. "No. But she's the best mommy she knows how to be."

Hannah drops the blanket and sits up, staring at me through her tears. "I think I like Louise better. She smiles a lot."

I chuckle hollowly. "Not everyone can be the best at everything, Han."

She purses her lips and nods. "You're not the best

at hide and seek." She begins to smile, and I feel a small piece inside of me heal again. "I find you *all* the time!"

I lean toward her and quickly grab her foot, pulling her toward me. She squeals. "C'mon, Squirrel. Mister Paul is waitin' to see his best girl." I hoist her over my shoulder while she squeals and slaps my back.

"Put me down!" She yells through her laugh.

I bounce down the hallway, jostling her a little, and listen as she laughs harder. "I might not be the best hider, but I am the best brother, right?" I ask, pausing at the top of the stairs.

"Yes!"

I right her so I can hug her, her small arms go around my neck and she presses her cheek to mine.

"I love you, Riley."

"I love you, too."

I jump from step to step, listening to her giggles. It makes the anger back away, so it's almost nonexistent.

"Now, we have a few glasses to fill, don't we?" I ask her as I reach the bottom and set her on her feet.

She sighs dramatically as if she were out of breath. "I guess," she agrees and skips toward the kitchen.

When I look up, I realize I'm not alone. A pair of tear filled, brown eyes are staring at me from a few feet away. Her gorgeous smile and dimple remind of what it felt like to kiss her.

I feel my lips turn up into a smile before I even think to smile at her. "Hey, you."

She takes a step toward me. "Hey, Best Brother," she teases.

I look down to the floor as the meaning washes over me. She witnessed mine and Hannah's exchange. I wasn't really expecting an audience for that.

"My brother, Luca, used to make me say that all the time." She chuckles. "He threatens me though, says if I don't say it, he'll give me a swirly."

I laugh. But I don't feel the humor I'm supposed to, the humor I'd probably feel any other time. "I gotta go help Han, come on." I wave her to follow me. Her shoes click softly behind me.

"Where's Louise?" Miss Denise asks.

"She'll be down in a few," Jack answers.

"Hey, Han. You ready to show off your pouring skills?" I ask as I step onto the deck.

Hannah is perched on Mister Paul's knee already. She smiles widely and reaches for the pitcher.

Grabbing the glass nearest her, I hold it as she pours.

"You did a great job, kiddo!" Mister Paul encourages.

"Riley taught me," she says proudly.

She slides the pitcher my way, and I finish pouring the lemonade as Jack clears the two places for Mom and Ted. Audrey sits next to Mister Paul and starts folding one of the napkins.

"We have a bit while the burgers cook, if you kids

want to go play or watch TV you can," Louise announces as she steps out onto the deck. I glance up to her as I set the empty pitcher down. Her hair is now pulled tightly on top of her head, earlier, she had it loose to her shoulders with one of those toothy clips holding her hair away from her eyes. I also notice she's wearing makeup, earlier she wasn't wearing any. Maybe that's what she was doing, finishing getting ready.

I frown and turn away from her.

Women are weird.

"Han, you wanna go swing?" I ask.

"No! I wanna stay with Mister Paul!"

Mister Paul laughs and hugs her. "How about this? You and I go swing and let the grumpy teens sit in the grass and do nothing."

Hannah turns around to Audrey, seeing her fold the napkin. "Are you grumpy?"

Audrey smiles. "I'm not grumpy." She folds the corners and then carefully puts it in her palm. "Hold out your hand."

She does as instructed, and Audrey drops the napkin creation in her hand. "What is it?"

"A frog. They're prettier with paper, but he still sort of looks like a frog, don't you think?"

"Ri! I'm holding a frog!" she squeals in delight.

I chuckle. "Want to see if we can catch a real frog?"

"Ewww! No!"

Audrey laughs, and I find myself feeling strings of

happiness return. The events of this morning flow through my mind reminding me that happiness is fleeting.

"Do you want to learn how to make your own frog? We can make some paper frogs while the adults cook," she offers.

"Not yet."

"Okay, let me know when you're ready." She smiles sweetly at Hannah and then glances toward me. "I'm gonna go wrestle your brother into a happier mood."

Hannah laughs.

"Don't find any more mud," Miss Denise scolds.

"I won't, Ma. We'll be around." She stands and walks past me to the steps leading to the backyard. "Come on, grumpy," she teases as she bops down the three wooden steps.

Following her lead, I jump down the steps and land next to her. "Do you really think I'm grumpy?"

She snorts. "No. I think you're a tad frosty, but that's just you."

I shrug and lead the way around the side of the house.

"Why'd Jack take away extra plates? Was someone else coming?"

I swallow. "Last minute cancelation."

"Oh. That's too bad."

"Yeah," I mumble and add a shrug. "It is what it is."

We reach the front yard, and I sit in the grass next to the sidewalk.

"Is Coach Page staying on next year?" she asks.

"He said he is. But I know he's gonna retire soon."

"He's been old for forever," she agrees.

She sits about a foot away from me. I want to tell her that she can sit closer, but I can't get the words out.

So I say nothing.

"I'm taking Alice muddin' tomorrow," she says quietly as she brushes her fingers through a tuft of grass in front of her.

I snort. "You're not serious."

"I am," she says with a smile. As she pulls a blade of grass, she glances over to me. "Remember that dress I wore on my birthday?"

The yellow dress, I remember it like it was yesterday. I could hardly focus on anything but her.

"Yeah," I choke out and try clearing my throat.

"That's why I get to take her muddin'." She holds the blade of grass between her thumbs, cups her hands, and holds her thumbs to her mouth. Her lips part and a loud noise, that almost sounds like a duck call, replaces our momentary silence.

As much as I want to be her thumbs right now, I can't get the image of her in that yellow dress out of my head, and both do odd things to the guilt swirling inside of me.

"Food!" Jack yells from the back of the house.

"I thought we'd have more time," I mutter with a frown. I'm almost thankful we don't have more time, but another minute just to watch her play with the grass would have been alright.

We walk back to the deck and take our seats, opposite each other.

"Thank you for coming over, we're celebrating our three year anniversary. I'm not one for big parties, and neither is Louise, we just wanted some special people to celebrate with us," Jack says.

Louise stands beside my father and holds his hand. "And we agree, there's no one more special than you guys to Riley and Hannah. You've always looked out for them, and that makes you special to us as well. Thank you for everything you've done without needing to."

"Dig in," Jack announces.

Autopilot takes over my functions.

Part of me wants to correct them and their thinking. My mother has done plenty for Hannah and me.

The anger that they didn't even mention her in that sense is replaced by the anger of knowing how right Jack and Louise are. Paul and Denise have been amazing to us, they never needed to be as generous, but they were.

With the feeling of fire in my chest, I glance across the table to Audrey. She's gripping the handle of the spoon that's shoved in the potato salad, but it's her smile and warm eyes that cools the fire inside.

She is more important.

She is special.

My lungs squeeze, limiting my supply of oxygen.

I take as deep a breath as I can to calm myself down.

Three on three, run the puck… I flip through the plays in my head and think about training, school, finding a job, anything, just to breathe well enough to eat the food I managed to get on my plate.

Embracing 18 Years
Audrey & Riley

Chapter 31

Audrey

How long can you go on being silent? I stare out over the grassy hill in front of the school as I get lost in my thoughts. The answer to that question changes for me. It depends on what I'm supposed to be silent about. If it's a secret present, I stay silent until I'm allowed to burst. If it's not my secret to tell, forever. If it's something that will lead to harm or injury, until I find the right person to tell.

If it's Riley...

It's been one year and twelve days since he pucked me in the gymnasium and kissed me. It's been six months, three weeks, and two days since he tackled me in the mud.

I've been waiting for him to say something.

To show something.

He's had plenty of opportunity, too. At Jack and Louise's three-year anniversary, we went off on our own before and after dinner. At Hannah's seventh birthday party, he and I sat next to the present table while she and her friends played in the ball pit at Bazinga's Arcade. My brother and my parents have held bonfires and cookouts that he's attended, we went job hunting together more than once, and the list goes on. The only thing that happens is that we get close, then awkward, and then suddenly we're discussing the inner workings of an escalator or how a megaphone works.

It's not just his fault.

I glare at the stupid clouds that seem so happy today.

I've run away from him at least ten times since he called me out on it in the mud.

But he hasn't tried. Well, he held my hand for the first time three weeks ago as he drove me to school on our first day of senior year. I thought for sure we would talk or that he'd hold my hand again at some point.

I can't stay silent forever.

What do I even say, though? I'm not even sure what I feel or think anymore. I'm torn up inside with the need to know what we are and if there can ever be anything more than this awkward thing we can call our friendship.

I fear bringing it up. What if he can't get anything out? He's nearly passed out on me more times than I can count. Once in the garage, the only time he blacked out, it was enough for me to never want to see it happen again. So when his chest moves exaggerated and his face turns sheet white and eyes seem to beg for help, I shut up about whatever it was and change the subject to distract him.

The bell shrills, alerting the end of the day and reminding me that this is the third day this week I haven't paid attention to Mr. Kellerman's Politics lecture. I quickly gather my stuff and follow the line of zombified students to the door to leave.

"Don't forget! You have four days to complete your debates," Mr. Kellerman shouts as we exit his room.

I internally groan. It's far too early in the year to be having such elaborate assignments.

When I walk out of the room, I weave through the full hallway of students, doing my best not to run into anyone.

"Aud!" Riley yells from...somewhere deep inside the belly of students.

I thrash my head around, trying to find him as I stand on my tippy toes to see over other students. "Riley?" I shout, hoping he can hear me.

A warm hand glides over my forearm a second before Riley's smiling face comes into view.

"Hey, ready to get out of here?" He asks.

I'm driving him to school until he gets his car inspected on Friday. Which means, I have to take him to practice and then home. "Almost, I've gotta grab some books from my locker."

He holds up a finger and digs in his book bag. "I have English and history here, you have your politics, and I stopped and grabbed your Marketing stuff and notebooks just in case. Oh, and you can use my chemistry book. Is that everything?" He glances to me expectantly, and all I can think of is how he's taking care of me.

I nod once, wishing that he was wrong and had forgotten something, but he didn't. He thought of me, paid attention to my classes, and saved me a locker trip. My insides claw at my heart, reminding me to speak up and use my words to figure out what's going on.

"Great!" His shoulders sag even though he smiles, like he was actually worried he had forgotten something.

"Come on, let's get you to practice," I say over the crowd and nod in the direction of the doors, politely ignoring the nagging feeling in my gut. Letting him lead the way, I clutch my books to my chest and push myself closer to his back. The cologne he uses is still strong, and it tugs at my heart.

It's one of my favorite scents, close behind mud, snow, new shoes, and saw dust and grease.

As we leave the building, he slows his pace to walk beside me.

"First game is Wednesday night."

I glance at him sideways. "I know."

"You won't miss it?"

I raise an eyebrow at him. "I think I've only missed one in the last four years. Why would I miss this one?"

He shrugs a shoulder and stops at my passenger door. "Just..." His glance falls to the ground and his chest rises and falls heavily. "Be there."

I nod, but he can't see that. Unlocking my door, I chuck my stuff into the backseat and lean over the console, unlocking his door. "I'll be there," I whisper as he sits.

He clears his throat and plays with the strap of the seatbelt. "Will you be alright during my practice?"

I smile at him. "I'll be fine. I've got plenty of work to do."

The silence that falls betweens us is awkward, it feels too stiff.

The urge to say something to him becomes overwhelming. I maneuver my car out of the busy lot and down the one-way road to leave the premises.

If I could just ask him how Hannah is doing, or his mom...maybe this pain will end, too.

The pain of silence.

It almost feels like the calm before a storm, and with Riley, that can mean an ice storm. Not something I'm willing to face again. I think I've had deeper conversations with Alice's cat than Riley lately.

I frown and glance over to Riley as I turn onto Main Street. He looks like he always does; blond, shaggy hair that falls to the top of his eyebrows, blue eyes, dimpled chin, and wide, square jaw. I glance back to the road so I don't crash. But the torment I see in his eyes is more present today than it has been in a while, not since I had to help him carry his mom to her room, not since we cleaned his house from his mom's intoxicated destruction.

Flipping my left turn signal on, I wait for the truck to pass so I can pull into the rink.

"Near or far?" He asks so suddenly that I startle and double tap the gas pedal before smoothly turning into the parking lot.

"Depends," I say, confused. "You? Near or far?"

"How about... home or new places?"

"What's your definition of home?" I ask as I pull into a spot.

"I want your definition and answer. I already know mine."

Putting my car in park, I run my tongue over the fronts of my top teeth while I think of how to word my answer. "Home isn't a place. It's more of a feeling. So long as I have that feeling, I could go to Italy without a translation dictionary and be fine."

He smiles brightly, the kind of smile that exposes his teeth and puts a shine in his eye. Seeing that, I smile in return.

I must've said something right for a change.

Grabbing my books and his book bag, I let the silence fall between us again.

"Yo, Captain!" someone yells from behind me. I jump and spin around to see the boy that made Riley so mad last year. I look at him, really look at him, half expecting him to say something ignorant again, or something that implies Riley and I are more than we are. But he isn't looking at me. He's jogging towards us, but looking past me, to Riley.

"Alex," Riley says with a nod as he shuts my trunk lid.

"My mom wants me to give this to you," he says, digging an envelope from his pocket. "I don't know what it is, but she said it's a thank you for helping me out."

I watch them curiously, not having any idea what he's talking about.

"It wasn't any trouble. You would've done the same for me if I was in your position."

He shakes his head. "I don't know, man. You never need help with anything." A chuckle cuts through his lips. "'Cept your anger, maybe."

Riley's posture straightens and the smile falls from his face. "What are you talking about?" he asks gruffly. I can tell he's teasing Alex, but it's very subtle. His frozen glare is only half sincere.

Alex takes a half step back. "Nothin'," he mutters.

Riley cracks a smile and winks at him. "Gotcha."

Alex shakes his head and tries to relax. "Let's go work over the freshmeat."

They start walking, so I follow.

"You know I can't condone that. You got to cut the newbies some slack."

Alex stops suddenly, and I almost slam into his hockey stick. "You didn't cut *me* any slack! You still haven't, and I'm first string with you this year!"

Riley turns around, walking backwards. "I'm the captain, and your attitude gets you in trouble." He nods his head at me, silently asking me to speed up. I walk around the stunned Alex, catching up to Riley again.

"I'm gonna work on that, Riley," he says softly.

Riley gently places his hand on my shoulder. My heart flutters and my cheeks heat almost instantly.

"You've got a lot of work to do," Riley responds. He takes the book bag from my shoulder and carries it for me. The spot he touched still feels warm but now I feel the loss of contact and remember just how long it's been since he's touched me in a way that was more than friends.

Riley opens the door and holds it for me and Alex to pass through. Alex winks at me before jogging down the stairs. I raise an eyebrow at his retreating form and wait at the steps for Riley, so I can get the book bag back from him.

"See ya in a few," he says softly and winks.

I hold my hand out.

His eyebrows pinch together as he glances from my hand to my face in an expression of confusion mixed with humor.

"Book bag?"

He smiles and nods. "Oh, right." He places the straps in my waiting hand, but doesn't walk away.

"Go on, you need to practice for Wednesday's game."

His eyes connect with mine, drop to my lips then back to my eyes again. "Wednesday."

My stomach flutters higher than my heart. "Quit bein' weird and go practice before Coach chews you out."

He winks and jogs down the steps toward the locker room.

Wednesday must be really important. I wonder if a

scout will be out to look at him. I frown. He would tell me about something like that, right?

I mean, having a scout out could mean something excellent for his future. Whether it's a college scout or one from an association, it could be good for his future.

When he disappears behind the swinging door at the end of the hallway diagonal to where I'm at, I work my way to the back row of benches. The further away I am, the less distracted I'll be and, hopefully, be able to concentrate on the dumb project Mr. Kellerman assigned.

Chapter 32

Riley

Focusing through practice proved difficult, but listening to my mom and Ted talk about whatever they're talking about is worse.

Wednesday, things will change, and I'm hoping for the better.

"Riley!" My mother shouts and snaps her fingers. "Where are you, son?"

"Um, in the kitchen," I answer confused.

She frowns. "You could at least pretend you're happy to be spending time with me. You barely see me anymore, thanks to your father. What have you been up to?"

I clear my throat. "Sorry, Mom. I've just got a lot to think about."

"You wanna participate during dinner? I cooked this food for you, and you haven't even touched it." She frowns at me, fork poised in the air, pointing to my plate.

I glance down to my plate. The lasagna noodles look too yellow and the meat and cheese look grey. My stomach recoils and I glance over to Hannah. Thankfully she's pushing globs around her plate.

"Can I be excused? I have some work to finish up before cleaning up dinner."

She smiles softly. "That's my good boy. Thank you, baby."

I nod and take my plate to the counter. I'll dump everything in the trash later. Hopefully Mom and Ted don't get sick from it, but it honestly wouldn't surprise me.

I rush up the stairs and dart into the safe haven my room provides.

Digging through my desk drawer, I find the brown box I hid in the second drawer months ago. Still resting in the back corner under team flyers and notebooks filled with random notes from old classes. I stuff everything back in the drawer and carefully set the box in the center of my desk.

Closing my eyes, I say a silent prayer that no one found it while I was away from my room or the house. As I lift the lid, I crack an eye open to see if it's still inside. The plastic puck and my pocket knife are still safely tucked inside. I breathe a sigh of relief and open my eyes fully.

Dumping the contents of the box on my desk, I gently flip the blade of the knife out of the built in sheath.

It won't be ready today and I still need to pick

something up for it to be complete, but I'm positive this is the one thing I'll get right.

I just have to make her believe me, and that counts on me finding the words.

R

Coach Page blows his whistle, long and loud. We all stop and skate to the bench. It's our last practice before Wednesday's game.

"We're gonna practice a five on five offense to defense scenario," he announces and holds up his dry erase board. "For this drill, Silk, Jackson, Humphrey, Hopkins, and Carter, you'll start as offense behind Van Luit. Smith, McHugh, and Jefferies, you'll be passing at the neutral line. Newton and Zumbrum, you're their back up. You are the reds," he says, pointing to me. "And you guys grab a white jersey from the box. On my whistle, take your places. Second whistle starts the passing of white's three and red sprints to opposite end. Third whistle, red rushes Van Luit. Red, when you reach the net, circle back and switch to a defensive position. Warlocks are going to be tough to beat tomorrow!"

"Warriors can beat them!" the team shouts in response.

"Go!" He blows his whistle and we all take our position.

"Don't let Jefferies score," I mutter to Todd.

"Don't trip and lose the lead, Silk," he taunts.

I grin at him, and he shakes his head.

Coach blows his whistle again, and my four and I

start our sprint to the boards.

As I approach Andy McHugh, Coach blows the whistle again. I inhale the sweet scent of the ice and let it fill my lungs, hardening my veins. Digging my blade into the ice, I give myself another boost and sail for the net, circling behind it and passing my red wearing teammates. “Faster!” I yell as I control my footing to sprint after the whites.

Looking ahead, Andy passes to Alex, who tries to gain a shot on Todd in the absence of defense.

Coach blows his whistle as Rob, Pat, and I reach our positions.

“Again!” he shouts.

I pop my mouth guard out and chew on it as I circle behind the net and slice beside Todd.

“Allen needs to control his footing. He was wild and sloppy on the pass back up. That’s what the hold up was. He skidded into Dan,” Todd says, flipping his face mask up.

“Game’s tomorrow, if Coach puts him in, he’s gonna have to figure it out,” I spit. Todd narrows his eyes at me. My natural reflex to push the weakest link out is still present this year. In all actuality, he’s not our weakest link. He’s just too slow for this type of play. “Hump!”

“Sorry, Riley,” he mumbles around his mouth guard as he stops beside me.

“No worries, Hump. We can’t be great at everything.” I shrug and bump the butt of my stick off his shoulder pad. “Look straight ahead,” I instruct him. His eyes warily find mine, no longer looking at his feet. I nod, hoping to encourage him to look ahead. As his head turns away from me and toward the far side of the ice, as I let him in on a secret Coach Page told me years ago. "Keep your focus on something immoveable in front of you. Your peripheral vision will pick up movement but your focus will be on the object in front of you. Just don't over-think it and don't give up."

He's silent for a moment. "What if I trip? I nee-,"

"Stop thinking."

He purses his lips and glances back at me. "What do I do when I have to turn?"

"Find a new focal point."

"That's just so-,"

"Stop thinking, just try it once. Don't worry about how fast or slow you are."

He nods. "Thanks, Captain."

I grin and slide away, taking my position on the other side of the net and wait for Coach to start the drill again. I close my eyes and take in the scent of the ice, preparing for the drill.

One more day.

My anticipation, adrenaline, and nervousness soars, taking the place of confidence and calm.

Coach sounds his whistle, and I sluggishly start my sprint. I've got to focus if I want to get past this drill, make goals, and win tomorrow. I need to focus on those things in order for my plan to work.

Swallowing everything and shoving it all in a box in

my stomach, I dig my blades in the ice and grit my teeth as I push forward.

R

"You adjusting alright?" Coach asks me, leaning against his truck outside the rink.

I shift my weight from foot to foot. "Yeah, it's different but okay." My eyes find Audrey's car four spaces away from Coach's.

"I'm glad you're getting along with Jack. He's been beside himself lately."

Chewing on my cheek, I ask a question that I've been wondering about for a year now. "Have you always stayed in contact with my dad?"

He smiles. "Yes. But before you get angry with him or me, there was a reason I didn't tell you or set something up for you two to hang out."

I nod, waiting for him to continue.

He rubs the sleeves of his jacket and looks at me with sincerity. "When things went south with your parents, I figured it'd be like any other divorce of my player's parents. There would be some anger or sorrow to deal with, and confusion from the child. I also figured there would be some other problems with practices or even games because when there's two homes the child travels between, sometimes things get messy or forgotten, and sometimes parents make it a big deal."

"That didn't happen with me," I remind him.

"No," he says, shaking his head. "That didn't happen." He glances to the building for a moment before continuing. "The first thing I noticed was you and your reactions to little things. I didn't know that your dad left or that you hadn't seen him since. All I knew was that you were hitting the ice harder, you were training harder, and you were studying more. You completely immersed yourself in hockey and school. For an eleven year old, that's something unusual. My own son at eleven was more into video games and getting into trouble with his friends, not studying, training, or staying home with his sister. I didn't know what happened, but I thought it was amazing. You always had potential to be great, but this meant something else."

After Jack left, he's right, I ignored anything that wasn't hockey, school, or home. That was the first time I shut Audrey out, I think. She was struggling with her brothers leaving for college and my home was falling apart. It took her a few days after Jack left, but she walked over to my house in the middle of the night and finally got me to talk about what happened.

That's just what she does. She doesn't like silence.

"It was the third game that I noticed your dad wasn't in his usual spot behind the Jacob's. I called your house to talk to your dad, I worried that something bad happened. Your mom told me Jack left and that you'd be leaving hockey and not returning because of the abandonment." His eyes find mine. "Let me tell you, as a father myself, hearing those words… I got angry. I've known Jack since we were about your age. It didn't sound like him at all. I found your dad not long after that. He was staying at the motel the next town over, and he looked like crap. I'll save you the details, but he wasn't in a good way at all."

The wheels turn in my head. Jack had said something about how he wasn't okay for a while. I guess that makes sense.

"He said he left Sue and that she was angrier than he's ever seen her." He puts a hand on my shoulder. "I'm sure you can piece together the rest of what happened, but the reason I didn't tell you anything... that's a bit complicated. Your dad didn't want to get me involved, he feared that Sue might try something to get me fired, and then after she petitioned the school, by law I wasn't even supposed to be talking to Jack."

"I get it. It sucks, but I get it. Thanks for telling me," I say, ending the conversation so I no longer hold Audrey up.

"Jack says things are going good, but he worries about you," Coach says, stopping my retreat.

Raising an eyebrow, I turn back at him. "Why would he be worried about me?"

Coach's lips form a straight line and his jaw shifts side to side for a split second. "We've all noticed odd things about you. Jack, all of us really, we just worry that you need some extra help," he admits.

My chest tightens. "I'm fine."

"Look, I'm no expert, and neither is my wife, but she thinks you have anxiety. If that's left uncontrolled you could run into some problems-,"

"I said I'm fine," I snap, cutting him off. "I'll see you tomorrow for the game." Walking away from him, I make a mental note to call Jack and tell him that I'm fine.

I really am fine.

I will be fine.

One day.

Chapter 33

Audrey

The atmosphere in the arena does not match how I feel at this very moment.

Families are cheering their child and team on, friends are taunting the other team's fans; it almost feels as high energy as an NHL game with all the chirping going on. It feels weird, this isn't how things normally go at our games. But the Warlocks are tough and from a larger city than us in our little hole-in-the-wall town.

I mostly feel confused, outside of the odd atmosphere in the arena. Riley has been saying "Wednesday" the last two days.

Well, it's Wednesday, and there's been only more weirdness than usual. His normal pregame jitters were through the roof this morning when I picked him up for school and he only got more spacey and jumpy as the day wore on. When I asked him if he was okay, he told me that I had to pay attention to tonight's game.

I am paying attention.

He is not.

The ref announces the end of our timeout and the team takes the ice, Riley included. My stomach churns. I haven't even looked at the score yet, but I'm almost positive we're losing.

The puck drops in the face-off zone, and Riley turns the puck over to a Warlock. His body stiffens but he chases after the puck.

"Are you really not going to acknowledge my presence?" Alice mutters beside me.

I startle and stare at her. "How long have you been sitting there?"

She snorts. "Only since the game started."

I tear my eyes away from her and focus back on the ice, looking for Riley. "He's playing like crap tonight," I say. "Why did he make a big deal out of watching this?"

"Well, Todd kiddingly told me that-,"

"Kiddingly?" I glare at her for distracting me, and with poor grammar.

"We're not talking about my grammar, we're talking about Riley," she snaps. "Anyway, Todd was *joking* around with some of the guys today and said that Riley was going to choke on the puck tonight."

"That's not a very nice joke."

"Well, from what I understand, he's been very distracted lately," she coos and bumps my shoulder, once again pulling my attention from the ice.

"Alice, what is that supposed to mean?"

"You, my dear. He's been distracted by you."

I scoff. "Hardly."

"You've been watching him play, yeah?" I nod. "So tell me, where does he keep looking?"

I furrow my brows in confusion and glance back to the ice, searching for him. "I have no-," I stop speaking as my eyes lock on his. His cold blue eyes are staring directly at me instead of on the puck. Anger bowls over my confusion and I jump to my feet and slam my hands against the boards. "Are you stupid?!" I shout at him but I know he can't hear me.

"You really didn't know?" Alice chimes.

I turn my glare to her. "Really? You think I'd condone him throwing away a game that scouts could very well be at, for what? For him to stare at me like he's never seen anyone so-,"

Alice waves her hand in a circle, silently getting me to finish my sentence.

"No. No. I cannot be the cause of this sloppy playing." Without another word, I tug my keys from my pocket and storm away from her.

"What is he thinking?" I grumble to myself as I stomp up the stairs toward the front entrance.

Nearly everyone to my left jumps from their seats and shouts, "Yes!"

I halt my retreat and turn around to see what happened. The score buzzer sounds and glancing to the scoreboard, I see we scored. Warrior's two - Warlock's two. I peer around the tall man nearest me and scan the ice. Riley has one leg in the air, wigging his hips, and thrusting his stick in the air.

"What is he doing?" a woman near me asks with a laugh.

He's doing a one armed, one legged, booty shaking dance, just like I dared him to last year.

I watch as Riley turns toward my seat, the one I vacated. His feet are now both on the ice. I'm too far away to see his facial expression, but if it's anything like how I feel right now, I'm betting it's bad.

Swallowing my guilt, I take the steps two at a time to get back to my seat.

"That didn't take long," Alice cheers. "I don't know much about hockey, but I know that Riley scoring is a good thing... Why do you look like someone stole your four wheeler thingy?"

Without taking my eyes off of Riley's back, I answer her, "He danced."

If she responds, I can't tell. It wasn't after a win, but it was after he scored. That has to mean something.

Is that what he wanted me to see tonight?

My mind races trying to figure out the code breaker or a way to solve the dancing riddle.

The players file out and Riley and a Warlock meet at center ice with the ref. Riley's stance seems more relaxed than it has been.

This is good.

The puck drops and he slams the blade of his stick against the puck, sending it sailing to the left side, and his shoulder slams into the Warlock before he spins to open for a pass. I hold my breath as I watch him sprint down the ice.

This is Riley.

He's got his game back.

A

"Audrey!" Alice hollers.

"Shut up. Hockey!" I respond. Sitting on the edge of my seat, I glance between the clock and the players.

"I'm heading out. I'll see you tomorrow," she says in my ear and pats my shoulder.

I nod but don't take my eyes from the game. There's thirty seconds left on the clock and as long as they can fight off the Warlocks, we can win tonight.

A particularly tall Warlock slams against Riley, nearly knocking him over, but he regains his footing before his glove can touch the ice.

I jump to my feet. "Get him! Go!" I scream and tap the glass.

My eyes find the clock, twenty four seconds left. That's too much time.

Riley glides through a grouping of Warlocks, snapping the puck and sending it sailing deep in Warlock zone. My heart races, matching the speed of the puck, and I jump up and down in excitement. If the Warriors can keep the puck in Warlock zone, they'll be golden and we'll come out with a win tonight.

I find Riley again, this time, he's looking at me. I point at him then to the puck, hoping he gets my meaning. He winks and checks a Warlock away from the puck. Allen taps the puck away from Riley and the Warlock and passes it to Robert Hopkins, a Warrior. My stomach lurches as I watch Robert taunt two Warlocks by keeping the puck just out of their reach.

The three beat buzzer alerts the end of the game.

"Let's go Warriors!" chants through the area, and I join in.

Riley slices to a stop in front of me. I hold one finger to glass, our tradition, but he doesn't remove his glove.

He spits his mouth guard into his glove and shouts something. I shake head and point to my ears, telling him I can't hear him. He nods, points to me then to his eye, and smiles as he skates backward.

The teams line up for their show of sportsmanship. Riley cuts to the front of the line, his usual spot, and starts moving forward. Tapping the gloves of the Warlock players as he glides along, my eyes don't leave his form until he circles behind the teams.

Wildly, I search for him between the players and the coaches. The blade of a stick bounces in the air just beyond the players. I follow it until I connect it to a person. Riley is dancing again, one arm in the air, one leg lifted, and hips shaking. He switches legs to keep his balance before he straightens and stops in front of me again.

He dances.

Again.

My lips pull up into a smile and a laugh bubbles from my chest.

"You're not a chicken," I mouth through the boards.

Chapter 34

Riley

I silently place my bag in Audrey's backseat.

"So, um..." she drawls and jingles her keys in her hand.

"Milkshakes?" I suggest.

She chuckles quietly. "Yeah. Of course."

Sitting in the passenger seat, I watch her as she starts the ignition. I open my mouth, but I feel my chest tightening. Jack's words replay in my mind, "Embrace it." Taking a deep breath and closing my eyes, I envision ice, my blades scraping and gliding across it.

Slowly, she pulls out of the spot, and my chest loosens its grip on my lungs with the same momentum.

Her radio is playing softly, diluting the stiff silence between us. I open my mouth, but nothing comes out. Frustrated, I stare out the window and let my mind go completely blank, like the sky tonight. There's not one star lighting the sky. There's no hope for the night, and that's exactly how I feel.

“Um, yeah, I need a medium vanilla shake and a…” Audrey trails, tapping my shoulder. She mouths “chocolate,” and I nod. “And a medium chocolate shake too, please.”

The lighting of the parking lot gives me the opportunity to check Audrey’s reflection in the window. She seems…at peace. I’m not sure. She doesn’t look upset but she doesn’t look happy either.

After putting our shakes in the cup holders, we’re off to our spot near the park. As the streetlights space out further, my opportunity of seeing her reflection in the window fades. By the time I have the courage to face her again, we’re pulling into our spot at the park. With a resigned sigh, I grab my shake and meet her on the trunk of her car.

The silence between us is thick with things unsaid. My eyes seem to be sucked into a gravitational pull, straight to her eyes. Nothing matters, not the chill in the air, not how quick-paced my heart is racing, and certainly not the frozen cup in my hand.

Her cheeks suck in as she takes a pull from the straw and a second later, she peeks at me from the corner of her eye.

One second, she wipes her mouth with her delicate hand.

Two seconds, her eyes flit away.

Three seconds, the corner of her mouth turns up into a tight smile.

Four seconds, a laugh breaks the silence between us.

Five seconds, I’m lost.

"Would you stop it?"

I clear my throat. "Stop what?"

"Staring. It's unnerving."

I smile. "I can't help it."

I'm not even lying, and it feels good to be able to tell her the truth without my lungs seizing up.

"So..." she drawls, flicking the tip of her straw. "You danced."

"I did." My chest starts to clench. "I danced for you," I whisper.

Her honey colored eyes flit back to mine. I feel her breath. It's hot and moist against the chilled air swirling around us.

"Why, Riley?" She asks, eyes searching mine.

I take the deepest breath I can manage.

Please, lungs, brain, let me speak.

"Have you ever felt like you were a glass figurine?" I ask, the stupidity of it, true or not, reminds me of Louise's angels that she decorates the house with. "Everything going on just pushes you to the edge of a cliff, and you know that if you're knocked down, the landing would shatter you?" Everything gets fuzzy for a moment and to distract myself, I take a sip of the frozen chocolate in my hand. The cooler temperature reminds me of the ice. Ice is relatable. It's unforgiving but freeing. Focusing on that, I continue. "I'm unbreakable with you."

I can't look at her.

One second, I can't hear anything but my own heartbeat.

Two seconds, a warm hand grazes the back of my hand.

Three seconds, coconut and lime mixed with a touch of ice fills my senses.

Four seconds, she rests her head on my shoulder.

Five seconds, I can breathe.

"I don't view myself as a figurine, or you, for that matter. We're seasons, and we're opposites. I'm spring, and you're winter. But together we're autumn, and I can live with that."

The ice around my lungs seems to melt at her words. *Together we're Autumn,* I chuckle at her words. In a way, she makes sense. I don't think we're one whole season. I'm not as strong as winter can be, or as harsh, but I understand why she feels that way.

"I can live with autumn, too," I agree and move my arm to wrap around her shoulders.

She picks at the plastic lid on her milkshake, and the tapping noise echoes through the silent park.

"Do you-,"

"Can we-,"

We melt into laughter at our timing, and just like that, I feel peace. With her, I can just be me. I can let go of everything. All I have to remember is that she's my balance and my strength.

"I'm sorry," I say. "Go ahead."

"No, you're fine. Do you want to walk around? I feel like I've been sitting all day," she explains.

I nod. "That'd be cool." We slide off the hood and start walking through the gravel parking lot.

"What were you going to say?"

I peek at her from the corner of my eye before answering. "Can..." my words get caught in my throat. I take a sip of the milkshake and focus on the coolness filling my mouth. After I swallow, I try again. "Can we try being an us?" I blurt before my lungs seize.

A chuckle escapes her lips and she grips my hand with hers.

I open my mouth but nothing comes out.

She turns into me, stopping me in my tracks, and looks up at my face. The streetlight gives her skin an unnatural golden glow as it hides the freckles dotting her nose and cheeks.

"I would like that very much," she finally says. Her smile grows wider, and I feel myself smiling in response. She ducks her head back down, but doesn't leave. "I wasn't sure if we would ever give our relationship a name-,"

"A name? It's not a pet, Audrey."

She lets go of my hand and slaps at my chest. "I don't mean like that," she says, peeking at me through her eyelashes. "I meant...like if we'd ever be an us, a couple-,"

"Oh-,"

"Yeah. I was afraid to say anything, or do anything.

So, I did nothing. I figured when you were ready, you'd say something, and if not, I'd know that I was wrong in thinking that I was important..."

I tune out as she continues to ramble. I made her afraid to speak up? She thought she wasn't important?

I lean down and press my lips to hers. Her lips feel just like they did before, soft and silky, only this time they're cool to the touch. With my free hand, I cup her cheek and stroke over the place where I know freckles lie with my thumb. I sigh and pull back from her again, but leave my hand resting against her skin.

"I'm sorry," I whisper. "I never meant for you to feel unimportant because you are very important to me."

Her lips purse as she takes a step backward. "I always say stupid stuff," she mutters.

Part of me wants to snatch her hand and pull her back to me, but another part of me wants to let things stay just like this. It's the part of me that says to run away. The part that makes me feel like continuing this with her is a disaster waiting to happen. I'm not good enough for her.

You're just like your father, always taking the coward's way and leaving. You'll never have a lasting relationship because of your lying, coward father. Remember to thank him *for that.*

There's ice in my head, ice in my lungs, and ice in my heart.

I am not my mother's words.

Am I?

Chapter 35

Audrey

Getting a handle on my emotions is like telling Hannah to stop being so cute. My cheeks hurt from smiling for so long.

I peek over to Riley again. His eyes are staring off into the distance, brows furrowed, and lips pursed.

In hopes of getting his attention back to the present, I clear my throat. No change.

"Hey," I say carefully and place my hand on his arm. "What's goin' on?"

His eyes, ice blue and full of an emotion I can't quite name, search over my face. "I'm good."

I try to hide my frown from him. "Okay." If the lines of friendship weren't crossed, I'd be sitting here telling him he's a liar, or trying to make him smile and laugh because I'd already know what's on his mind.

This is a problem.

"Are you okay?" he asks, pulling me from my thoughts.

"What?" My brows pinch together in confusion as I glance back over to him. "I'm grand. Why do you ask?"

He smirks at me. "You...growled."

My eyes pop wide. "No, I didn't."

"You did."

"I'm as good as I can be right now," I explain slowly.

He nods and sighs before looking off into the distance again. "What does it mean to be in a relationship like this?"

"Umm..." I was not expecting him to ask this.

"I don't mean...I don't know. I just know that I've never done the relationship thing-,"

"I don't think it's too different from our friendship," I offer. "Sure, we get to kiss whenever we want, but we're still us. We're Riley and Audrey."

He grins. "Whenever we want?"

I bump his side as we walk back to my car. "You know what I mean. Why are you asking anyway?"

He tugs my hand, spinning me in front of him and wraps his arms around me as the glare from my headlights beam against our side.

Bending his knees, he shrinks to look me in the eyes. "I'm not sure," he says, shrugging a shoulder. "I've only dreamed-,"

My pocket buzzes. "Hold that thought," I say with a frown. Sliding my phone out of my pocket, I almost feel like I'm betraying him, but no one texts me on game nights unless it's an emergency. I have a text from Mom wondering where I am. Checking the time, I note that I have five minutes until curfew.

"Shoot, Ri, we gotta go!" I shout in a panic and run toward my door. Thankfully, he follows me just as quickly.

"I can walk back from here. Text me when you get home, promise?"

I frown and watch him open the back door. "No, get in, I'll take you."

After a moment of silence, he closes the door and opens the passenger door.

I'll be late, and likely get in trouble, but at least I can make sure that he gets back to his mom's before curfew.

A

Pulling into my driveway fifteen minutes late, I know I'm in trouble. Part of me doesn't even care and a smaller part of me realizes that this could be very bad for my near future.

Riley is my boyfriend.

I let out a giddy squeal before pushing open the door.

Mom and Dad are sitting on the couch watching some weird show about living in other countries.

"Hey, I'm home and I'm really sorry I missed curfew," I announce, hoping they'll take it easy on me.

Dad raises an eyebrow and turns his attention my way. "Your mom and I talked about your punishment already." He pauses, possibly for dramatic effect because he enjoys that sort of thing.

"My punishment…"

"There's a list on the fridge for you. You can only leave the house for work or school until the list is complete."

My mouth falls open and I scramble to the kitchen. "I have to help Riley the rest of the week! He needs a ride to and from school and practice while his car is still in the shop! What am I supposed to do?" I shout and flick the light switch on in my rush to the fridge.

I yank the solitary paper from the fridge so hard the magnet pops off and clatters to the floor. There's only three things on this list.

- Wake up at 3:30 A.M. and eat breakfast with Dad

- Hug us. We love you and want to be a part of your life considering we brought you into it

- Promise and follow through to having lunch with your annoying parents once a weekend

I read the list, then reread it three more times to be sure.

"Aud? Did you find your list?" Mom hollers.

I silently walk back into the living room. "Are you serious?"

"Do I ever joke about a punishment?" My dad deadpans.

"This is…" I start to say how stupid this punishment is, but I stop myself. This is actually a cool punishment. "I'm really sorry for being late," I say sincerely and lean down to hug them both.

"I love you, baby girl. You had us worried for a minute," Dad whispers.

"I love you too, Daddy."

"Next time, just let us know," Mom says.

I grin and pull away from them both. "Well, I would have called or sent a text… but I didn't even notice the time until you texted me."

"Warriors win?" Dad asks with a crooked smile.

I nod. "And then we had milkshakes and…"

My mom sits forward. "And…"

"Riley asked me out!" I squeal again and let out a giggle.

My dad rolls his eyes. "'Sakes, I'm gonna have to have another talk with that boy."

I snort.

"Let them be," my mom tells him.

"Denni, you can't-,"

"Paul, I am-,"

"No daughter-,"

"We'll talk later."

"You're darn straight we'll talk later. And, I'll have a talk with Riley while I'm at it."

I laugh at Dad. Mom's so going to kick his butt. You can see it in the annoyed way she glares at him.

"You should probably get to sleep, Aud. Breakfast will be early," she reminds me.

I hug them both once more and jog down the hall to my room. Glancing at my punishment one last time, I smile before I dig my phone from my pocket.

? Riley

:) ?

:) Riley

I let out a sigh of relief and drop to my bed. He didn't get in trouble.

I'll need a ride to school, but Jack said he'll drop my car off so I'll have my car for practice. Riley

I frown. I really enjoyed going with him to practice. It helped with my hockey fix.

I respond with an okay and lie down on my bed.

The strangeness between Riley and me isn't exactly new, but I'm still not used to it. I know something is going on with him. Still. I've thought things were getting better since he has his dad in his life, and in some ways, I guess he is better. In other ways…he seems sadder, scared. Like tonight when he told me he feels breakable without me. I've always thought of him as strong and steady, he is ice; a permanent winter.

I need to figure out what's going on with him, but how do I get him to talk?

Three A.M. will be here before I know it, but I can't help but think there's something I should be doing that's more important than sleep.

Climbing off my bed, I start up my computer and wait for it to boot while I pull out my notebook with my plan for staying back with Hannah.

My plan is changing again, but I'm not sure how.

Chapter 36

Riley

Riley," my mom hollers from the bottom of the stairs.

"Coming!" I respond, grabbing my backpack from the top of my desk. Last night when I got home, I packed up the puck and hid it in my bag. Hopefully I'll be able to finish it soon. "What's up?" I ask as I jog down the steps.

"Just making sure you have all your stuff you need to take back to your fathers." She sniffs and purses her lips. Thursdays she's always particularly nasty.

"Yes, I packed up my backpack last night-,"

"The clothes I bought you stay here," she snaps, cutting me off.

"I know, Mom."

"Good. I know you like the clothes I buy you better, I don't want *them* to wash them wrong or ruin them. I know they'd cut up those nice pants I just bought you."

"Mom, you don't have to worry about my clothes. I

do the laundry here and over there," I explain. Louise expressed that she was shocked at my knowledge of laundry. She felt that I thought they'd make me do my own, so she was upset with how to handle it. I explained that I do the laundry out of habit, someone needs to wash the clothes, and I don't mind doing it if it helps everyone out. We're still on a standstill about me cooking meals and making lunches for Hannah. She feels that it should be her job, and I just feel like I've done it for years, it's weird to not do it.

"I know you think I'm being stupid, but if I don't keep your clothes here, you'd never return to me," she whispers and tears fill her eyes.

I hate to see her cry. "Mom, I'll always come back to you. Don't worry. I love you."

She smiles, all traces of tears gone in an instant. "Good. Tuesday we're having your favorite dinner! You should stop by after school. Maybe we can rent-,"

"Mom," I interrupt her. "You need to talk to Jack about that." Frowning, I walk past her.

"*His* decision will be no because he doesn't care about your wellbeing the way I do. Don't forget, he left us, I never left!"

I ignore her words. She keeps yelling, but I can't listen to her anymore.

I wish my parents never would've split up six years ago. If they would've stayed together, I wouldn't have to split days or deal with dramatic Thursdays. Hannah wouldn't have to keep half her life a secret. When she talks about Jack or Louise, Mom goes ballistic, and Hannah hides in her special place. It usually takes a good hour until she calms down enough for me to coax Hannah out of her closet. Hannah's learned now to be quiet about her feelings for Jack and Louise.

I am worried because Mom has been especially strange toward Hannah lately. They have secret meetings in Mom's room. Hannah won't tell me what's going on, I imagine girly things, but nothing is amiss. Just transition days are awful in both houses. Jack and Louise seem quieter until Hannah starts screaming or crying about something small. I don't know what to make of any of it anymore.

Grabbing Hannah's cereal box from the cupboard, I place it on the table in front of her chair and move to get her a bowl. As I finish getting Hannah's breakfast together, Mom mutters from the living room.

I pick up Hannah's backpack from the laundry room floor and check to make sure she's got everything she needs for school and this coming week. Behind her folder is her favorite pair of pajamas. My heart sinks. If Mom finds this, there's really no telling what she'd say to Hannah. Picking up her orange nightgown, I slip it into my hockey bag.

Glancing to the clock, I see I have two minutes before Audrey gets here. Just the thought of her has me smiling, again.

"What's that stupid look for?" Mom asks harshly as she walks into the kitchen with her arms crossed.

I shrug a shoulder and put my duffel bag strap on my shoulder before snatching up my backpack. "Nothin',"

Mom nods once. "I love you to the moon, baby boy. Have a great week with your dad."

My eyebrows raise as her words wash over me. I hope this means she's accepted what's happening.

"Just because there's a silly court order that says you travel between home and his house, you're old enough to say no, to stay home." I am old enough to choose. "Think about that while you're at school. Hopefully your father will at least allow you to come back home early. A week is too long to be away from you."

I grunt noncommittally and shove out the front door. If Hannah has better luck this morning, it'd be a miracle.

R

I drop into the seat next to Audrey in the cafeteria. Dealing with my mom this morning left me exhausted and my classes so far haven't helped.

Audrey yawns. "I don't know how I am still awake."

"Don't yawn," I groan at her and then yawn.

She smiles. "Sorry, can't help it."

"Why are you so tired today?"

Her smile stays plastered on her face but she looks away from me. "No reason really, I just stayed up sort of late. Why are you so tired, Captain?"

My teeth clench together as I hold back the truth of what happened this morning. "Just an exhausting morning." I keep my eyes on her as recognition makes a connection. She knows I'm holding back, just as she did. We both notice what we're doing and look toward the front of the cafeteria.

Part of me wonders what happened that she stayed up so late. Did she get in trouble with her parents? Did she fight with Greg about something stupid again? It doesn't even matter what happened.

What matters is she doesn't tell me anything.

I let out a sigh and slide my hand into hers. There's no drama, no guilt, no competition, not with her. I glance at her from the corner of my eye. She's staring at our linked fingers resting on her leg, and she's smiling. She's smiling hard enough that her dimples show, and I swear her freckles are brighter than they were a few moments ago.

"What are you lookin' at?"

"You."

"Stop it," she says before turning her head away from me again. Her long brown hair falls over her shoulder, shielding her cheek from me.

I gently rub my thumb over her knuckle. "Are you working Saturday?"

"Yes and after work Billy and Sarah are coming over for a bonfire with Greg. Wanna come over and keep me company?"

"I'll talk to Jack and see what's planned, but I'm hoping to be able to get out for a bit. I was gonna ask if you wanted to get dinner somewhere..."

She looks at me and frowns. "I'm working 'til eight."

A moment of uncertainty passes between us. It's a moment filled with hope and disappointment. It only lasts a second, but it's long enough for my mother's words to start creeping back in.

She squeezes my fingers. "Apple Fest is this weekend, should we go to that on Sunday? Might be fun."

I smile and my mother's words become a hushed whisper in the back of my mind. "I'll see what I can do this weekend, for sure."

Through the rest of lunch hour, we sit in our not quite comfortable silence. I stop myself ten different times from asking her questions. Would she answer any question I ask? Why would she? I'm just this dumbass guy she's kind of dating.

Maybe my mom is right, to an extent. I'll never have a lasting relationship with anyone. Except Hannah. I'm not a perfect brother, but I'd do anything for her. Her nightgown in my practice bag is evidence of that.

Audrey smiles at me and takes a drink from her lemonade.

I can't hurt her.

Will I?

Am I now?

Chapter 37

Audrey

"You and Mr. Silk looked quite cozy at lunch yesterday," Alice says, trying to coax information out of me.

"Yep," I answer her around a yawn.

She glares at me and throws a straw at me. "So...are you official or not?"

I pick up the straw and set it on the counter. "We are."

"But..."

"No buts," I say with a shrug.

"Why aren't you excited? This is what you've wanted since we were in fifth grade and boys became more than just cootie goblins."

I smile. "I'm plenty excited. Just exhausted."

She groans. "Has there been late night phone calls? Visits?"

Rolling my eyes, I walk to the other side of the counter and wipe down the table. "I got in trouble after the game and as a punishment I have to wake up at three A.M. to make breakfast for my dad. And eat with him, too."

She drops her pen to the counter. "What?"

I let out an airy chuckle. "My parents are weird sometimes. I guess they knew I'd miss curfew and thought up this weird punishment, but it's cool, too. I don't know, Alice. I kind of like it, but I'm not used to getting up this early and with everything else..."

"What's everything else?"

I ignore her question and wipe down the other tables before glancing to the clock again. "Is it too soon to flip the sign?"

"Go ahead. I don't think anyone is coming in the next two minutes. We won't lock it yet, just in case. You're avoiding my question."

"I know." I flip the sign from "Open" to "Closed" and start flipping chairs so we can mop the floor.

"I'm waiting."

Without answering her, I head to the back and grab the bucket.

"Out with it!" She yells from the swinging door. "What's everything else?"

I sigh, dropping the soap back on the shelf and shutting off the water. "I don't know what I'm doing."

"Um...you're going to mop while I count out the drawer?"

"Yes, smarty. *That*, I know. Just...after high school."

"Last I heard, you were thinking about studying for a degree in teaching. Which, I never got to say how odd I thought that was. You're more outdoorsy...and you kind of suck at teaching."

"That was before. Now, I don't know." I leave out the part where I don't know because Riley hasn't mentioned where he's going or where he'd like to go. He hasn't mentioned if scouts were at any games. And we haven't talked about where I'm going since I told him my plan was to be sure I stayed close by for Hannah.

After Jack came back around, I decided that I would send other applications out, rather that just the ones close by. I chose a few of the ones Riley talked about before...but I couldn't remember them all and I still don't know if his plans changed.

If it weren't for this annoying wall between us, I'd know.

Alice and I finish our closing routine and lock up.

"I'll see you Monday, and Aud?" I glance at her over my shoulder, hand still raised in a half wave. "Get a good nights sleep and I'm sure you'll figure it out. Maybe you should talk to Riley or your mom." She opens her car door and drops inside.

Talk to Riley... Yeah. That'll happen.

If I can figure out how to talk to him again.

A

I sit in the grass next to Sarah and enjoy the

warmth from the fire. “Did anyone remember marshmallows?”

Greg nods. “Yeah, they’re in the kitchen. I’ll go find some sticks.”

“I’ll grab the marshmallows!” Sarah shouts and jumps to her feet. “Aud, you need a blanket or anything?”

I shake my head. “A bottle of water would be great though.” She nods and skips into the house.

Scootching closer to the fire, I hold my hands out, greedy for heat.

“How was work, Dahling?” Billy asks.

I grin at him over the fire. “It was pretty slow, Mr. Wedding Singer,” I tease him using a brand of Billy Idol for his song, White Wedding.

Billy snorts. “He’s my Idol!” he shouts in a girly. “I hear you’re dating Riley.”

“Yes,” I answer shortly, waiting for him to say something stupid.

He purses his lips and his jaw works, as if he’s chewing on something. “So, is Riley your Mel, Andrea, or Robert?”

“You spend too much time on Wiki-pedia to find ways to annoy me.”

“Not really. I used to surf the internet looking for ways to annoy you, but Audrey Hepburn was an amazing woman.”

“You’re on the verge of sounding like my dad.”

He stands up, grabbing the iron poker and stirs the coals, sending hot, loose ashes into the sky.

I slide away, surely gaining grass stains on my backside.

"I'm not obsessed. I think it's cool they named you after her, even if I don't see a resemblance."

"You're not the only one."

"I brought out some water and some tea, just in case the water doesn't wash down the marshmallow," Sarah announces.

"Tea sounds good, Babe," Billy snatches a glass from her hand.

She glares at him.

"Water is fine. Thanks Sarah," I assure her.

Greg sits down in his chair and slides his pocketknife from the cargo pocket in his pants. "I'm only stayin' out here for ten more minutes, I've gotta shower before Westgate comes on."

"No wonder your sister has a date and you don't," Billy jibes. "Watching your weekly Soaps aren't getting' you laid-,"

"Gross," I mutter, untwisting the cap on the water bottle and crinkling my nose.

"It's a good show, and you watch it too, idiot," Greg fires back.

"He's got you there," Sarah interjects.

I fall silent as they bicker and joke around. The heat wrapping around my fingertips soothes the chill that was there, but seems to enhance the chill in my feet. Repositioning myself, I rest my feet on top of the cinderblocks circling our fire pit.

"Hey, Sweetie," Sarah whispers. I glance to her, my movement jerky because I don't know how long she's been beside me. "We're gonna go in for an hour, will you be alright with the fire?"

"Yeah, go watch your show. I'll be just fine." I try smiling, hoping she doesn't worry. I probably should go inside, but the heat feels too nice to waste.

"Come on!" Billy yells. "You'll miss the start!"

Sarah chuckles. "Such a girl." She pats my leg and stands up. "Greg left the sticks on his chair and the marshmallows are beside you." Without waiting for my reply, she rushes to the house and disappears.

As my toes heat up, the urge to roast a marshmallow consumes me. Pulling myself to my feet, I grab a stick from Greg's chair and note that he's already burnt the sap off. Ripping the marshmallow bag open, four topple out, one dropping right into the fire pit. I frown and pick up the other three, blowing the dirt off and impaling one on the end of my stick.

The marshmallows feel hard and cold, almost frozen, but the flames in the fire don't care. As I rotate the stick, the marshmallow starts to turn a beautiful golden color. I sit down on my knees and blow on the gooey glob on the end of my stick.

If only something could do this to Riley.

He's frozen. It's not just his nickname. He's frozen inside himself, and freezing everyone out. He did it to me. I'm still on the outside, shivering and cold, waiting for him to thaw and let me back in.

As I bite the roasted marshmallow, my mouth fills with heat, and as I swallow it, my insides heat up.

Maybe I need to be more like the fire. I turn my attention back to the flames and watch as they lick the wood, drying out every ounce of moisture and consume it.

Fire can't be frozen.

The only thing he can do is douse me out, but only if he thaws.

Everything begins to fall into perspective.

I am the one who changed. I allowed his kiss to change me when I never should've let that happen. Involuntarily, I suffocated my own personal fire with all of my silly insecurities.

I turned myself into the ashy existence I've become.

Ashes are so much like dirt but different. A mask. I haven't been hiding behind the dirt that keeps me free. I've been hiding behind my ashes and they've been keeping me in place instead of setting me free the way dirt does.

If I don't act like the fire that I am, he'll never know that I choose him.

I need the ice to melt and soothe my fire so I stay on the path of healing and away from destruction. I don't want to be like this fire. I don't want to destroy anything to fuel myself.

My path is with Riley. Always with him.

Chapter 38

Riley

My phone rings, shrilling through the quiet in my room. Picking up my phone, the name I see on the screen invokes a smile that I feel deep in my chest as well as on my face.

Audrey

"Hey, you. How was work?"

"I need to see you. Now."

I sit up on my bed. "What?"

"Obviously, you couldn't come over for the bonfire, but can I stop by for a few minutes?"

"Um…I guess that's okay?"

There's ruffling in the background and a male voice tells her to make it quick.

"Who was that?"

"Billy. He's put out because I'm making him miss

his show to sit by the fire."

"I take it you're leaving now then?"

"I'll be there in like five minutes." The line goes dead. I stare at my phone in bewilderment. She's never hung up on me before.

Sighing, I stand up and head out the hallway. Listening for voices, I try to figure out where Jack is hiding out. He wasn't happy with what Hannah had to say when she got home from school yesterday. She started repeating things that our mom has said over the last few days. "You don't have to listen to them." "They don't love you, Princess." "They only wanted you with them to hurt me."

She's been hearing this sort of stuff for a while, but only just now repeating it and acting on it.

Angry voices down the hallway spark my attention.

"Sue, that's enough!" Jack shouts.

Annoyance bubbles in my gut.

"Gee, because you're married and your husband probably heard what my wife just heard."

Confusion replaces the annoyance.

"Our children, they are why I called you, not to discuss the cleanliness of your parts. Hannah is acting out against us here and her teacher sent a note home with her that she's-,"

Silence fills the air. I hope they're done. Walking toward the kitchen, I poke my head around the corner.

Louise is sitting at the table, staring at the ceiling

with her hands folded on the table. She looks unsure of what to do. I don't see Jack anywhere, so I step forward and clear my throat.

"Louise?"

She startles a bit. "Riley, you should be working on your homework."

I nod. "I'm finished. Um...Audrey called. She wants to talk to me about something. Is it alright to sit on the porch with her a bit?"

She frowns and glances behind me. I turn and find Jack with the phone still pressed to his ear.

He places his hand over the microphone. "Don't leave the yard. Make sure she leaves in enough time not to miss her curfew."

I smile my thanks and dart out the door.

Headlights splash against the grass before her car pulls to a stop in the driveway.

Meeting her halfway, I pause and let her reach me.

She surprises me by twisting her arms around my neck and melding her lips to mine in an instant. My surprise quickly vanishes and I wrap my arms around her waist, relaxing against her.

One of her hands slides into my hair, and I suck her bottom lip into mouth for a moment before peppering her lips with light kisses.

"This is a surprise," I whisper between pecks.

She smiles. "Is it a good surprise?"

I linger on her lips and nod.

As she releases me, she grabs my left hand in hers and pulls me to sit in the cool grass next to her.

"What's this about?" I ask.

"There's a lot of reasons for my visit," she says vaguely.

I smile. "Not just making out in the yard?"

She ducks her head a little. "No, that was a bonus." She rubs her pant leg with her free hand before facing me again. "How are you doing with going between houses?"

"Good, I guess..." I lie.

She frowns. "I used to know these kinds of things. You used to tell me how Hannah was doing in school, who her favorite teacher is or even what her favorite game at the old daycare was. We used to talk about what your Mom and Ted were up to. I've always known that things with Sue were on the abnormal side and sometimes dangerous..." her voice trails and she look up to the streetlamp across the street and squints. "I haven't forgotten any of it. I haven't forgotten the random times you've mentioned doing laundry or dishes or cooking. I can only guess how things are going now. Part of me wants to believe that things are better since Jack came into your life." She levels her gaze on me again. "But I know different." Her free hand presses to her chest and the hand in mine, squeezes my fingers. "I've seen the sad way you look off into the distance and I remember each time I've felt that you were pushing me away to avoid talking to me. I see what happens when things get...honest between us. Like now," she says, her eyes plead with mine. And it's then that I realize my breath is coming in waves and my heart is pounding so hard I can hear my pulse in my ears.

"Talk to me. Please."

My mouth opens, but nothing comes out.

"It's okay. I'm not going anywhere." She shifts, sitting on her knees. Her hand comes to my cheek, gently stroking. "That's the other reason I came." She pauses, taking a deep, shaky breath, but keeping her eyes glued to mine. "I'm not letting you go on without me."

All oxygen dispels from my lungs. Her touch, it's magic. "You're not staying behind anymore?" I whisper, remembering her plan of staying back for Hannah. Her change in our unspoken plan of going to college together, coming to mind. It started as a joke a few years ago, but became something I depended upon. When she shakes her head, I let go of her hand and circle my arms around, pulling her in my lap and crushing her in my arms.

Her arms squeeze my shoulders. "I'm here whenever you're ready to talk. I won't force you, but I won't sit back and watch this hurt consume you either." Her hot breath tickles my ear. "You can't live without love, Riley."

The old fight stirs in my mind. But this time, two words banish my mother's insults. *Embrace it.* My father told me that once. When you find someone who changes you, embrace her. *I am.* I think in response to my father. I finally am and I don't intend to let go.

Ever.

I walk into the kitchen to get a drink and notice my father sitting at the table with his head in his hands.

"So, you and Mom fought tonight..." I say before I can think better of it.

His head pops up from his palms. "Uh. Yeah. How much did you hear?"

I shrug. "Not enough to make sense of it honestly."

"Trying to co-parent with her is proving difficult," he admits and stares at the face of the table. "How's Audrey?"

"She's good," I say with a smile. "We're going to Apple Fest on Sunday, if that's alright."

He grins. "That should be a fun time. I always enjoyed Apple Fest."

"Is there anything I can do to help with Hannah?" I ask. He might think its crazy, but he doesn't know just how much I've parented Hannah in the past. I'm the one who taught her her ABC's and to count and tie her shoes. It's never come up, but I think now might be a good time to tell him.

"I don't know Riley, it's like she has a second personality sometimes. I'm not sure anyone can help with this, besides a therapist." He shrugs. "Do you need to talk to a counselor or anything? I can-,"

I frown. "No, I'm fine. I don't think Hannah needs to see one either. I'll talk to her and find out what's going on."

"Riley, that's really not necessary."

"Jack, I don't think you understand my relationship with Hannah. I'm the one who's always been there for her, I'm the one who parented her-,"

"She's had your mom-,"

"Mom didn't really do anything with her." I shrug. "Someone needed to teach Hannah everything so she could go to school and get by in general."

"Your mother didn't..."

I shake my head. "Let me talk to her before you make any decisions. Sometimes she acts weird over the silliest things, but it's usually something that means the world to her."

His shoulders sag with the breath he expels. "I'm not arguing any more tonight." His fingers drum on the table. "Do you need any money for Apple Fest?"

My mouth drops. "Um. No. I -,"

"Riley, it's okay. I want to give you some money for it. I have a lot to make up for and this is one small way I can." He leans forward and digs his wallet from his back pocket. "I missed out on sending you to carnivals and teaching you to drive, please let me help you for the Apple Fest. Get some hot cider for you and Audrey while you walk around." He slides a twenty across the table and taps it. "If you'd feel better about it, you can pay me back later. I trust you, Riley, but I also want you to have a good time with your friend, like teenagers are supposed to do."

My eyes widen and I look up to his soft eyes. "She's my girlfriend."

He laughs. "In that case, do you need more than twenty? Dates can run expensive. Maybe you'd like to try your hand at apple dunking to win her a prize?" he pulls another twenty out.

"No, no." I shake my head. "That's too much. I

don't need your money."

"Riley, it's just money."

"Just money? I guess you have more money than Mom. But, I don't need you to give me money. I don't need anything from you."

He sighs. "I'm sorry. I just don't know how to make you happy."

"Not by giving me money when I don't deserve it." I stand, prepared to storm back to my room.

"You deserve more than you realize, Riley. What you've accepted isn't always what you deserve. Please, take this money and have fun for a change. You're released from being the responsible adult for a day. Relax and have fun on your date."

I turn in place and stare at him.

"Louise was right about you," he says softly. "You're too young to be this old." He slips the bills into my hand. "Riley, I'd like to help you in any way I can. I don't know what it is, but I know something is bothering you. Louise and I have seen it for a while now. Please, if you won't talk to a counselor, talk to one of us or even Audrey."

My chest, vise grip tight, seems to turn itself inside-out and I barely notice he leaves me in the kitchen. Sitting on the floor, I stare at my jeans while I try to regain my breath.

Coach said anxiety. Is that what this is? Do I need help?

Chapter 39

Audrey

Things aren't good," Riley mutters into my shoulder. I hold my breath and freeze my entire body. I don't want to do anything that would make him stop. I can't even believe I had the courage to say everything I just did. "I feel like I'm ready to snap but I don't know why. Every day it's something different."

I don't understand, so I say nothing and wait for him to continue.

He pulls back and stares into my eyes. "I've said it before, I feel unbreakable with you."

I release my breath and search his eyes. "The strength comes from you, not me, Riley."

He shakes his head. "I know that, but you make me realize it. It is you."

I smile. "Riley, we'll get through this. Whatever it is that's crashing around you, it's not who you are."

He closes his eyes and rests his forehead against

my cheek. I brush my hand through his hair, enjoying the rubble of that stupid wall between us. I demolished it with just a few words. It took a while, but I'm not letting that wall rebuild. It's painful on the other side.

"My mom and dad punished me for missing curfew after the game," I mutter into his hair. His shoulders tense and I feel his jaw work like he's getting ready to say something. "It's okay though, I only have to wake up before the sun and have breakfast with my dad."

Riley pulls back and stares into my eyes with a bewildered expression. "That's your punishment? Not cleaning the truck? No banning of the four wheeler? No yelling?"

I smile sadly, his mom's idea of punishment was always low blows, and I'm not sure how Jack punishes him or if he even does. My brows pinch together. "My parents are weird, that's for sure. But the punishment works in their advantage. I have to spend more time with them and remember to hug them. I think they know what they're doing. It's not even been a week yet but I already feel like my dad and I are close like we were when I was Hannah's age." I shrug.

He looks away thoughtfully. "It sounds nice having normal parents."

"I'm sorry, I didn't mean-,"

"Hey." His hand reaches up and brushes my hair from my face. "I didn't say that to make you feel bad for telling me. I'm glad you did. It just makes my resolve stronger. I won't be like mine, ever."

I smile. "You're thinking about your future, aren't you?"

A tepid smile graces his lips. "Not really." He

glances back to the door of his dad's house. "I feel like I owe someone an apology."

Someone... Hannah? Louise? Jack?

"Have any scouts been to your games yet?" I ask to distract him from his parental issues.

"I haven't heard anything yet. Have you sent any applications out?"

We discuss a few colleges, and I realize that our plan is still our plan. I'm hoping Lady Luck is on our side and allows us to go to the same college, but neither of us heard anything.

I can feel the ice melting. It soothes my fire. Relaxing against Riley, I shift off his lap and sit next to him.

"Jack doesn't want you to miss curfew. You should probably go," he whispers in my hair.

I frown. "Are we still going to Apple Fest tomorrow?"

"Yeah, I'll pick you up after lunch."

I smile. "Good. I'm having lunch with my parents. Perfect timing."

He chuckles. "I intend to have lunch with Hannah tomorrow since she was at her friend's house today. Hopefully I can set her straight."

Pulling back I search his face, studying his frown. "What happened with Hannah?"

"Sue," he says chillingly as he walks me to my car. "Don't worry, she'll be alright. I'll make sure of it."

A

"This is nice," my mom compliments.

I set the table and made us each sandwiches and scooped potato salad for us. "Lunch is served."

My dad pats his stomach. "I hope there's more potato salad in the fridge."

I smile. "Yes, I imagine you'll finish it off before I'm back from Apple Fest."

My mom laughs. "He'll probably finish it before you leave."

"How are things with Riley?" my dad presses.

I grin without meaning to. "Its better now."

My mom raises an eyebrow at me. "You were feeling off about him before?"

I shake my head. "I don't know how to explain it. I had epiphany last night and tested my theory. It worked."

My dad stops, fork hovering near his mouth. "An epiphany? Testing your theory? Audrey..."

"Relax, Dad! It was nothing." I purse my lips, finding the words to explain it. "You know how you've known someone for so long, you pick up on the little things they say...faces they make."

"Like your dad right now...mouth agape and brows furrowed. He's confused and shocked. And I'm going to take a shot in the dark and say that cause is because of you sounding like an adult." As if on cue, my dad turns and slowly glares at my mom.

"Hush," he manages.

"Like that," I agree. "I've known Riley for so long that I know something is eating at him. He wouldn't tell me freely, and I was afraid of pushing him away when he pushed me. My epiphany was that he was afraid to tell me because of the way I've been reacting to him. I changed, because I'm dumb-,"

"Because you let him push you out when normally you're the only one who can reach through the ice and thaw him out," my dad says, pointing his fork in my direction. "That's very...mature." He shoves his fork in his mouth and lowers his gaze to his plate.

I take a bite of my sandwich and chance a glance at my mom. She's staring at me with her mouth hanging open slightly. "What, Mom?"

She quickly closes her mouth and returns her gaze to her plate. "Nothing, Aud. Thank you for this meal."

I shrug. "I actually think this is the coolest punishment. I like this."

Mom snorts.

"The only thing that would make this any better is if you knew how to bake Grandma's sweet potato pie," my dad muses.

"I can't bake," I protest.

"And I've tried her recipe six ways from Sunday, she took that secret to heaven," my mom says carefully, gently stroking his forearm.

He shifts his arm so he can hold her hand. "I know." He smiles at Mom. They silently communicate, or they just don't need to say any words. Everyone misses Grandma, but it was Dad's mom. You don't let go of that pain.

My parents can weather anything, I'm sure of it. The strength they have together isn't like tug-of-war, it's shared.

If I have learned anything from them over the years, it's that love is the best strength anyone can give you. It's needed in life, because without it, the existence of life is bleak and painful.

Chapter 40

Riley

Hannah sits across the table from me, looking rather upset.

"What's wrong, Squirrel?"

Her eyes dart to mine then away quickly. "Nothing."

I snort at her lie. "Your soup and cheesy toast are getting cold."

"It's *grilled cheese,*" she corrects me with an adorable glare. Not even a year ago, grilled cheese was her cheesy toast. "I'm not five anymore."

"I know that."

"I can take care of myself!"

I frown at her. "You can't, Hannah. Yes. You're a big girl and can do-,"

"I just wanna go home!" Tears come to her eyes.

"Hannah, do you remember the promises I've made you?"

A single tear escapes her eye. "You'll break them all."

I close my eyes, trying to push away the anger she's coaxing. "Have I ever given you a reason to think that?"

Her glare drops to her plate and she pokes her sandwich. "It's too brown."

"Do you want mine? I'll trade you."

"No."

"Why do you want to go to Mom's so badly?"

"All of my stuff is there," she mutters. "She lets me be me and doesn't force me to do anything."

"Like...clean up your room? Or, your orange nightgown?"

Her eyes grow wide.

I cross the room and dig through my bag, pulling out her nightgown that I forgot about until now. "I found this in your bag. I put it in mine so you wouldn't get in trouble."

She launches from her chair and barrels around the table, bee-lining for me. I quickly kneel down and open my arms to her.

"Thank you!" She squeals in delight, giving me a quick hug before snatching her nightgown from my hand. "It smells like you."

I purse my lips. "Want me to wash it? Sorry about

that."

She laughs. "It doesn't stink. It smells like ice and your spray stuff. I like it. It's safe."

I smile at her. "Alright, can we eat now?"

She nods and skips to her chair. As we eat, she tells me about how this girl in her class, Jenny, is mean to her because every other week her clothes aren't right. "She said I'm a goodwill advertisement on Monday. Whatever that means."

I frown. "What's Jenny's last name?"

"Harris," she tells me and rambles on about how she tried getting the girl back for embarrassing her but the teacher caught her and then called Jack. She also missed recess because of whatever happened.

I'll have to have a talk with Andy Harris. He's new to the team this season. Whatever Jenny is saying to Hannah, it's something that the girl has heard elsewhere. There's no way a first grader can be that mean without coaching or hearing it from someone she respects.

"You know Jack and Louise care about you, right?"

"Sure. They care about you, too."

I nod. "Why are you being cold to them?"

She drops her spoon in her bowl and slouches, eyes falling to her lap.

"Hey...what's goin' on?"

"I don't wanna tell you," she whispers.

I get up and walk around to her chair. Kneeling

beside her, I brush her hair from her face. "Come on, Squirrel, this isn't like you. What happened?"

She mashes her lips together and shakes her head. Instead of keeping her eyes and hands on her lap, she grabs my hand and her eyes fly to mine. She gets up, tugging me to go with her.

I follow her up to her room and sit on her pink bed, pushing her purple pillow back to the head of her bed.

She opens her closet door and starts digging through her toy box. When she emerges again, she's carrying her wooden jewelry box. It's the one I found for her fourth birthday. She used to put Barbie shoes inside of it, but I'm guessing it has a new purpose now.

Silently, she climbs on her bed and sits toward the back, plopping the jewelry box in front of her. "Mommy said she was proud of me, that I showed her I love her best." She opens the lid just enough to fit her hand inside and tugs out a silver rectangular object. "So she gave me this." She pushed toward me. It's an iPod. Shock fills me, followed closely by anger.

You're old enough to stay home. Mom's words ring through my head. She's working on Hannah, trying to get her to hurt Jack purposefully.

"How did you show her that you love her best?"

She shrugs a shoulder. "I don't know. But she told me that if I ignore Jack's dumb rules this week, she'll take me to get my ears pierced!"

"You can't keep this, Hannah."

"But it's mine. Mommy gave it to me," she argues.

"For the wrong reasons, Hannah. Keeping that and

anything else she gave you is wrong. She's telling you it's okay to hurt people," I nearly shout.

Hannah flinches. "She said you'd act like this! She said you'd take Jack's side! She's not wrong, Riley!"

I swallow my anger and sigh. "Hannah."

"No! I never should've trusted you!" she screams and hugs her jewelry box filled with uselessness.

Holding my resolve, I face her again. "I know how you feel. She's my mom, too. Think about the way it makes you feel to be mean to Jack and Louise. I know you don't like it."

She still glares at me, but her hold on her the box loosens.

"If it makes you feel bad inside, how do you think it makes them feel?"

She looks down to the box and her iPod. "I like this stuff though. Mommy said not to show Jack or Louise. It's supposed to be our secret."

"Why'd you show me?"

She looks away from all of it, to the wall. "I don't know."

Fear consumes me. If she continues like this, it could be trouble for her. "Want to come with me and Audrey to the Apple Fest?"

She turns and looks at me. "You're not supposed to bring me along on your dates, Riley."

"Who said this was an actual date?" I scoff.

"I saw you guys kissing last night. I'm pretty sure

sisters don't go on dates. You guys are gross." Her nose scrunches.

I laugh. "Come on. Get dressed. You'll have fun and you won't be grossed out. Promise."

I can see her weighing the options.

"I'm supposed to call Mom today."

"We'll call her together on the way to Audrey's."

She frowns. "Can we call her tomorrow after school?" Now I frown. "Fine, after the festival, she always makes me feel bad. I don't want to feel bad at the festival."

My heart feels like it's in a blender. I can't do anything to save her from this hurt. I can only help her manage it after it's done.

This must be similar to the way Audrey feels when I hurt.

R

I watch Audrey and Hannah holding hands a few feet in front of me, laughing and pointing at the people bobbing for apples.

"Come on!" Audrey yells. "Let's try!"

"No!" Hannah protests, but doesn't stop Audrey from pulling her in the direction of the line. "Can we try the Apple Smasher first?"

Audrey grins and spins around to me.

"Apple Smasher sounds more appealing," I say, agreeing with Hannah.

She shrugs. "Let's go then! Hannah's arms need to be filled with apple goodies!"

Hannah stares at Audrey in wonder as she's pulled through the crowd.

The scent of apple and cinnamon makes my stomach growl. I'll definitely need to take a break from the games to try out some of the many snacks the vendors have.

"My first Apple Fest was when I was about your age," Audrey tells Hannah as we wait for three open spots at the smashing table.

"Really? Why didn't you go when you were younger?"

Audrey laughs. "Well, your brother found a gooey apple with a worm in it when we were at pre-school and he threw it at me."

Hannah turns and looks at me. I shrug. "That's so gross!"

"Anyway, it took me a few years to realize that not all apples are bad. So I begged my brothers to take me with them. They won me as many prizes as they could and probably fed me a good ten pounds of apples, too. It's a brother's code, I think."

"What is?"

"To spoil their baby sisters and see how much she can eat before she explodes."

Hannah laughs and nods her head, her golden curls bouncing with her enthusiasm.

I dig into my pocket and pull out enough bills to

cover the three of us for this game and hand it to the guy in the apron.

"Smash as many apples as you can before the buzzer goes off. Don't be fooled though. These buggers are quick. Smash them all for the big prize!" He shouts and hands us mallets.

"What's the big prize?" Hannah asks him.

"The rainbow apple tree," he answers, pointing to the ceiling.

Her eyes enlarge and a smile beams from her face.

I'll be here all day if I have to but she will go home with one.

"You'll get two," Audrey promises, and I glance to her uncertainly. She just winks.

We played Apple Smash four times. Hannah got her two rainbow trees that are almost as tall as she is, and she got three laughing apples.

"Food," I grumble.

Audrey smiles at me. "Fritters?"

Hannah bounces. "That sounds good! What are they?"

"Fried dough with yummy apples chunks inside," Audrey answers and tugs Hannah in the direction of the vendor, leaving me to carry the rainbow trees.

After we get our snack, we pick a table to sit at and stuff our faces. Hannah sees a friend from school and ditches us for a few minutes.

"I hope you don't mind I brought Hannah," I tell

her, reaching over the table and stroking the back of her hand.

She grins and peeks over to Hannah chattering away with her friend about how her brother won her the "coolest trees."

"I love that you brought her along. I miss spending time with her. It's been a while."

"She was worried about tagging along on our date. Said we'd be gross." I mimic the face Hannah gave me earlier.

"It's the best date." She leans over the table and pecks my cheek.

"Don't let Hannah see or hear that," I tease.

"Too late," Hannah grumbles and flops on the bench beside Audrey.

I laugh.

"Wanna ride Applesauce?" Audrey asks.

"But we're eating!" She shouts with shock written all over her face.

Audrey shrugs. "It's not enough to fill you up."

Hannah thinks about it. "Only if I sit in the middle."

"You know, Squirrel...you're not that big. I can still reach over you to kiss Audrey," I tease.

She rolls her eyes. "Eww!"

Audrey laughs, throwing her head back. "Let's hurry up then! No more down time, that's when your brother is tempted to be gross." She sticks her tongue out at me, just like Hannah.

Chapter 41

Audrey

Riley and I sit on the hood of his car after his Monday practice. I don't mind that we haven't said anything this time. It feels good to just be with him and have his arm around me.

"She's been buying Hannah off," he mutters.

I backtrack through my memory, trying to figure out if we stopped a conversation at some point today or yesterday. Coming up short, I turn and look at him. He's frowning, staring at the sky.

"What are you talking about?"

He glances to me, pain in his eyes. "My mom, she's giving Hannah gifts every time she hears about her being a brat to Jack or Louise."

I swallow. "That's not right."

He shakes his head. "Not at all. Hannah knows it's wrong, but I don't think she's going to stop. Ma-, I mean Sue, has power over her still. After we dropped you off, we did our weekly call to Sue and she laid it on thick to me that I won't go back early, I'm positive she was laying it on thick to Hannah, too. Hannah was in tears by the time we got home. And you know how short the drive is from your house to Jack's."

I frown. "What can we do to help Hannah?"

His eyes search mine for a breath. "Be there for her. We can't stop Sue's actions, or Hannah's." He shrugs. "She's getting bullied at school from the way Sue makes her dress and then she's guilted into being a brat to Jack and Louise."

"I hate to say it, but maybe more time away from Sue is for the best."

He clucks his tongue. "I thought about that. But I can't let Hannah go over there and not know what kind of crap she's exposed to. Jack and Louise aren't perfect, but they don't tell us to be jerks to anyone."

I smile. "You like Jack and Louise."

"I don't know. Maybe. I guess. I don't feel as wound tight there as I do with Sue and Ted."

"Hey, Sue is your mom and Jack is your dad. You can call them that, even if you're mad at them."

"I'd rather not."

"Well, are you thinking of a plan? Anything?"

"I don't know. I'm not sure what I can do."

"Have you talked to Jack?" He shakes his head. "Maybe you should try that first."

Silence falls between us, neither of us sure what to say.

Leaning my head on his shoulder, I try to think of a

way to help him through this.

If love can provide strength, I wish to give him enough to endure the struggle he has to go through.

I slide an arm behind his back and drape the other over his lap as I reposition my head to fit in the crook of his neck. He reacts instantly. His arms circle around me, squeezing me closer to him.

I don't need words to know that he needs strength. But it's the only thing I'm unsure of how to give to him.

A

My phone rings, pulling me from my research.

"Hello," I answer without looking.

"Hey, lil' sis!" Luca hollers into the phone.

"Hey, Luc, what's up?"

"Just calling to get some sibling love," he says with a laugh.

"Aw, I love you, Luca!"

"I love you, too. Guess what?"

"Um... you're wearing a purple bra?"

"Oh! So close!" he drawls with a snort-laugh. "No, I'm gonna propose to Addy."

I lean against the back of my computer chair. "Really? I didn't know you guys were *that* serious."

He's silent for a moment. "I didn't know until recently."

"Well... are you sure?"

"Yeah," he whispers. "I really am."

I think about the last time I talked to Addy, it was the day after my birthday and she called me. She explained that she was so terrified to give away the surprise that she waited. "She seems sweet. But I haven't had the opportunity to meet her yet."

Luca groans. "I know. You and Greg haven't met her, but I promise, she's the one."

"How are you so sure of this? I mean, your favorite sister hasn't even met her. She could be a closet gold digger!"

This time he really laughs, a full, deep, hearty, bellowing laugh that bursts through the speaker. "We're visiting in two weeks. I plan to propose before we leave."

"Oh," I breathe. "Will you do it...here?"

"Kind of... We're coming to Riley's game and then afterwards we're gonna treat you all, Riley included-,"

"Riley and I always do shakes at our spot if they win-,"

"If they lose, you are coming to dinner with me. If he wins, I'll change my plans. Maybe we can all go to your spot?"

"Uh," I mutter and think. "Milkshakes and sitting on the trunk of a car overlooking a creepy graveyard. Gee, Luca. That's so incredibly romantic. I hope the man of my dreams takes a number from your book."

He groans. "Can you change your plans this once?"

I snort. "It's our tradition, but I'll talk to Riley for sure. Why is it so important we are there?"

He clicks his tongue a few times. "I have a major announcement. And then, depending on how she reacts to that, I'll propose to her. But if she takes it badly...I need you and Riley to buffer the panic or tears, or whatever happens."

I tap my pencil against the spiral rings on my notebooks. "You've definitely piqued my curiosity. What's this big announcement?"

"I know you'll love it no matter how Addy reacts."

"You're buying me a puppy."

"No-,"

"You're buying me a puppy and a new ATV?"

"Aud-,"

"You're buying me a puppy, a new ATV, *and* you're moving back to good ole Dalesburg!"

"I'm not-,"

"Please? I won't tell!"

"No. Not happenin'."

I growl at him. "You suck."

"Shut up short stack. How's my Scooby holdin' up?"

I grin. "He's fabulous. And I haven't gotten stuck yet. But, I did put a rip in his ear when I was trying to teach Alice the basics of steering."

"You did that already? Why didn't you tell me?"

I laugh. "It slipped my mind, but I'll send you the pictures."

"You better. I'll see you in two weeks, okay? Addy should be calling in a few minutes and I need to get the nerves out."

"Hey."

"What?"

"I love you!"

"I know. I love you, too."

The phone clicks off and I text Riley Luca's question. A few minutes go by and my phone buzzes.

I suppose, as long as we get a milkshake wherever we go or on the way home. I wonder what his news could be? Riley

I chuckle at his insistence of milkshakes. I can't really blame him. We've done this for about 5 years. My mom made the mistake of starting that, but it was a good one.

Milkshakes, yes, and I have zero idea about his news. He wouldn't even give me a hint.

LOL. He never does. Why'd you bother asking? Riley

Meh. He was teasing me with shiny new info.

After a few texts, I end the conversation for the night, I really need to finish my homework. Three A.M. will be ugly.

A

A tap on my door pulls me from my homework. I look up to the time and see that it's 3:45 A.M.

"Crap," I mutter and jump to my door. "Sorry, Dad."

"I thought you overslept," he explains.

I smile sleepily. "No. Finishing up homework."

"How about we do cereal?"

"Okay, I'll get the bowls."

Through the quiet of morning, we walk through to the kitchen in silence. While I grab the bowls and spoons, he pulls the milk from the fridge and grabs a box of cereal from the cupboard.

"How much do you guys have left to do?" I ask Dad about his work. They're building a municipal building for the state.

"There's about two weeks worth of work left if the weather cooperates." He pours his cereal in the bowl. "It's boring stuff, I'm sure you don't want to talk shop."

I grin. "Not really. Just thought I'd ask anyway."

"Luca and Sean are coming home soon," he says with a knowing smile.

"I know. Luca called me last night."

He stares at me blankly. "Should've known he'd talk to you."

"I wonder what his news is."

I glare at my bowl. "I don't know. He wouldn't tell me."

Dad chuckles. "Me either."

"I know what I want to do after high school," I blurt before shoving my spoon in my mouth.

Dad looks at me startled. "Oh yeah? What's that?"

I finish chewing and swallow before answering. "I want to get into family law or social work."

He takes a drink of his coffee and as he sets it back on the table he opens his mouth. "Are you sure? You'd have to separate your personal feelings from the cases you encounter. You could meet an abused little girl that reminds you of Hannah, and you'd have to keep yourself professional."

I nod. "I know. But I know I need to be in this type of work. I wasn't good with psychology last year so counseling is out. I know I want to help people."

He purses his lips. "Are you sure you want to do family or children? There's other ways of helping people you know."

"I've given it a lot of thought, Dad."

"I thought you wanted to be a teacher and go to school around here?"

I shrug. "I am not a very good teacher, just ask Alice."

He laughs. "Poor girl. I thought she was going to break in half at the sight of all that mud. It may have been that Alice wasn't a very student."

I shrug a shoulder and steal his coffee from him. "I saw a lot of what Riley and Hannah have been through and are still going through. You know it has a name?"

His brows furrow as he reaches across the table to grab his coffee back. "What has a name?"

"What his mom is doing to them. It has a name. Parental Alienation. It's a form of mental abuse that in most cases gets overlooked by the system. I think someone that worked with Jack's case was familiar with it and was able to help some, but no one can really stop it from happening. That's why I want to get into the field. I'm familiar with the signs now that I know about it." I look into my dad's eyes and slide his coffee closer to his hand. "I want to help someone going through that very thing, and other things. I want to help families. Everyone deserves to have a loving family."

"I think you'll do good things in the future, baby girl." He nods once and then stands to take his bowl to the sink.

I really hope I can do good things in the future. Now I just have to wait to hear back from colleges and talk to Riley about all of this.

Chapter 42

Riley

I sit in my car, waiting for the courage to walk inside that house. The pinecone wreath seems to laugh at me from its perch on the green painted door. It's heard many autumn fights in the last few years. It knows what I've heard and what I haven't. That fact makes me glad the wreath isn't able to speak.

Glancing to the clock, I realize I've been staring at the front door for only five minutes, though it feels like hours.

I open my door, stretching my legs out. Holding my breath, I stand and listen, waiting for any sign of what kind of mood my mother is in.

I didn't come home early.

Instead, I'm here on Thursday, my scheduled day. Part of me thinks that it's crap we have a schedule like this, but right this very second that part is as quiet as the house.

Walking toward the front door, I take a deep breath and say a silent prayer that my mother is in a decent mood.

I count to ten and open the door.

"It's about time you show up," she rasps from the living room as I close the door.

Entering the living room, I see her sitting on the couch. Her hair is a mess, shirt half buttoned and un-tucked from her stained dress pants. I swallow the hope I had previously.

"I know, but this is the scheduled da-,"

"I've been waiting since Tuesday. You made a fool out of me," she growls and stands on wobbly legs. "Ted left me for a drunken bar slut, said that he couldn't deal with my kids anymore and couldn't deal with not drinking whenever he wanted to. You didn't come home. Go eat your dinner." She staggers past me, heading for the stairs. "And get comfortable, you're not leaving anymore to go to Jack's. He's ruining you."

I take a few steps toward the kitchen and the putrid odor of rancid meat welcomes me home. As acid climbs its way to my mouth, I slip my phone from my pocket. Hannah can't see this.

"Riley?" Louise answers.

I cough. "Where's Jack?"

"He ran out to the store, is everything okay?"

I take a deep breath and instantly regret it. Spinning on my heels, I rush back out the front door to retch.

"Are you sick? Where's your mom? Riley?"

I spit once more. “Sorry about that.”

“Where’s your mom, honey? Maybe she’ll-,”

“She’s probably passed out already. Look, you guys have to get Hannah from school. She can’t come here.”

“Honey, that’s a court order violation. Your dad could lose you guys or be held in contempt of co-,”

“I know that. But this is bad. Tuesday’s dinner is rotting on the table, the trash is over flowing, Sue is drunk and passed out, and apparently Ted left and isn’t coming back,” I rush to explain. “I can’t let Hannah be here with this crap. If you guys won’t take her I’ll call Mr. and Mrs. Jacobs.”

Things are shuffled in the background, followed by the distinct jingle of metal that can only be keys. I breathe a sigh of relief.

“I’ll go pick her up at the bus stop so the school doesn’t alert your mom’s attorney right away. But I want you to come home, too.”

My gut twists, and not because I need to vomit again. “I’ll get you guys in more trouble.”

“Your safety is more important than the court order. You aren’t safe there. I’m sure your father can call an emergency meeting with the lawyer.”

“I understand your concern but I promise, I’ll be fine tonight. I just don’t want Hannah to witness any of the mess. She’s seen so much before...and been through so much...it might trigger-,”

“How much of a mess? What might be triggered?”

I lean against the outside wall. “I’ll come over this

evening to explain, after I've cleaned the kitchen, living room, bathroom, and checked on Sue."

"Riley, you're scaring me." Her voice trembles. "Just...be careful and I'll see you soon."

"I'll be fine," I promise her. Her paternal-like worry leaves me feeling unhinged.

I take a deep breath of fresh air and enter the house. On my way in I yank the pinecone wreath from the door. This thing doesn't need to see or hear anymore autumn disasters in this house.

That, and it smells a heck of a lot better than half the house.

R

I open the front door to Jack's and stumble inside, forgetting about the lip.

"Oh my god! Riley! Are you okay?" Louise shouts, leaping from the recliner with her arms out like she's trying to catch me.

I straighten, catching myself before she reaches me. Shooting her a quick smile, I turn and close the door. "Sorry, I forgot about the lip on the door."

She mashes her lips together and tries not to laugh.

"That's my boy," Jack says, entering my line of sight. "Graceful on ice but clumsy as hell on dry land."

"Oh, you boys." She waves us both off. "Now-,"

"I made curfew," I offer them both, knowing it's still pretty late. Hannah is hopefully sleepin. I don't want to rehash this with her.

Jack steers us to the kitchen. “Okay, what happened after your phone call to Louise?”

I sit down in my normal seat and explain how disgusting everything was when I got home, and what my mom said before stumbling up the stairs. “I cleaned everything up, did a few loads of laundry then went to check on her. She had thrown up in her sleep, so I cleaned her up and changed her sheets.”

Jack looks calm, except for his eyes. His blue eyes turned icy at some point and it’s enough to chill me to my core.

Louise looks sad. But I can’t tell why.

“It’s not the first time I’ve come home to a disaster, but it’s been a while since Hannah has seen that kind of thing,” I explain.

“What don’t we know about?” Louise asks while she grips Jack’s hand. It’s either for strength, compassion, or protection. But Jack doesn’t seem any calmer with her hand on his.

“A couple months after you left, Mom started going to the bar. I only assume that because she would come home later and later, always reeking of alcohol, cigarettes, and sometimes vomit. Sometimes she wouldn’t even get the chance to close the door before passing out on the floor,” I say and look down to my own hands that are clenched in a fist. My knee bounces uncontrollably and my lungs start squeezing. “I was eleven, and acting as man of the house. I cared for Hannah after school, I made sure to pack her lunch pail and bag for day care, then preschool, and then for kindergarten, and I still do it all when we’re at her house.”

A chair scrapes against the floor, and I flinch. Taking a deep breath I continue. "She started seeing some guy, I thought she was happy. She seemed like it and even started doing things moms do… cleaning the house when she was off work, paying the electric bill before the shut off notice, giving Hannah baths… Then we met him. We got to meet Ted. I never liked him. The first time I saw him he said, "So this is the kid that's supposed to be my new son? Damn. That sucks." But when he saw Hannah, he was over the moon. I hated him."

Feet slap against the floor, someone is pacing, I think.

I swallow the bile that's starting to rise. "Ted and Mom drank. A lot. After a few weeks, the house started looking like crap again, the pink notices started arriving again, and one day I caught Hannah trying to drink from a vodka bottle. I took care of Hannah, like I did after you left. I made sure to write out mom's checks to pay the bills and update her checkbook balance. I got really good at forging her signature too.

"Then they started fighting. Sometimes Hannah and I would get so scared that we'd hide together in her closet. Mom became clumsy, like she was walking around on a tight wire or something. She shut the cabinet door on her hand, ran into a doorknob… Then it stopped, out of the blue, it all just stopped. Ted wasn't coming around, Mom was paying for bills on her own, and she started buying us school clothes and supplies. She refused to pay for my hockey stuff, so I had started doing odd jobs around the neighborhood to save my money for it. The third time we went to states, we won."

"I remember that. That was four years ago or so," Louise adds.

I nod without looking at either of them. "Todd's parents were throwing this big party, it's the only time Audrey and I didn't do our milkshake tradition." I take a deep breath, and pray I can get it all out. "Audrey had photos to drop off for Mom so she went over... I will never forget the sound of her scream." I close my eyes, letting the rest of the memory consume me, and rip out of my chest and mouth. They have to know now. I can't stop. "I ran over scared out of my mind. It was a scream that meant something more than a snake or wormy apples... It filled my feet with cinder blocks but I still beat everyone to my house. Audrey was still screaming when I reached her, and Mom and Hannah were covered in blood. We thought the worst."

Louise hiccups, and Jack comes over to my side, resting a heavy hand on my shaking shoulder.

"I'm sorry I wasn't there," he mutters.

As if he said nothing, the words pour from my mouth. "He almost killed her, and she took him back. He could've killed Hannah, and Mom still took him back. Married him, too." I mutter even though my chest is aching and breath isn't reaching my lungs or head. "If Hannah would've seen what I saw...she'd be in her safe place right now."

"Riley, honey, can you hear me?" Louise says in the distance.

Memories haunt my vision, taking over my senses. I see the blood and the motionless bodies. I hear the screams and I feel my own terror.

This is not where I need to be. This is not real.

Audrey.

Audrey is real.

Not screaming.

Laughing. Freckles. Dimples.

Everything goes black and silent.

Chapter 43

Audrey

It's been two weeks since Luca called.

One week and three days since I got a phone call at midnight saying Riley was taken to the hospital.

One week, three days, and eleven hours since I had to retell the worst night of my life. That I had walked into Riley's house to see what Ted left behind in a drunken rage; Hannah and Sue. Telling what I knew about that night to him and Louise was not something I ever planned on doing, and especially not when Riley was getting a CAT scan done.

One week and two days since I broke down on Riley when he told me he had suffered from a severe anxiety attack that led to him blacking out and almost breaking his nose on the edge of the table.

And...

It's been one week exactly since Sue barged into Jack's house without knocking.

One week since Sue yanked Hannah by the arm off of Jack's couch making Hannah yell and cry.

Once week since I told Sue I hated her for what she's put Hannah and Riley through.

One week since Sue slapped me across the face.

One week since Hannah and Riley watched the police escort their mom from Jack and Louise's property.

And now, my mom and dad, Hannah, Jack and Louise, and my brothers and Addy are watching Riley skate ... Like nothing ever happened.

Someone in a blue jersey trips Riley with the blade of his stick. I jump from my seat and slam my fist on the boards. "Come on! Tripping!"

Addy chuckles. "Is she always like this?"

"She's a hockey baby," Luca tells her. "Go Warriors!" he shouts, jumping to his feet as one of our players recovers the puck and rushes out of our zone into neutral ice at the center.

Addy seems okay, as nice as she was over the phone even. I just don't really care to be around anyone. Luca asked if I was alright, but Mom told me not to tell him until after they left. "Distance is best with that sort of news." I guess she's right, but I can't stand lying to Luca. He's always had my back. Luca drove six hours home the night that I found Sue and Hannah on the floor because I couldn't calm down or sleep. And now I'm lying to him.

The end of game buzzer goes off.

Warriors tie Groves.

"Ugh!" I half yell and drop my forehead to the board in front of me.

Riley leads the sportsmanship chain, tapping gloves as usual and before I know it, he's slicing to a stop in front of me. I grin, even though I try really hard not to. He pops his mouth piece out, letting it hang the corner of his mouth and smiling so hard his eyes squint. He does what he always does, he tugs one glove off and presses his hand to the board. I join my palm to his.

"Go shower stinky!" I holler.

He winks at me before waving to our families before catching the line of Warriors exiting the ice.

"Aud," Luca says in his overbearing, brutish, brother tone. "What was that?"

"What was what?"

Addy chuckles and quickly covers her mouth with her hand.

"Uh...that cute, little, dreamy-eyed thing you just did. That's what."

My dad and Jack start laughing as Louise and my mom usher Hannah and everyone else to stand. Luca steps around Jack and Dad to stand next to me.

"I have no idea what you're talking about. I only told my boyfriend that he stinks."

"Sis," he sighs, trying not to smile. "He probably does stink."

"We'll meet you guys out at the cars."

"Do you guys do milkshakes for ties?" I shake my

head. "Why do they even allow ties? That's stupid."

I snort. "You're tellin' me, but I don't make the rules."

"Really quick, do you like Addy?"

I peer at my brother. Six foot, thick neck and shoulders, scruffy face, eight years older than me and he looks like my answer has the power to break him.

"Honestly, I think she's alright and she seems to really care about you," I confess. The fact that she's waiting at the end of aisle has no affect on my answer. "I've just been in a bad mood. Stress from classes and what not."

He breathes a sigh of relief. "Good. I'll probably send everyone to the restaurant since you guys will probably take a bit."

I shrug. "Not that long. After games Coach is usually pretty quick about letting them out, unless they lose. Which they didn't, they -,"

"Tied," we say together.

He nods and squeezes my shoulder. "I've missed you short stuff."

"Me too, Scooby Doo."

I sit back down in my seat and wait for Riley to exit the away locker room as Luca greets Addy at the end of the aisle by putting his arm around her shoulder.

I'd be lying if I said I wasn't still curious and worried about what Luca's news could be. Whatever it is, he's worried about Addy's reaction, too.

A

I keep glancing at Luca throughout dinner. He makes no move, and there has been no announcement thus far.

"He'll say whatever he has to say when he's ready." Riley whispers in my ear as if he can read my mind.

I smile shyly at him and bump my shoulder to his.

After the waitress clears our dinner plates and Luca orders us dessert, that I probably won't eat, he finally clears his throat and sits up straighter.

"I know someone here, Audrey," he coughs around my name, "is wondering why I wanted everyone here. Jack, thank you for tagging along too, it's been great to catch back up with you. But I want to do more than just catch up. I wanted to let you all know that I've accepted a job in Dalesburg as game commissioner." My attention flies to Addy's face. First, her mouth drops open, but then, she smiles and squeezes his hand. "So you'll all be seeing me a lot more."

Congratulations are shared but through it all, Addy stares at Luca with a glassy eyes.

"I'm so proud of you, Luca," she says.

"Yeah?" he drops out of his seat and pops open a black box that seemed to materialize from thin air. Our mom and Louise gasp simultaneously. "Would you join me in PA as my fiancé?"

She cries and nods with her hands over her mouth and everyone at the table cheers.

I smile at my brother, and feel a silly, traitor tear escape my eye as I release my own breath. It takes me a minute, but I'm glad she said yes, almost as glad as I am that my brother will back here.

Even if I'll be leaving the area for college, I'll see him more than I would've had he not come back home.

I suppose it's only a matter of time before Sean moves back, too.

I glance to my other brother. He and Greg are thumb wrestling, already bored with Luca's display. I laugh at them and lean my head against Riley's shoulder. His arm comes around my shoulders, and I snuggle closer to him in our oversized booth. His lips touch the top of my head for a moment before he starts talking to my dad about the absurdity of ties in high school hockey.

A

I knock on Jack and Louise's front door. Riley usually meets me out here on the porch but I guess this time he got distracted with something.

The door creaks open slowly and Hannah peeks out. "Audrey!" she yells and quickly launches at my waist in a hug. "What are you doing here?"

I grin and pat her back. "I'm here to see your brother."

She frowns. "Oh. He's with our dad. *Not* arguing."

"They're not arguing?"

"That's what they say," she says with a shrug and waves me inside.

I follow her inside and hear Riley talking loudly, not quite a yell.

"See…they're arguing."

I grin. "Well, not all disagreements are arguments or a fight."

"I guess, but they don't sound happy, it sounds like they're arguing to me."

"Do you have any construction paper?" I ask her.

She taps her pointer finger to her chin and her eyes flit to the ceiling. "Yes! One second!" No sooner are the words out of her mouth, she's running up the stairs.

"I know what they suggested, but it's still not going to change my mind. I'm fine," I hear Riley say down the hallway.

"I think you should at least try it," Jack argues.

Hannah thunders down the stairs. "Got it!" she runs over to where I'm standing and hands me a stack of construction paper in various sizes.

"Let's go into the kitchen and I'll teach you something really cool."

She rushes into the kitchen, flicking on the light and jumping into a seat at the table.

"Where's the scissors?" I ask her. She points to a drawer, and I retrieve them. "Okay, do you know how to make one of these rectangles into a perfect square?" She shakes her head no. "Alright, we'll start by getting two rectangles to squares. Choose a color."

While I wait for Riley to finish his conversation with

Jack, Hannah and I make origami frogs.

"Watch this," I say, pressing the backside of my frog down against the table and releasing my finger quickly, making the frog hop.

She squeals and laughs. "My turn!"

I laugh and watch her make her frog hop. Movement on the other side of the room catches my eye. Riley is leaning against the doorway to the kitchen, watching us. I wave at him and he nods with a smile.

"Let's make more! I want an army of frogs!"

"Do you remember how to make them?" I ask her.

"Maybe."

"I'm going to go talk to your brother, you get started and before I leave I'll pop back in and see how you're doing. Sound good?"

She nods and flicks through the construction paper.

I walk over to Riley, and he holds his hand out to me.

"You and Jack okay?" I ask as we reach the front door.

He lets out a breath and his shoulders sag. "Yes, no. I'm not really sure."

"What were you not fighting about?"

He snorts. "It wasn't a fight. It was a healthy disagreement. Therapy."

"Therapy for...?"

"Me. I can't talk about certain things. It's not that I don't want to, I just can't. My body doesn't let me." He shrugs. "If my body doesn't let me talk about that stuff to people who matter, why would it be different for a stranger?"

"Maybe it would be different if you don't know the person. Riley?"

He glares at me. "I don't want to talk about this anymore."

"I'm sorry." I hold my hands up in surrender. "Have you heard anything back from any colleges yet?"

"I got a rejection letter." He tilts his head to the side and looks into my eyes. "You?"

"Nothing yet." I let out an annoyed sigh. "I know what I want to do though."

"Yeah? I don't have a major yet. I wonder if I'll be able to play hockey with an undecided major." He snorts. "What's your plan?"

I dig my fingernails into my palm and tell myself it's okay to tell him. "I'm leaning toward social work but maybe something in family law."

His face becomes a mask, void of all emotion. I suck my top lip into my mouth and grind my teeth against it while I wait for him to respond.

"That's really cool," he says and looks up to the sky. "I don't think I could do anything like that."

"Well, your goal is to make it to the NHL not torture yourself with legal terminology."

"And if I make it, will your career allow you to

come to my games?"

"When you make it, I'll be right there every single game, no matter what my career is and no matter what our relationship is," I promise him.

"You'll have to make a living somehow," he reminds me. "Miss too much work for me and you'll run into problems with work."

"You are important to me, Riley. When the time comes, I'm sure we'll work something out. For now, we just have to wait for acceptance letters and take everything else day by day." I smile at him, and he smiles back.

Feeling the cool breeze against my bare cheek, I shiver. Riley tugs me closer to him and puts his arm around my shoulders. The silence surrounding us is comfortable, and my thoughts remain on the future.

Chapter 44

Riley

I'm not exactly sure what happened with the emergency restriction between Jack and Sue, but Hannah and I haven't seen her for weeks. Hannah apologized to Jack and Louise for being so mean to them, and even gave Jack the treasures Sue rewarded her with.

As much as I want to know what happened, I'm relieved Hannah no longer has to deal with the turmoil I've endured and she only began going through.

Audrey and I have been sailing through our togetherness. Minor hiccups here and there, but nothing we can't handle. She tries talking me into seeing the therapist Jack's family doctor suggested, but I won't budge.

Picking up the plastic puck, I push the flap I carved and watch as it pops open. I smile at my handy work then frown because I don't have anything to fill it with.

The last game of the season is this week, and another scout is coming. In the last four weeks I've had three offers to play at three different schools. But even that doesn't excite me as much as what I have planned for the last game. Audrey and I plan to go to the same college, thankfully, so after the season is over we're going to sit down and figure out what yeses we have in common.

I pull my wallet from my back pocket and count out three tens, a five, and eight ones. Forty bucks won't get me much, and I haven't had the need to get a job since Jack has been paying for everything, so I won't be getting any more money anytime soon.

Stuffing my money back in my wallet and pushing everything in my pockets, I jog out of the room, looking for Jack or Louise.

Laughter from the living room draws my attention. Jack is laughing at something, and I hope it's just the TV and not a phone conversation.

In the living room, Jack and Louise are watching TV, thankfully.

I clear my throat. "Um, J-Dad?"

Jack looks at me and smiles. I know he caught my stutter and I also know he won't call me on it.

"What can I do for ya?"

"Can I talk to you...outside? Maybe?" I shift my weight from the heels of my feet to my toes nervously.

"How about my office? We won't need to throw on layers," he offers as he stands.

I was actually hoping for the cold to help me figure out the right words to use to borrow money.

"Okay," I agree, feeling that if I don't do this now,

I'll never do it.

I follow him into his office, and he closes the door behind me. I've only been in here a handful of times, but it smells just the same as it did before, pencil shavings and pine wood cleaner.

"You look nervous, son," he points out the obvious. "What's going on?" He braces his hands on the back of his computer chair.

"I need to borrow some money," I say quietly.

"Okay," he pulls out his wallet. "How much?"

My mouth drops open in shock. "You're not gonna ask what its for? Or lecture me about having a job? Or-"

"Riley, relax. You said borrow. I know you know what that means, and I've told you before, I trust you and I know that when the time is right, you'll get a job."

I flounder even more. "I could have a job, already. Bussing tables-,"

"But you don't need it. I said I'd help you with anything you need-,"

"But this isn't-,"

"One hundred?" He questions pulling bills out.

"Who has that kind of cash on hand?" I spit out in my shock. He finally drops his wallet to his desk and looks at me. "You're just going to hand me money, of that amount, and not ask why?

"Okay. What do you need to borrow money for?"

I frown and glare at him. "To buy a ring."

Jack's eyes grow wide. "You're ki-,"

"A promise ring," I emphasize the word promise.

"I assume this is for Audrey." I nod. "Do you know her ring size?"

I chew on my thumbnail and shake my head. That's something I didn't think about.

"Wait here," he says and swiftly leaves his office.

How do you get a girl's ring size without them knowing?

The door pushes open and Jack reenters the room with something in his hand. "Now, it's a little old fashioned," he says. "But it's beautiful."

My teeth grind together as I stare at him in confusion.

"Go on, open it."

I flip open the red box. On a cushion is small gold ring with a blue gem shaped like a teardrop. Closer inspection of the ring reveals leaves etched into the gold.

"What is this?" I ask, astonished at how much I think Audrey will like it.

"It's nothing fancy, just gold plated and a sapphire." He shrugs. "It's something I found when I cleaned out my parent's house. It was your grandma's, but I don't know the story behind it."

"You want me to give this to Audrey?"

"We can go check out what the jewelers have if you don't like it," he offers.

"I didn't say that. But it was grandma's," I argue.

"Right. I have tiny, delicate fingers and a dress to match it," he deadpans. I close my eyes and laugh as I picture him trying to wear a dress. "I'm a guy, I kept it because I figured you or Hannah would find a use for it before I ever did. It's not worth much, like I said, it's just gold plated."

"Together we're autumn," I mutter as I stare at the ring again. The blue teardrop could be a rain drop, and gold leaves...it's autumn forever on this ring.

"What?" He asks.

"Nothing," I answer and pull out the hockey puck from my pocket.

Jack laughs lightly as he leans against his desk. "You're giving it to her in a hockey puck? Oh, you so know the way to her heart."

I grin. "Who keeps the puck?" As I say it, I realize that we've been playing this game for nearing two years.

"You like older women, you realize this right?" He claps my shoulder as I transfer the cloth and ring into the puck.

I shake my head. "Shut up, it's only four months."

R

The last game of the season is Senior Night. Each senior on the team chooses two escorts. It's usually the parents. But I'm being different and Coach said I could. I chose Jack because he's the one who allowed me to dream big when I was little. He developed my love of the game from his own love for the game. I also chose Audrey, because if not for her, I probably would've quit after freshman year.

I stand at the start of the carpet that leads to center ice where Coach Page waits with honors for Seniors. Audrey is on my right and my dad is on my left.

"I feel so out of place," Audrey mumbles, tugging the hem of that yellow dress.

"You think you feel out of place?" My dad questions. "Try wearing a bowtie."

I laugh at both of them. "Hey, it's supposed to be my night."

Audrey slaps the pad on my shoulder. "Why'd you invite me to escort you? Louise would have *loved* this honor!"

Leaning down, I give her cheek a peck. "Because I love torturing you, and you're important, too."

She mashes her lips into thin line. "I'll get you back for this whole dress thing. Alice and my mom have cameras, everywhere!"

Jack groans. "How many pictures are they taking and how many silly faces do you know?"

"Game on," Audrey promises.

I look to the ceiling. "You guys, I swear. It's not that bad being seen with me on ice."

"No one said that," Jack responds. "We just like making things tough for Alice and Denise."

Finally, Coach begins his three-sentence speech as

practiced and then announces my name followed by my escort's names.

"Don't you dare let me trip," Audrey whispers harshly and clutches my arm with a grip of death.

It's too hard to mask my face into the frozen glare I've worn when on the ice for as long as I can remember.

After us, the rest of the Seniors and escorts are called out and Coach gives us our awards. While he gives his closing, I pull the plastic puck from my left sleeve.

"I promise, I'll always keep your heart, but it's your turn to keep the puck," I whisper and place the puck in her hand.

Coach dismisses us and two kids from second-string follow us while rolling up the carpet.

"I'll see you guys after the game!" I shout and jog to the locker room.

Todd greets me behind the swinging door. "Well?"

"I did it," I mutter, suddenly feeling like I need to puke, I double over.

Todd laughs. "You know she loves you."

I lift my head to look at him. "I guess I should've told her I love her before this."

"What?" his smile drops. "You guys haven't..."

I shake my head. "I'm an idiot."

Coach claps his hands. "Alright fellas! I know you're all itchin' to get out there and kick some Cougar tail..."

I share a worried look with Todd before paying attention to Coach for the last time of my high school career.

R

After the brutal game, that we barely won, I'm so afraid to face Audrey that I hang back in the locker room, congratulating each teammate on their way out.

Alex comes over to the doors.

"Good game, Kid."

He smirks. "What the heck are you still doin' here?"

I shrug. "Sayin' goodbye to the team. She's all yours next year, and I'll know if you screw it up. Trust me, you don't want that."

He shakes his head. "Don't you worry about me or the team, Silk. Go out there and get your woman." He looks at me pointedly. "She's smokin' in that yellow dress."

I glare at him. "Do we need to rehash this again?"

He slaps my shoulder. "No. I'm getting' you out the door since your boy Todd is bein' butthurt about it." He bends and grabs my duffel. "Come on Captain. You've said your goodbyes, you're clean, and you know that I'm not the same kid that I was two years ago."

I frown at him. "You're making a pretty good start at bein' Captain."

He shoves my duffel into my chest and points to the door. "Don't make me get Coach."

Laughing, we both exit the locker room. Audrey paces at the end of the hallway. I stumble to a stop when I see her. The yellow dress hugs her chest and billows to just above her knees. Her long brown hair is now piled into a messy bun and she's gripping the plastic puck in her right hand.

"Good night, Audrey," Alex sings, announcing his presence. But she doesn't see him, she sees me first.

"Yeah, night," she mumbles to him while staring at me.

I search her face, looking for any sign of what she's feeling right now. But her face is void of anything I can go on. She's been working on her poker face.

It's time to face the music, I tell myself, and force my feet to move.

The closer I get to her, the corners of her mouth turn up in a smile, and when I'm standing in front of her, her smile is full blown, dimples and teeth. I close my eyes and feel myself smile in return.

"Mister Silk, what is this?" She asks, holding out the puck.

"It's our puck Miss Jacobs."

"Uh huh," she agrees. "And inside of it?"

I suck my lips into my mouth and bite down for a second. Grabbing her hand, I pull her to the steps so we're out of the way of the last few teammates.

"It's a promise ring," I whisper to her.

She pushes on the tab to open the puck and stares at the ring. "I completely missed the game. I missed everything. You ruined me tonight."

I worry my lip and glance out to the ice. "I'm not a mind reader, Aud. What do you mean?" My lungs shrink in size.

"It fits my finger perfectly, too. I'm not even sure how that works, but I've tried it on about fifty times since I opened this thing by accident."

I glance over to her. "Aud-,"

"It's so pretty-,"

"Audrey, you're killing me."

She peers at me over the puck. "I think, traditionally, you're supposed to say it first. But you're a chicken. I love you."

I laugh and lean close to her. "I love you, too."

Cheers from behind us startle us both. I groan and drop my forehead to her shoulder.

She moves slightly. "Alex! Isn't it beautiful?" She shouts.

"I told you, you were supposed to say it before you gave it to her!" Todd hollers.

With the team behind me, and probably Coach, I kiss my girl.

Epilogue

"Welcome to Pittsburgh!" The announcer blares over the giant speakers. "Here come your Pittsburgh Penguins!" He goes through and announces the starting players in alphabetical order. I scream and jump up and down for everyone. "Riley Silk! Number fifty one!"

I scream my heart out. My husband has done it. He made his dreams come true, and I couldn't be prouder than I am this very moment.

Hannah and Louise each squeeze my hand, probably trying to calm me down so I don't give birth to our baby girl during his first game.

"Remember, if you get overexcited we drag you out," Louise reminds me.

I smile at her. This woman has been through hell with Riley's mom and even him and Hannah, but she stuck with them. Jack and Louise celebrated their ten year wedding anniversary last week.

Hannah is a hormone filled, beautiful fourteen year old that has more admirers than she can bat an eyelash at. For now, she only has eyes for her brother's Captain. Thirteen years her senior, Taylor Payne is her Prince

Charming, she doesn't even care that he's married. Taylor is hers. And it pisses Riley off, so she makes shirts that say "Mrs. Payne" and flirts with him every chance she gets.

My family is great, all back in Dalesburg. Luca and Addy got married after Riley and I graduated high school. Greg finally got a girlfriend last year, and Sean announced that he's gay and has a partner of four years, Toby.

Riley refuses to talk to his mom, Sue. She's been in counseling for a year now and has been sober for two months. Hannah speaks to her occasionally, but refuses to see her yet. I can't say I blame either one of them. The woman stole Riley's childhood. Louise and my mom reminded me that I'm no better than Sue if I don't encourage Riley to think about speaking with her.

Last week, I told him that he has a heart big enough for both of his parents, and he told me that he has the mentality of a guy starting his NHL career. Meaning, he's far too nervous for parental crap. I did make him promise to think about it and maybe after the season is over he can call her.

Five years ago, on March twenty eighth, Riley and I secretly got married. Two of his teammates went with us and we got married in an adorable, little white church. We had been in college for a few months, sharing an apartment, and some insanity came over us. His teammate, Jordie, knew the pastor at the church and drove us two hours out there. Our parents still think we got married two years ago. Our first wedding is by far my favorite of the two. No dresses, no drama, no decisions, just us and happiness and blue jeans. My mom was pretty ticked at my big wedding when I wore jeans and chucks under the dress she chose for me.

Hannah and I jump from our seats and scream at the tops of our lungs when Riley scores his first goal, the first goal for our team putting us in the lead.

Before I took my maternity leave, I worked with a law firm in Harrisburg Pennsylvania. I am a mediator, my priorities lie with the children and finding the truth and best possible options for them. When my maternity leave is over, I'll be starting here in Pittsburgh. My close experience with Riley and Hannah when they dealt with Parental Alienation, and still are, has helped me enlighten lawyers, judges, and parents of Parental Alienation and the affect it leaves on parents and children. Not everyone gets a happy ending. I glance to Louise, she claps and smiles as she watches the boys skate. She lost her son, she never got the chance to reconnect with her son.

Rubbing my stomach, I glance away quickly so I don't burst into tears for the tenth time today.

A home opener win is a grateful blessing for your first NHL game, and my husband achieved that and his first NHL goal tonight. I was so excited that Louise threatened to tell Riley how many times I jumped and swore at the refs and opposing team.

By the time we reach our home away from home, I'm ready to collapse.

My cellphone rings before I reach the bed.

"Hello?"

"Dahling!" Billy wails. "That was some game!"

I laugh and set my purse down on the counter. "Sounds like you're havin' a party!" I shout through the phone, hoping he hears me.

"Sarah and I may have thrown a little shindig in Riley's honor." He laughs.

I laugh, too. He and Sarah have three kids and finally tied the knot a few months ago.

"So, is Riley your Mel, Andrea, or Robert? You have to answer me now."

I grin and look at Riley. The years have done him good. His hair is slightly darker now, and a bit shorter than it was in high school. His nose has more bumps from fighting, and he's letting his beard grow for me and my wild pregnancy hormones. My favorite feature has not changed. His eyes, the deep blue sea that rests behind his lids is still present.

"He's my Riley," I answer Billy and endure another few minutes of teasing.

"Do you need anything?" Riley asks me for the fifth time since we left the arena.

I smile at him. "Only your magic fingers."

He leads me to the bed and helps me get comfortable.

"You know, I am pregnant but I'm perfectly capable of getting onto a hotel bed."

He laughs huskily. "I know, but I'm feeling pretty invincible right now. Let me have this."

I raise my arms and allow him to remove my shirt so he can massage my back. "You kicked a-butt tonight, Babe."

"Aw, that was almost a quarter in the swear jar," he teases and gently rubs his fingers into sore muscles in my back, and I moan in response.

"You should hear some of things I've heard tonight," I say.

"Anything good?"

"You have some admirers."

"I bet I'm married to one of them," he says softly in my ear, gently rubbing his chin stubble on my bare shoulder.

"Maybe a little," I tease.

"Are you turncoatin' on me, Mrs. Silk?"

I turn my head and look into his deep, blue eyes. Waves of blue drown me in love. "Never."

He brings his lips to mine, delighting me with his scruff and warm lips. "I love you."

I grin and run my fingers against the hair on his cheek. "I love you, too."

Our baby kicks, and I jerk upright very quickly.

Riley lies down beside me, resting his head on my thigh and rubs my belly. "I love you too, Danielle."

The End

Playlist

A Twist in my Story - Secondhand Serenade

All Over the Road - Easton Corbin

Between the Raindrops - Lifehouse Ft. Natasha Bedingfield

Breaking Inside - Shinedown Ft. Lzzy Hale

Good to be Alive - Skillet

Hate & Love - Jack Savoretti

Jacob's Ladder - Mark Wills

Lego House - Ed Sheeran

Life - The Avett Brothers

Life in the Pain - SafetySuit

Lost in You - Three Days Grace

Love - American Authors

Love Whiplash - Jayme Dee

Move - Thousand Foot Krutch

Mud - Jerrod Niemann

Mud on the Tires - Brad Paisley

Rain is a Good Thing - Luke Bryan

The Way Around Is Through - Live

Times Are Hard - Redlight King

Unbreakable - Framing Hanley

What If - Five For Fighting

What was I Thinkin' - Dierks Bentley

White Wedding - Billy Idol

A Note From The Author

Thank you for purchasing your copy of Pucked. It means a lot to me to be able to shed some light or education on something that doesn't get a lot of attention.

In this story, a few heavy topics are touched. There are several scenes involving alcohol and minor drug abuse. Always, if you need help with drug or alcohol abuse for yourself or someone else, please look into support and help in your area. I would offer a number to call, but there are so many that are geared for specific areas or countries. Search the internet for your local hotline, or contact your doctor or hospital for a referral. For teens and youth, a guidance counselor or an adult you trust could help with this information.

The heaviest form of abuse in this story is Parental Alienation. What is Parental Alienation? Parental Alienation is defined as a form of emotional child abuse where one parent vilifies or belittles the other parent to the child to plant a seed of distrust or hatred toward the parent. Its intent and effect is to destroy the present and future relationship between a child and the alienated parent.

In some cases of Parental Alienation, the abuse starts

while both parents are together.

At eleven, a girl notices her parents don't seem quite as happy as she remembers them being before. Tension is thick and noticeable, but she isn't sure if it's a new thing or if it's always been there. She's always been a daddy's girl, since he's the fun one. Mom is always stressing out, grumpy, and doesn't seem to want to be around the girl very often. She knows she's not the best daughter, a bit of a brat sometimes, but if her own mother doesn't want to be around her, then why should she torture her?

Over the next few years, the girl fought with her mother constantly over trivial things and did things purposefully to hurt her mother under the guidance of her father. Her father called her mother names like, "Witch from hell," and "Satan," among other hurtful, demeaning things. The girl was careful to hold in anything that could be linked to "acting like the witch," to not displease her daddy.

One night, while she was supposed to be sleeping because she had school in the morning, her father came into her room with a notebook and a pen. "Sweetie, things are going south between your mom and me." She nodded, knowing they weren't happy for a long time. It was bound to happen at some point. "You're old enough to tell a judge which parent you want to live with. You know I'll buy you anything you want, cigarettes, alcohol, a cellphone that Mother would hate..." She smiles. "And you know that if you stayed with *her* you'd never be happy. She'd call you fat to your face instead of behind your back." The young girl glares at the wall in the direction where she knows her mother is sleeping. "I need you to write two letters, sweetie. One to the judge, stating you want to live with me, and the other to your mother."

When he left her room that night, she did as he advised. She wrote two letters; one to a judge and the other to her mother. She did not sleep until they were both finished. When she finished the letter to her mother filled with all the reasons she hated her, she left it on the table for her mom to read.

The parents did not divorce. In the years that followed that night, things got worse between the mother and daughter. Until one day she saw her father in his true light and began to see her mother in her true light. She witnessed her father spew lies about her in to adults she respected. He bought inappropriate gifts for a few of her friends and witnessed moments that made her question if she even knew the man she loved and called "Daddy." She saw all the lies her father told her and everyone else. In her observations, she kept all the information to herself and began to withdraw from spending time with him, choosing her friends instead. Still, she feared hurting her father and loosely held onto the façade of hating her mother. For years, she tried to accept both of her parents and their individual flaws. Her parents divorced after she turned eighteen and by the time she turned twenty, she had no relationship with father at all. He was angered that the girl enjoyed a relationship with the "Witch Mother." - An anonymous story.

Not every case of Parental Alienation is the same. In some instances, the abuse is introduced during and after divorce.

Two sisters watched their parents fight as their home life and family fall apart. Their father left their mother, leaving them with their hurt and angry mother. Through the years, the mother would tell them stories twisted with hate and lies about the father. She would remind them that he doesn't love them like she does, that he lies, that all he does is hurt people. She told them, "Your father is a drunk, a lowlife," and "Men are good for nothing." The sisters believed their mother and showed their dislike of their father through words, ignoring him, and even refusing visitations. Over the years, the watched their mother use men for money, only to discard them when she felt they could offer nothing more.

As the sisters came into their adulthood, the oldest sister was encouraged by loving friends to contact her father. With guard and hesitation, she contacted him and found that he wasn't as bad as she was told. He had his flaws, but he was caring toward her and her children. He wanted a relationship with her and her growing family, nothing more and nothing degrading. She tried to encourage her sister the same way her friends encouraged her, but she was unsuccessful in her efforts. The younger sister needed money for something, she would contact their father but refuse anything other than money. - An anonymous story.

The abuse in Parental Alienation can be so strong that it can brainwash a child. The affects are lasting and sometimes never heal. It can start with parents, as exampled above, or from a step parent, guardian, or grandparent undermining the parent to child relationship with intent to damage the bond between them. If you feel like you are in a similar situation, there are steps you can take. Minors, you can seek your guidance counselor, an adult you trust, a priest, even your physician. Parents, the best advice I can give for these situations is keep the line of communication open between you and the child. Find an attorney with experience in cases that deal with Parental Alienation. For more information on how to help or what to do, please visit: paawareness.org

You are never alone.

Rachel Walter

Acknowledgements

Randy, my wonderful husband, without you I wouldn't be able to write with the same amount of passion that I have now. I don't have the words to thank you properly for everything you do from dealing with me and my work stress to every ounce of support and encouragement you give me. I love you.

To my family and friends, thank you for loving me through the process of this book. Thank you for providing me distraction when needed and when unwanted. Thank your for answering my random questions when I had them. Most of all, thank you for being you and not at all psychotic or creepy. Big shout to my kids, thank you for encouraging me to finish this story and being there to give me inside the teen mind answers, y'all are the best stepkids I could ask for and I love you three to pieces.

My betas, critiquers, editor, and proofreader, you guys are the absolute best. Thank you for questioning phrases, words, reactions, and pushing me to be better in my craft. I appreciate every single thing you do. Thank you for taking the time out of your lives to help me. I couldn't do what I do without you all.

Regina Wamba, thank you so much for creating the beautiful cover for this story. You never fail to impress me with each and every cover you create for me and all your clients. Love you tons and I cannot wait to give you a tackle hug!

Mark Prego, thank you for answering my questions regarding high school ice hockey.

To every person who contacted me regarding Parental Alienation, thank you for sharing your stories. I hold your experiences near to my heart.

To every blogger and author who shared updates, teasers, the cover and blurb, and the release announcement Thank You! Dusti, a very awkward squeezy hug for everything you've done to help and encourage me!

Dani Morales. You are a friend, an ear, an organizer, a supporter, a beta and so much more. Without you, Riley wouldn't be who he turned out to be. Thank you for pushing me to write this story during moments of weakness and doubt. Dani + Riley = Forever!

My biggest and best thank you will always be saved for my readers. So, THANK YOU. Thank you for choosing Pucked as your latest read. I really hope you enjoy it. Keep telling your friends about every book you love and if you have the time, leave an honest review where you purchased your copy.

About Rachel Walter

Rachel is a wife and mother from Central Pennsylvania. Her favorite season is fall, for hockey, changing leaves, pumpkin everything, and bonfires. She's also a coffeenista with an insomnia problem. When Rachel isn't playing with the people inside her head, making her family believe she belongs in the loony bin, she enjoys spending time with her family, friends, species confused cat (he believes he's part dog, love him), and finding new books and music to fall in love with.

Regarding writing, her first love is Young Adult Paranormal, but she's venturing outside of her comfort zone and opening up to writing more genres.

More from Rachel Walter

Available Now

Young Adult Paranormal Romance

The Soul Mate Series:

True Connection (Book One)

Soul Promise (Book Two)

Adult Contemporary Romance

Pocono Valley Romances:

A Message of Flowers

Coming Soon:

The Soul Mate Series:

Twisted Destiny (Book Three)

(To Be Announced)

A Pocono Valley Romance:

Catching Breeze

(To Be Announced)

Just for Fun

The next few pages are for blackout poetry! Once you've created your poem, take a picture of it and upload it to Twitter, Instagram, Facebook, or whichever social media you're into and use the hashtag #Pucked4Life

There's enough pages to let a friend play, too.

Have fun!

The last five minutes of study hall are always the slowest, but today, the hands on Mr. Theiss's old-fashioned clock seem to stand still. I stare out the window, waiting, wishing I were free from this place and already home.

The sun peeks out from behind the gray clouds that have cast our little town in the shadows for days.

Life is like the weather. Rain, like our emotions, builds up along the streets of our hearts, softening the earth of our souls, creating mud. Though messy, mud is the glue of our decisions. It cements our personal changes. It's not permanent, because when it rains again, you'll need to restructure, rebuild, change, and just like our decisions in life, nothing lasts forever.

But in the mud, there's freedom, relief, hope, and even a sense of peace - a mask.

Hiding behind masks is human nature. Even I hide behind a mask to keep others out, to shield my feelings and thoughts.

When it rains, for me, it's a time to reflect, and when the sun shines, drying the residue and warming my soul, I know I'll begin to heal. Temporary or not, it's still a relief to know that even a small solution is on the way.

The bell shrills, startling me from my thoughts. I burst from my seat and work my way to the door.

It's been raining for two days straight on this side of the Susquehanna River. School just ended, and the brightness of the sun feels like a long lost friend has finally come home, making an unusually warm autumn day.

My mother.
For letting a man break her down so badly that she can't function properly.
She gets another.
She's forgotten that she's a mother. I'm not old enough to care for my baby sister properly, not in the parental way she deserves. I still need a mom, but at least I'm old enough to figure things out on my own.
My mother gets another puck just for hurting my baby sister by ignoring her like she does. It smashes into the wall.
Another puck with her face, because it's her fault that Audrey wants to stay here. Audrey can see that Hannah needs a mother. So why can't Mom see it?
I kick the bag again, lining up another row.
She gets one more, for bringing another man into our house, causing a whole different world of shit for us.
I tap a puck forward, glaring at it.
This one's for Ted.
I purposefully miss the net this time. Smashing the puck into the wall so hard I hear it crack as it rattles across the floor.
One more for Ted.
His alcohol addiction nearly ended everything I know and love in one night with his drunken rage.
My mother gets another puck. This one's for bringing the man that beat her, almost to death, in front of my baby sister last year back into our home. I purposefully crash it into the wall again.
I smash yet another into the cement wall.
For bringing the man who hit my baby sister because she wouldn't stop crying, back into our lives.
Todd.
For asking my Audrey out and kissing her.
My stick hooks around the last puck.
It gets my face.

I roll over and put the puck next to my Pittsburgh Penguins puck that the team signed two years ago, and the puck Riley, Todd, Rob, and Derrick signed as a joke.

It wasn't too long after the joke puck that the worst night of my life happened. Riley's team won that night. It was the one win that we didn't do our milkshake tradition. We went to Todd's party instead. Everything started off normal, fun even. Riley was enjoying himself with the team.

My mom had given me photos from the county game to give to Sue, Riley's mom, so I told Riley that I was going to pop over and give her the photos.

When I walked into that house, I thought death was circling like a vulture. I've never seen that much blood before in my life. And Hannah's little body...

I dropped the photos and screamed at the top of my lungs. I was rooted to the spot just inside the doorway. We still don't know how I ended up with blood on me.

I know Riley feels guilty, that he should've been there to protect them, should've pressed charges for his sister's sake. But it fell on Sue. She wouldn't push it, and told the doctors and police she didn't know who it was.

A shiver runs down my spine, resting in my lower back. I snatch my phone from my back pocket and send a quick text to Riley. A lone question mark. It's our code to see if the other is okay.

We came up with this when we each got our phones a few years ago, after his dad left and when my brothers were leaving for college. If he responds with a smiley face, he's good. Anything else would mean that I stop in after work and sneak around to the back yard, so we can talk behind the shed. If it were reversed, he would come over and meet me in the garage. Before we had our cars, it was more difficult to accomplish, but luckily we don't live too far apart.

The longer I stay here with him, the more hurt I feel. But this isn't about me. It's about my friend who needs me. I chew on my cheek for a moment. "Let me make a phone call. I'll be right back." I push myself off his floor and slide my phone out of my pocket. I send a quick text to Candy, asking if she can cover for me for a few hours. When she responds with a yes, I call my dad.

"Hey sweetie, where you at?" He answers.

"I'm over at Candy's now. Is it alright if I stay here for dinner?"

"I don't see why not. Just be home by ten."

I smile. "Thanks Daddy."

After ending the call with my dad, I quietly push Riley's door back open. His head is buried in his hands, so I quietly take my seat on the floor next to him.

"I'm tired of hurting," he mumbles.

Tentatively, I place my hand on his shoulder. "What can I do?"

His hand slowly reaches for me, landing just above my knee. "Don't leave me."

His voice begs me to stay. But I can't stay here with him. I'd get in so much trouble. "I can't stay."

"Please," he whispers. He sits up and looks at me, tears in his eyes. "Everyone good leaves me. Don't leave me."

His chest heaves.

"I have to go home in a few hours," I argue lightly.

He takes a deep breath and glances to the ceiling. The storm inside of him seems to pass for the moment.

"Who can tell me the lesson Romeo and Juliet teaches us?" the English teacher asks.

I tap the eraser of my pencil on the edge of the desk.

"Riley, what did you learn from Romeo and Juliet?" Annoyance colors her tone.

I raise my eyes to meet hers. "That love kills you."

A few gasps and snickers follow my words.

"Why do you say that? It wasn't love that killed them-,"

"They held the illusion of love higher than the physicality of living. Love killed them. Regardless of the torment each experienced, they both chose wrong. You can't live with love-,"

"Love isn't an illusion, it's a feeling from your heart and soul," Audrey interrupts me. I don't look at her. I refuse to allow that. "They faced their world without each other and couldn't stand to live without the light of love. They were doomed from the start-,"

"Holding love higher than life is for fools," I interrupt her. "What's the point of life or the "feeling" of love if it only breaks you or kills you? Life is meant to be lived."

"This, class..."

I tune out. I can't listen to anymore or participate. Succumbing to the numbness is easier than dealing with a discussion about love.

It's pointless.

He doesn't need to see these idiotic tears. I hate me for exposing this to him.
Pity will spew from his mouth, and then I'll lie and say I'm okay. I can't stand lying to him.
But the need to get away from these tears, from him, from myself, it's too much. I shove his chest again and using my feet, I try sliding away.
His arms frame my head and shoulders like a cage, and my heart stops as the tears fall faster. My heart releases the sob and I can't stop it.
"Audrey," he whispers my name right into my ear, the same way he did before. The same way that made me kiss him.
It takes everything inside of me not to look at him.
Slick fingertips touch my cheek, and my breath freezes in my lungs under his touch.
"I'm sorry," he whispers. "Please, let me try again."
My chest heaves, expelling yet another sob, and I shove him again.
"Audrey," he whispers again, this time he uses his fingers to tilt my face toward him.
Looking into his icy eyes and seeing hope reflecting in them, I clamp my teeth on my bottom lip to try and slow the tears. I can't imagine what he sees. If it's anything like what I feel then it's weakness, tears, doubt, and fear.
He lowers his face closer to mine, and my eyes widen.
His lips touch my top lip and his fingers cup my cheek as his thumb works to release my bottom lip from my teeth.
My eyes flutter closed as I press my lips against his. I reach one arm up and place it on his wrist.
My heart, the stupid organ I wanted to feed to the birds, explodes into a thousand dancing leprechauns inside my chest.
When my breathing returns to normal and my tears slow, he pulls his lips from mine and drops his forehead to mine.

I take the deepest breath I can manage.
Please, lungs, brain, let me speak.
"Have you ever felt like you were a glass figurine?" I ask, the stupidity of it, true or not, reminds me of Louise's angels that she decorates the house with. "Everything going on just pushes you to the edge of a cliff, and you know that if you're knocked down, the landing would shatter you?" Everything gets fuzzy for a moment and to distract myself, I take a sip of the frozen chocolate in my hand. The cooler temperature reminds me of the ice. Ice is relatable. It's unforgiving but freeing. Focusing on that, I continue. "I'm unbreakable with you."
I can't look at her.
One second, I can't hear anything but my own heartbeat.
Two seconds, a warm hand grazes the back of my hand.
Three seconds, coconut and lime mixed with a touch of ice fills my senses.
Four seconds, she rests her head on my shoulder.
Five seconds, I can breathe.
"I don't view myself as a figurine, or you, for that matter. We're seasons, and we're opposites. I'm spring, and you're winter. But together we're autumn, and I can live with that."
The ice around my lungs seems to melt at her words. *Together we're Autumn,* I chuckle at her words. In a way, she makes sense. I don't think we're one whole season. I'm not as strong as winter can be, or as harsh, but I understand why she feels that way.
"I can live with autumn, too," I agree and move my arm to wrap around her shoulders.

Made in the USA
Middletown, DE
17 October 2015